Confessional Politics

Women's Sexual Self-Representations in Life Writing and Popular Media

Edited by Irene Gammel

Southern Illinois University Press
Carbondale and Edwardsville

Library of Congress Cataloging-in-Publication Data

Confessional politics : Women's sexual self-representations in life
writing and popular media / edited by Irene Gammel.
p. cm.
Includes bibliographical references and index.
1. Literature—Women authors—History and criticism. 2. Literature,
Modern—20th century—History and criticism. 3. Women in literature. 4. Sex in literature. 5. Autobiography in literature. 6. Feminism
and literature. 7. Women in mass media. I. Gammel, Irene, [DATE].
PN479.C65 1999
818'.540809492072—dc21
ISBN 0-8093-2254-4 (paper :alk. paper)   98-29739
ISBN 0-8093-2253-6 (cloth :alk. paper)   CIP

828 GAm

The paper used in this publication meets the minimum requirements of
American National Standard for Information Sciences—Permanence of
Paper for Printed Library Materials, ANSI Z39.48-1984. ∞

To Annette

Contents

Contents

Acknowledgments

The genesis of this book is as diverse and polymorphous as the topics, genres, and fields covered in it. *Confessional Politics* is situated at the intersection of autobiographical studies, women's studies, literary studies, performance studies, and media studies. I would like to thank all the contributors for bringing such rich variety to the topic and for charting new territories with an exciting variety of projects. More importantly, I would like to acknowledge the depth of their theoretical contributions in examining and advancing feminist scholarship and thus enabling new critical perspectives on confessional politics. I would also like to thank them for providing support and ideas for the editorial process itself.

Confessional Politics is deeply indebted to others whose traces and scholarly influences are inscribed in this work: Judith Butler, University of California; Richard Cavell, University of British Columbia; Rita Felski, University of Virginia; Paul Hjartarson, University of Alberta; Linda Hutcheon, University of Toronto; Sherrie Innis, Miami University; Marlene Kadar, York University; Claudia Kotte, Universität Münster; Nancy Miller, CUNY; Linda J. Nicholson, SUNY; Hiltraud Schmidt-Waldherr, Frauenforschung der Fachhochschule Fulda; Sidonie Smith, University of Michigan; Patricia Srebrnik, University of Calgary; and Janice Williamson, University of Alberta. For editorial suggestions and support, I am grateful to the following persons: my colleagues in the Women's Studies Programme and the Department of English at the University of Prince Edward Island, in particular Elizabeth Percival, Elizabeth Epperly, Geoffrey Lindsay, and Richard Lemm; Miriam Gogol, SUNY; Lorraine Janzen Kooistra, Nipissing University; Nicole Neatby, University of Prince Edward Island; Marie José des Rivières; Karen Smythe, Dalhousie University; Henry Srebrnik, University of Prince Edward Island; Gretchen Wilson, writer; and Jean Wilson, McMaster University. Warm thanks go to Don Mason for editorial support and for preparing the index with great care. I have been fortunate in my team of research assistants: Sara Underwood, whose editorial and formatting skills were invaluable; Tracey Noftle, whose energetic professionalism was a delight;

and Kim Tanner, whose heart and soul touched each and every aspect of this project. I would like to thank the anonymous readers at Southern Illinois University Press for their enthusiastic support and extremely helpful comments and suggestions. I am grateful to copyeditor Elaine Otto and to the editorial staff at SIUP, in particular Tracey Sobol, John Gehner, and Carol Burns for their helpful and patient guidance through various stages of this project.

I would like to single out two persons without whom this project would not have been possible. Caroline Bayard provided the inspiration, the drive, and the generous intellectual support needed for the early stages of this project. My most deeply felt thanks go to J. Paul Boudreau, whose intellectual support, unwavering belief, and sensitive perception helped me push this project to completion.

I gratefully acknowledge the support of the Social Science and Humanities Research Council of Canada, as well as the University of Prince Edward Island Senate Committee on Research for generous grant support for this project.

In chapter 3, grateful acknowledgment is made to the following for the use of previously published material: *Tulsa Studies in Women's Literature* for material from "Breaking the Bonds of Discretion: Baroness Elsa and the Female Sexual Confession" by Irene Gammel and *Canadian Review of Comparative Literature* for material from "The Death of the Fairy-Tale Prince: Foucault, Feminism, and the Female Sexual Confession" by Irene Gammel. Grateful acknowledgment is also made for permission to publish excerpts from the typescript of Elsa von Freytag-Loringhoven's autobiography, Papers of Elsa von Freytag-Loringhoven, Special Collections, University of Maryland at College Park Libraries.

In chapter 4, grateful acknowledgment is made to the following for the use of previously published material: Women's Press for material from *The Bat Had Blue Eyes* by Betsy Warland; Véhicule Press for selected lines of "The Man Next Door" and "The Man Next Door II" from *Henry Moore's Sheep and Other Poems* by Susan Glickman; Libby Scheier for selected lines of "A Poem about Rape," "Jenny's Surprise, or, Complicity," "Nursery Rhyme, I," and "Jenny's Spring" from *Second Nature* by Libby Scheier and for selected lines of "14. Earth Per Verse, A Catalogue of Suspicions and Dreams" from *Sky* by Libby Scheier; Mary di Michele for selected lines of "The Primer" from *Luminous Emergencies* by Mary di Michele; and Goose Lane Editions for selected lines from "The Fall" excerpted from *Fables from the Women's Quarters* © Claire Harris, 1984. Reprinted with the permission of Goose Lane Editions.

In chapter 5, grateful acknowledgment is made to the Johns Hopkins University Press for the use of previously published materials from Elizabeth Wilson. "Not in this House: Incest, Denial, and Doubt in the White

Middle Class Family." *Yale Journal of Criticism* 8.1 (Spring 1995): 35–58. ©1995. The Johns Hopkins University Press.

In chapter 6, grateful acknowledgment is made to the following for the use of previously published material: Johns Hopkins University Press for material in *Theatre Journal* from "Women's Performance Art: Feminism and Postmodernism" by Jeannie Forte, from "Resisting/Performing/Femininity: Words, Flesh, and Feminism in Karen Finley's *The Constant State of Desire*" by Maria Pramaggiore, and from a review by Kathryn Heller; *Village Voice* for material from "Unspeakable Practices, Unnatural Acts: The Taboo Art of Karen Finley" by C. Carr; *New Republic* for material from "The Dope on Dana" by K. Lehrman; Michael Overn for material in *Tulane Drama Review* from "Letter to the Editor" by Michael Overn; University of California Press for material from *Hard Core: Power, Pleasure, and the Frenzy of the Visible* by Linda Williams © The Regents of the University of California, 1989; Vivian Patraka for material in *Discourse* from "Binary Terror and Feminist Performance" by Vivian Patraka; and Grove/Atlantic Inc. for material from "World Without End" in *Clit Notes* by Holly Hughes. Copyright © 1984 by Holly Hughes. Used by permission of Grove/Atlantic Inc.

In chapter 9, grateful acknowledgment is made to Universal Studios for permission to publish quotations from *Sally Jessy Raphael*.

Confessional
Politics

Introduction

In the wake of the growing power of twentieth-century feminist movements and feminist consciousness, women have reclaimed the authority to speak truthfully about their sexualities. Through diaries, journals, autobiographies, and case histories as well as popular fiction and performance art, they have articulated their sexual experiences in their own words and through this confluence have participated in confessional politics. Documentary films, TV and radio talk shows, self-help books, and magazines have further popularized this practice. More recently, news media attention to stories of harassment and abuse has given this practice an additional political twist, thus creating a heterogeneous genre that requires analysis and investigation.

While women have transgressed into the public domain with their personal stories, their sexual expressions are frequently read by the media and public as personal confessions. Indeed, the easy and often unquestioned association made between a woman's voice of sexuality and the confessional genre may account for the increasing media popularity of the genre. In life writing and popular media, the authenticating female body behind the speaking and writing voice somehow endows the woman's voice with an implicit realism and truth value, while frequently also providing a screen for reader projection and fantasy. The sixties feminist slogan "the personal is political" has further increased this trend, although the association of confession with sin, shame, and voyeurism has made many feminists weary of the practice.

The present collection probes the sexual confession as a gender discourse. If it is true that we are living in a confessional age, and that "telling all is in," as a popular article put it in its characterization of the nineties (Fillion 1994, 86), then the collection shows that the confession has become a specifically female discursive practice. From many different angles, the essays in this collection investigate the association of confession with femininity; they examine its function as a gender-specific discourse, as they probe its many feminized genres and subgenres. The articles demonstrate that in North American and European perceptions, women have become

1

the confessional sex par excellence. As Lori Saint-Martin writes in this collection, "The realm of the personal and sexual has always been literary for men (Saint Augustine, Rousseau, Michel Leiris, Henry Miller) and confessional for women (Colette, Erica Jong, Anaïs Nin)." Indeed, when men do confess their sexualities, they inevitably become feminized, as the last essay of this collection shows with Lorraine Janzen Kooistra's investigation of the cross-dressed confession as a subgenre of the female confession.

Thus the collection's more important concern is to probe women's participation in the larger domain of confessional politics. *Confessional Politics* investigates the many different ways in which women are subjected to confessional modalities in life writing and popular media and actively defy traditional confessional readings. Recent feminist archival research has brought to light a plethora of life writing, showing the experimental and creative energy with which women have negotiated their positions within the larger realm of confessional politics. Many "real-life" stories encode an awareness of the confessional reality principle, of possible appropriation and recolonization of their life stories; suspicion and skepticism mark their self-representation, signaling that theirs is not the unmediated cry from the female heart. Women encode boundaries and warnings, signaling their desire to create their own safe space in which to articulate their personal and sexual lives, while defying confessional entrapments. They tell and retell their personal stories by simultaneously enacting, and reacting against, confessional modalities that wish to contain them.

Women's awareness of the risks of confessional politics is typical of women's confessional interventions, both in life writing and in popular media. Beginning with a variety of representative genres in sexual life writing (including erotic diaries, journals, letters, and confessional fiction), before moving to a diversity of women's sexual self-representations in popular media (including performance art, public testimonies, and television talk shows), *Confessional Politics* shows that women's sexual self-representations are frequently appropriated and recirculated, resurfacing reframed and repackaged in film and documentary genres (including news media genres). Since the circulation of sexual self-representations confronts women almost inevitably with a confining frame, the essays in this collection examine how women, in turn, take charge of this challenge and experiment with ways of subverting traditional confessional readings, of dodging the conventional readings designed to contain them in traditional confessional paradigms. While the collection highlights the dangers of containment, its more important concern is to investigate the ways in which women creatively dodge and escape confessional snares. Deliberate play with the traditional confessional modalities is frequently at the heart of women's sexual self-representations. From a multiplicity of angles and positions, reflecting a multiplicity of written and popular genres, *Confessional*

Politics is ultimately concerned with the bidirectionality of the term *confession* for women: if the term implies women's subjection to confessional readings, it also serves to explore women's active manipulation of confessional conventions.

Confessional Readings: A Historical Perspective

The term *confession* is a problematic one for women, as it brings to mind its patriarchal history. Confession evokes its religious context—the image of the confessional and the priest. The black box, hiding the confessant from the eyes of the community and turning the confession of sin into a private act, was introduced through the Council of Trent in the sixteenth century. During the Middle Ages, Dante poeticized the Church's confessional ideology with its fundamental gender bias in the *Inferno*. In one of the most memorable and most frequently anthologized cantos, Dante has Francesca recall her life of passion and adultery. While Dante pilgrim is moved to tears by the tale of her intimate life, Dante poet, the composer of the *Commedia*, assumes the role of confessional reader and judge. He puts her in Hell, imposing legitimate punishment for her sexual transgression and superimposing the authoritative male voice of the poet (and of God) over that of the female voice.

If this medieval paradigm of confession most readily exposes the problematic aspects of sexual confessions for women, the secularization of the practice in subsequent decades did not dismantle its power dynamics, as Michel Foucault has amply documented in volume one of his *History of Sexuality* (1978). Where Dante taxonomized the religious sins of the flesh through a process of confessional readings, nineteenth- and twentieth-century social scientists and physicians further subjected women's lives to confessional readings, especially in sexology and psychoanalysis. Sigmund Freud institutionalized the paradigms of confessional reading in the in/famous case of Dora (alias Ida Bauer), whom he treated in 1900. In the course of her analysis, Bauer endeavored to articulate the ways in which she felt sexually traumatized, while Freud consistently re/read her story as a classical personal confession, in which a woman's word cannot be trusted but needs the hermeneutical expert to complete the act of truth telling. In Freud's confessional reading, Bauer became complicit in her sexual mistreatment. In her feminist revision of the case, Simone Tünnermann (1996, 138) shows how Freud denied and devalued Bauer's experiences, reducing them to sexually motivated unconscious desires for and fantasies about the man harassing her.

Confessional reading was also the fate of countless women writing sexual and erotic journals, letters, and diaries in the late nineteenth and early twentieth centuries, as male partners and lovers, frequently novelists and filmmakers, reshaped the material to make it fit their own version of female sexuality. Zelda Fitzgerald, wife of the flamboyant author of *The Great Gatsby*, was only one of many women whose unconventional sexual life writings were colonized as unprotected raw material for novels and more recently for films. *Jules and Jim* (Helen Hessel), *Henry and June* (Anaïs Nin), BBC's miniseries *Portrait of a Marriage* (Vita Sackville-West), and *The Lover* (Marguerite Duras) are but a few examples of the movie industry's predilection for applying confessional readings to women's written sexual lives. These confessional readings include omissions of transgressive elements (e.g., abortion in *Jules and Jim*); additions of misogynistic elements (e.g., a quasi-rape desired by the woman in *Henry and June*), and celebration of traditional institutions (e.g., marriage in *Portrait of a Marriage*). In these examples, women's voices of sexuality are not so much silenced as they are appropriated, tamed, and recolonized to fit patriarchal frames of reference. Like its religious and psychological predecessors, the confessional readers in the realm of fictional and cinematic art assume the roles of hermeneutical "experts," with the right and obligation to provide more truthful (male) versions of the female experience.

As these historical and recent examples show, confessional readings frequently entail a process of devaluation of the female voice. The female voice relating personal experience, like the sinner's and the patient's, belongs not to the realm of abstract and official *langue* but to *parole*, to familiar and intimate speech, and is thus characterized by a low degree of formality and authority, as it is perceived as ephemeral or trivial. Even when entering a more authorized form, as in the example of Anne Sexton's poetry, the confessional mode is dismissed as "raw," "narcissistic," and "unformed" (Keitel 1996, 334). Women's personal and sexual stories in life writing and popular media tend to make a dramatic splash when they first appear; they descend into the subconscious realm of memory only to surface later in more authoritative frames in appropriated and tamed form. Generally the traces of women's voices survive but under the name of a different author/ity.

A history of confessional readings has created the perception of women obsessively confessing their secrets, reinforcing stereotypes of the female psyche as fragmented and, what is perhaps even worse, as "needy." In western society, in which the self-sufficient, self-reliable bourgeois subject remains the ideal norm, confession easily becomes a measure of mental immaturity and emotional instability. "If you compress precious pieces of information into sound bites for people you don't know very well, it's like a one-night stand," we read in a popular American women's magazine warning against the "compulsion to confess" (Fillion 1994, 88). The impression of immaturity may be further reinforced by TV talk and self-help books prompting persons to "search for the inner child." The confession can become a solipsistic, circular exercise, slipping into what Nancy

Miller has called "a gesture of personal territorialism—a nationalism of the 'I'" (1991, xiv).

What is more, popular media actively participate in the construction of confessions, even while systematically devaluing them. The construction of confession in mass media, most recently in the case of Monica Lewinsky, is based on a process of selection and repetition, frequently perpetuating familiar pictures of female stereotypes, in particular that of femininity in bondage. Readers will also remember the lurid details of the case of Lorena Bobbitt, an American woman charged with cutting off her husband's penis with a kitchen knife after he raped and beat her. Through repeated replay, news media hyperexposed isolated sexual acts (battering, anal rape, etc.), while repeated images of Bobbitt's weeping, petite body, and selective memories, all restaged the role of the sexual victim. The coverage of such media events is generally accompanied by such negative epithets as "exhibitionism," "voyeurism," and "cheap entertainment." Framed by the electronic media in the last two decades, women's voices of sexual experience (including those speaking out and speaking up for their rights) are haunted by notoriety and low reputation.

Confession and Feminist Approaches

Given the polyvalence of the term *confession*, it is appropriate that the essays in this collection should adopt a variety of different approaches. To familiarize the reader I will briefly introduce a number of these approaches and modalities. The most influential recent theorist of western confession is the French historian Michel Foucault (1978). His iconoclastic approach to the western history of sexuality has been instrumental in popularizing the concept of confession. He believes that western society encourages confessions of sexuality because they are a powerful tool of social policing, of distinguishing between normal and abnormal sexual practices. Some essays in this collection turn Foucault's argument around and show that women do not so much confess as their articulations of sexuality are subjected to confessional readings by the social machine. Moreover, the term *confession* itself, as the collection shows, is characterized by a fundamental bidirectionality: women are subjected to confessional readings, but many women also use confessional conventions self-consciously, deliberately manipulating the confessional machine that wishes to entrap them.

Foucault's theory is, however, useful to conceptualize the power relationship involved in confessional politics. The confessional speech act is characterized by an imbalance between the confessor's power (to interpret, forgive, and console) and the confessant's impotence (in preventing his or her words from being turned against him or her). The confession has little authority of its own, but needs the voice of an authority—religious, medical, psychological, or legal—to legitimize it and assign it a truth value. It is this notion of confession as a power relationship that has preoccupied feminists and has led them to urge women to avoid the confessional genre. Confessing their sexualities and identities is seductive for women who have been silenced and condemned to speechlessness, argued Mary Lydon in the United States, but the voicing of female sexuality means that women's speech can easily become grounded in traditional parameters (1988). Many European feminists had paved the way for Lydon's suspicions, including Jutta Kolkenbrock-Netz and Marianne Schuller (1982) and Sigrid Weigel (1984), who have categorically rejected confessional modalities in European women's writing, arguing that they have little transformative value.

Other feminists, however, have come to reevaluate confessional practices. This revisionist approach was initiated in a chapter entitled "On Confession" in Rita Felski's *Beyond Feminist Aesthetics* (1989). Felski writes, "I use 'confession' simply to specify a type of autobiographical writing which signals its intention to foreground the most personal and intimate details of the author's life" (87). The feminist confession is community-building and empowering for women in that it allows them to speak out, but many women are caught in a narcissistic and obsessional confession, retelling the same painful story, unable to effect real change. In *Getting a Life: Everyday Uses of Autobiography* (1996), coeditors Sidonie Smith and Julia Watson cautiously insist on the transformative potential of the self-narrative (13–15), and so do most of their colleagues in a comprehensive collection of essays investigating the rich spectrum of autobiographical storytelling in American life and culture. As a flexible polytrope, the term *confession* surfaces in a variety of contexts: personal ads, psychotherapy, prisoners' narratives, and television talk shows.

Focusing on the recent confessional trend among first-person feminist theorists (most notably Jane Gallop), Susan David Bernstein employed the term *confession* because of its transgressive implications. "I prefer 'confessional' to 'autobiographical' or 'personal' because of the implication of transgression encoded in the first term," Bernstein writes. "I am interested in the intrusive 'I' as a rhetorical event; this textual moment carries the capacity to accentuate and overturn conventions of authority, particularly the pretense of objectivity as an ideological cover for masculine privilege" (1992, 121). Her most recent work, *Confessional Subjects*, a rigorous and important study of confession in Victorian literature and culture, however, takes the position that "confession is largely a site of coercion" (1997, 1); Bernstein deliberately refrains from "reading resistance per se in acts of women confessing" (2).

Confessional Politics presents a diversity of positions and opinions on the concept of confession within the larger context of women's sexual self-representations. Some essays in this collection continue to engage the term *confession* for women, but they do so with a significant departure, pointing to the women's strategic manipulation of confessional conventions. While Lydon, Felski, Bernstein, and others have introduced us to the complexity of the notion of the female and feminist confession, it is imperative now that we investigate the numerous pathways in which women channel, negotiate, and express their sexual self-representations within a larger frame of confessional politics. The collection shows that women frequently construct their sexual self-representations by actively manipulating confessional conventions and that, conversely, through reception, women frequently find themselves drawn back into spirals of traditional confessional readings. While this collection will highlight the many dimensions of confessional expressions, it also serves to investigate the powerful and provocative playfulness through which women actively shape and redefine their own boundaries in their sexual self-representations.

Moreover, the essays in this collection endeavor to establish a new genre that encompasses the articulation of female *sexual* self-representations. In distinction to the larger practice of autobiographical storytelling, these essays demonstrate that the telling of intimate life stories frequently moves beyond the language of authentic realism described by Foucault, Felski, and others and instead uses self-conscious rhetorical strategies that frequently approximate literary devices. The examples provided in this collection bear witness to the richness of linguistic, rhetorical, and performative strategies used by women in the telling of their intimate lives. To highlight women's active shaping of their sexual self-representations, recent feminist theoretical models form a backdrop in this collection's discussion of life writing.

While validating women's creativity in carving out niches for their sexual self-representation within the larger domain of confessional politics, many essays highlight the dangers of entrapment associated with the term *confession*. The negative reality principle of confessional politics requires women to distance and protect themselves, but the collection also shows that women manipulate confessional modalities to advantage, strategically dismantling its conventions from within. As the essays in this collection employ different theories—from discourse analysis, through performance theory, to theories of autobiographical self-representation, their unique differences all converge to highlight the core thesis of this collection—that women actively and strategically negotiate their positions and identities within the larger domain of confessional politics.

Confessional Interventions, Modalities, and Inversions

Confessional Politics investigates the creative ways in which women shape the telling of their sexual stories in order to resist, manipulate, and negotiate the confessional frames and practices designed to entrap them. To discuss women's engagement with the confessional process, we use the following key concepts as a structural device for the collection: *confessional interventions*, which signal women's abilities to disrupt confessional frames and unsettle the confessional reader's secure expectations; *confessional modalities*, which serve to investigate the power and limits of women's ability to maneuver and shift positions within the frame of institutionalized confessional politics; and *confessional inversions*, which describe a deliberate play with the very sexual identities imposed by confessional frames.

As confessional readings tend to devalue women's voices, a crucial element that characterizes women's confessional interventions is the creation of a "safe" zone in which women can articulate their sexualities without fear. The importance for a safety zone is best described by Anaïs Nin with reference to her erotic diaries: "By gradually building up this *shelter* of the diary, I built a place where I could tell the truth" (in Stone 1981, 159). *Confessional Politics* investigates a variety of strategies designed to create such safe zones. Women's confessional interventions involve an ideological rejection of shame, as shame is a central feature of the traditional confession (Tambling 1990, 70). "The Shame Is Over" is the title of Kate Millett's article in *Ms.* magazine (January 1975), a title echoed by many other sexual autobiographies, including Anja Meulenbelt's 1980 international best-seller, *De schaamte volar*.

This rejection of shame goes hand in hand with the goal to reclaim their authority to speak truthfully about their experiences and to create new spaces for the articulation of erotic pleasure in such forms as erotic fantasies (e.g., Nancy Friday's 1973 *Our Secret Garden*) or confessional autobiography. The title of Anja Meulenbelt's 1979 best-selling sexual manual, *Voor Onszelf* (For ourselves), is indicative of the goal of women's interventions. Meulenbelt writes that the book's focus is based on their own experiences and opinions. This book is "a gift to ourselves" and for other women reading the text (1979, my translation).

As traditional confessional readings almost systematically foreground and reproduce victims, *Confessional Politics* investigates women's interventions that explicitly defy the victim status even in their voicing of sexual trauma. While the primary motivation behind this sharing of a personal trauma, often after long years of silence, is the demand for a legal or social redressing of a sexual injury, traditional confessional modalities frequently jeopardize the women's desire for change. "Many women told us vehemently that they hate the term 'victim,'" write the collective editors of the anthology *Recollecting Our Lives* (Women Research Centre 1989, 22) and show that women reveal experiences of abuse, exploitation, disempowerment, by deliberately reversing the traditional power positions of the confessional genre. These strategies allow women to speak from positions of strength, even as they look back on past selves unable to speak.

However, the voicing of sexual experience, whether positive or negative, created a complex process of recolonization in popular media, highlighting the continued power of confessional entrapments. Indeed, women sharing coming-out stories, for instance, are acutely aware of the danger of being denigrated through the label "confession." Susan Wolfe and Julia Penelope Stanley, editors of *The Coming Out Stories* (1980), voice their concern about adequate protection and categorically refused to publish the stories in a "large, male commercial publishing house": "These stories were not written for 'mass' distribution and consumption—they were written for us" (xxiii).

If confessional modalities allow us to explore the omnipresent danger of confessional snares, strategies of confessional inversion reveal possibilities of playful disentanglement. Since the danger of confessional readings is increased in popular media (best-seller, TV talk, letters to the editor), women need to design continuously new strategies of resistance in their public voicing of sexuality. In the process of reclaiming their lives, women whose sexualities were traditionally dismissed under the rubric of "other" or "deviant" disentangle themselves from conventional snares through a process of confessional inversions, by using the very negative terms used to dismiss them in confessional frames imposed on their self-narratives.

Focusing on a specifically female discursive practice, the collection investigates confessional interventions, modalities, and inversions in a feminist context and advances a current debate on the value of women's disclosures and articulations of sexuality. All three concepts converge and overlap to show that women's participation in confessional politics is much more complex than the one-dimensional power play described by Foucault. *Confessional Politics* significantly expands and revises Foucault's confessional theories, by investigating the nature of the power relationship that exists between a woman articulating her sexuality and a reader interpreting the perceived "confession."

All three concepts help to illustrate the performative nature of women's self-representational acts, as they are meant to have an effect in the material reality of women's lives; they involve elements of role playing and theatricality, as women maneuver through different positions, roles, and settings. *Confessional Politics* examines the creative ways in which women manipulate the confessional framework, encoding their distance, creating double voices, transforming the genre from the inside out: through humor, parody, and satire; through fictionalizing strategies; through outrageous masquerades; through play and subversion; through various degrees of distance, ultimately struggling against the entrapment in patriarchal confessional paradigms. Frequently, the transgressive élan of their acts provokes further responses and efforts of containment, thus continuing the spiral of confessional readings. Many readers and spectators feel uneasy about the genre's characteristics: its transgressive sexual nature, its sometimes scandalous excess, and its breaking of the boundaries of normality. It is these characteristics which make it both fascinating and unsettling for its middle-class audience.

Confessional Politics, for the first time, brings together a diversity of feminist voices and critical positions on women's associations and connections with confession. Each essay will be framed by a short introduction, establishing its position within the larger collection. The collection analyzes representative genres in life writing (intimate diaries, erotic journals, and confessional best-sellers) and popular media (TV talk shows, letters to the editor, and performance art) and thus bridges the gap between the most silenced and the most voluble media. The essays draw on examples from North America (most notably the United States, but also from English Canada and Québec) as well as from Europe (Germany, England, France, and the Netherlands), revealing some of the confessional interventions, modalities, and inversions in their cultural specificity, but also identifying the patterns across different western cultures. Drawing attention to its institutional frame, *Confessional Politics* bears witness to the ubiquity and extraordinary diversity of this discursive practice, which requires critical attention, for it continues to shape women's cultural expressions of personal and sexual experiences.

Part One

Body Politics and
Confessional Interventions

The first section of this collection highlights the ways in which women take ownership of their erotic body pleasures and self-representations, actively constructing their sexual identities in life writing. Women have produced a rich spectrum of erotic expressions in life writing. This spectrum ranges from diaries written in secret, through confessional fiction written for publication, to autobiographical masquerades designed to shock partners and readers. Inscribing their awareness of the role and power of the confessional reader who passes judgment, women use a variety of strategies to encode significant distances, disruptions, and warnings. Investigating women's successes and limitations in avoiding confessional snares, part one introduces the reader to a variety of women's confessional interventions designed to disrupt conventional confessional readings: some women protect their sexual writing by strategically withholding information from the public gaze; some writers purposefully confuse the voyeuristic reader through a playful blurring of the boundaries between confession and fiction; and some women effectively subvert and parody the conventions of popular confessional genres. Through strategic confessional interventions, the very paradigms that encourage confessional readings are called into question.

1

Confessional Realities: Body-Writing and *The Diary of Anne Frank*

Marion Bishop

Anne Frank, one of the most famous diary writers in history, addressed her diary to an ideal female reader, an imaginary mirror reflecting her own growth. Encoding her resistance against the dangers of confessional readings, Anne eliminated sexually explicit passages from her diaries when she revised the manuscript for publication. Anne's hiding of the most intimate passages echoes the writing of many adolescents who write their sexualities in secret. But, given the extraordinary circumstances of her writing, Anne's intervention takes a significantly different twist. In the dialectics of writing, reading, and editing, Anne avoids the confessional reader's panoptic gaze and writes a safe space, which for her assumed a terrifying literality.

It is March 1944. The Frank and Van Pels families have been in hiding for almost two years. Anne and Peter steal away to the attic to talk about sex. On March 24, fifteen-year-old Anne confides in her diary:

> I would like to ask him if he knows what a girl really looks like there. I don't think a boy is as complicated down there as a girl. You can see exactly what a naked man looks like from photographs or pictures, but you can't with women. With them the sexual parts or whatever they are called are further between the legs. He probably hasn't seen a girl from so close, to be honest I haven't either. With a boy it's much easier. . . . With us it's all pretty much divided, before I was 11 or 12 years old I didn't realize that there were two inner lips as well, you couldn't see them at all. And the funniest thing of all was that I thought that the urine came out of the clitoris. (1989, 566)[1]

13

In this passage and others like it, Anne's body enters her text, as she narrates the physical intimacy she and Peter share, chronicles the onset and recurrence of her menstrual periods, and most strikingly, describes her own genitalia in explicit terms. However, most of these passages, including the one above, were excised from the first published version of her journal, *The Diary of a Young Girl* (1952) and were unavailable until her unedited diary was published.

The Diary of Anne Frank: The Critical Edition (Doubleday 1989) restores these passages and reveals a girl who is open in writing about her body, its changes, and her feelings about them.[2] *The Critical Edition* also suggests Anne's survival strategy for the two years she and her family were in hiding: living under conditions that required an almost complete renunciation of bodily instincts, movement, and expression, Anne discovered that the only way to have a body was to write one. And she did—using language so specifically corporeal she resisted not only the Nazi edict to silence and nullification but also cultural and linguistic norms that perpetuate the silence of women. In short, Anne's corporeally resonant response to Nazi oppression creates for her a linguistic body she can own: writing about the body becomes writing-the-body.

Although Anne's journal shares some characteristics with diaries of other individuals living in confinement, her use of specifically sexual writing to create a physical existence for herself is a point that other critics, such as Thomas Mallon (1984) and Jane Dupree Begos (1987), have failed to see.[3] Mallon explains in *A Book of One's Own* that the diaries of people he calls "Prisoners" are marked by "substitution, sublimation [and] transference . . . where the diary is a wish world." Further, he argues that for people living in isolation or a form of imprisonment, "diaries are not simply habits; they are attempts to create life" (251). He then reads Anne's diary as such an attempt, but also mentions her in his discussion of "Confessors," where he treats the confessional nature of adolescent girls' diaries disparagingly, even calling it "'Dear Diary' shit." On the other hand, Begos, a critic who has worked extensively with teenage girls' diaries, is respectful of Anne's record of the "awakening of love and the promise of womanhood" (Begos 1987, 70). But both of these critics wrote before 1989, working with the extensively *edited* version of Anne's text, ironically finding fault with and praising the significantly watered down material of *The Diary of a Young Girl.* With the backdrop of more recent studies by Sander Gilman (1988), Carol Gilligan (1990), and Sandra Patterson Iskander (1991), I propose to investigate the more specific issues and complexities of Anne's sexual writing.

But before the specifically sexual issues can be addressed, the story of how Anne wrote and revised her diary and how it came to be published in two such strikingly different versions needs to be told. Then I will explore the way Anne's sexual writing creates for her an existence through its connections to *écriture féminine*, and how in an unusual turn of events, a woman's most private writing—her journal—can come to have political implications. I will demonstrate that Anne, in effect, pushed against the boundaries of the confessional frame that Thomas Mallon imposes on such writing.

Many people are aware of the details behind Anne's journal: as German Jews living in Amsterdam during World War II, Anne, her father, Otto, her mother, Edith Frank-Hollander, and her sister, Margot—went into hiding in a small apartment above her father's spice warehouse. Another family, the Van Pels, with their teenage son, Peter, joined them. Approximately a year later, a local dentist, Friedrich Pfeffer, began sharing Anne's small room.[4] From June 1942 until August 1944, when their hiding place was raided by the Germans, they occupied this small space, never going outside, and surviving on food and necessities provided by friends. How they were discovered, so near the end of the war, is not entirely clear, but all eight were sent to concentration camps. Margot and Anne died at Bergen-Belsen in March 1945. Their father was the only inhabitant of this "Secret Annex" to survive the war.

Throughout the period in hiding, Anne kept a diary. However, sometime during the second year, she started revising it, probably with the hope that the revision would be published after the war. On the day that the families were taken away, Miep Gies, wife of Otto Frank's business partner and one of their caretakers, retrieved the diary from the apartment, intending to return it to Anne after the war. With the sad news of her death in the summer of 1945, Gies gave Anne's manuscript to Otto Frank. In an attempt to honor his daughter's desire to become a published writer, Otto published a portion of this manuscript in Dutch in 1947 under the title *Het Achterhuis* (The House Behind) and in 1952, an English translation was published as *The Diary of a Young Girl*. Assured by the statement printed in most editions that "with the exception of a few sections of little interest to the reader, the original text has been retained," readers believed the published version to be most of Anne's text (in Frank 1989, 166).

However, when Otto Frank died in 1980, he donated Anne's manuscript diaries to the Netherlands State Institute for War Documentation, where it was discovered that very little of Anne's original diary had been published: *Het Achterhuis* was a portion of Anne's own revision, edited and further cut by Anne's father and editors uncomfortable with some of its content and language. Sensing the power of the original document, this Netherlands agency published a Dutch critical edition of Anne's diaries in 1986 and an English translation with Doubleday in 1989. These texts juxtapose Anne's original text, her own revision, and the previously published version of her diary, revealing "a more rounded, a more detailed picture both of her development from a thirteen-year-old into a fifteen-year-old girl, and of her inner life and her progress as a writer" (in Frank 1989, 166). The differences between the two versions are most keenly seen in regard to the passages Anne edited out about her changing body and her growing sense of her own sexuality. Probably fueled by a need for privacy and a fear that her most intimate writing would be maligned or appropriated as "confession" if it were published, Anne excluded the most corporeal centered passages of the original manuscript from their revisions. Anne's suspicion that this body-writing would be misunderstood is entirely justified: too often, women's sexual expressions are interpreted from the male-centered perspective as confessional narcissism, self-absorption, and even titillation, typified by the frame imposed by Thomas Mallon. That her father and editor further excised materials renders even more visible the power of the reader in the shaping of women's sexual self-representations.

Michel Foucault has presented a model that analyzes sexual self-representations in terms of "confessions." While some of Foucault's insights apply to Anne's diaries, Anne uses strategies of sexual writing that seriously challenge the confessional paradigms outlined by Foucault. In *The History of Sexuality* (1978), Foucault argues that in western civilization, sexuality has become *the* topic that people must not discuss, but nonetheless feel compelled to do so. He places the sexual confession in the center of this paradigm, as a mode of oral discourse where confessors divest themselves of sexual secrets in the pursuit of truth that is never found, perpetuating a cycle of more and more confession in search of ever-evasive truths about the self. Further, he explains that the sexual confession is one of the few rhetorical situations where the listener, rather than the speaker, holds the power: "The confession is a ritual of discourse in which the speaking subject is also the subject of the statement; it is also a ritual that unfolds within a power relationship. . . . The agency of domination does not reside in the one who speaks (for it is he who is constrained), but in the one who listens and says nothing; not in the one who knows and answers, but in the one who questions and is not supposed to know" (61–62). Although these arguments are quite compelling, Foucault's assumptions are based on the idea of a confessor delivering a confession to a second party and, therefore, they do not have the same ramifications in Anne Frank's diary. Her strategic exclusion of the *sexual* passages from her revision suggests that in her original diary Anne is writing to herself as *primary* audience, deliberately dodging the gaze of an external reader in the process of revision and thus maintaining control of her sexual self-representations.

Although Anne had a secondary audience in mind for her revised text, her revision shows her constructing both private *and* public audiences, thus problematizing Foucault's theory in two ways. First, Anne deliberately refuses to deliver *confessions*, as she discloses her sexuality not to another person but to herself in order to gain a kind of corporeal-based self-knowledge. Second, the power dynamics usually at play in a sexual confession don't apply in Anne's draft and revision of her journal, because Anne's primary audience is herself: she is the "speaking subject,"[5] "the subject of the statement," "the one who listens and says nothing," and "the one who questions and is not supposed to know." Ultimately, this construction of herself as speaker *and* audience will generate power and authority for Anne, rather than taking or draining it.

In *Beyond Feminist Aesthetics* (1989), Rita Felski explores the feminist and political value of women's sexual self-representation by applying Foucault's terminology of the confession. Felski acknowledges that in a confession power resides in the listener, but her primary purpose is to explore the value of women's literary confessions and whether they can be of use to feminists politically (102–3). She also problematizes the genre in a way that is pertinent to Anne's journal. Echoing Foucault, Felski explains that a confessional autobiographer's constant purging in pursuit of truth becomes tiresome: "I write, therefore I am" becomes a vicious cycle, with the writer losing any political power in the process (112).

However, Anne's exclusion of sexually explicit material from her own revision suggests a strategic reworking of the confessional paradigm, as she intended specific materials to remain private or unpublished. Anne indicates in her diary that after a Dutch radio broadcast encouraged people to document their war experience, she became hopeful her diary would be published. The commentary to the critical edition of her diary cites this broadcast and subsequent journal entries articulating her desire to "publish a book entitled *Het Achterhuis* after the war" as the impetus for her painstaking revision and the bifurcation of private and public audiences it creates (Frank 1989, 61).[6] Anne's setting aside of certain passages as private separates the original version of her diary from the intended published autobiographical texts. Anne renders her sexual reality by deliberately resisting the confessional impulse to bare it all, thus maintaining control of her sexual writing.

The Cycle of Prohibition

Confined by Nazi terror to a life where her silence was not just figurative but also literal, Anne's sexual writing reads as a poignant attempt to render herself real—to use the symbolic in her journal to create the only kind of physical existence that was *safe*. Life in the Secret Annex involved what Foucault (1978) terms a "Cycle of Prohibition" of sex, sexuality, and bodily appetites, a cycle that leads to the figurative silencing of the body and sexual desire. Disturbingly, Foucault's description of this cycle can also be read as an actual, accurate description of the circumstances Anne faced in hiding: "Thou shalt not go near, thou shalt not touch, thou shalt not consume, thou shalt not experience pleasure, thou shalt not speak, thou shalt not show thyself; ultimately thou shalt not exist except in darkness and secrecy. . . . Renounce yourself or suffer the penalty of being suppressed; do not appear if you do not want to disappear. Your existence will be maintained only at the cost of your nullification" (1989, 84). Anne and the others in hiding could not go near their covered windows, could only eat food that was provided for them by caretakers, spoke only in whispers for the better part of two years, could not go outside, could not live except in literal darkness and secrecy. They renounced their names and identities in the outside world and became nonexistent in order to maintain their lives.

The journals are full of references to this literal silencing, references which demand a renunciation of all five senses and illustrate the terrible reality that was the Franks', the Van Pelses', and Pfeffer's existence. On the day they went into hiding, they quickly put up the curtains that covered the windows at all times. At night, when it might have been possible for a member of the Secret Annex to look out on the street from a darkened window, Allied air raids required the use of black-out strips in all the windows to prohibit any light from escaping. Not only could Anne not be seen but she could not see. Her journal mentions evening as a favorite time, for at twilight she could peer through the cracks in the curtains at the street before the black-out covers were put up. In this sight-reduced world, she also becomes fond of going to the attic, where she can stare out the skylight—her only unencumbered view of the outside world.

In addition to this prohibition on seeing and being seen was an absolutely essential silencing of their voices for fear of being detected. The hiding place was located directly above Mr. Frank's place of business, and although several of their most loyal caretakers worked there and saw the hiding families on a daily basis, many of the people in the warehouse below did not know there were people in hiding above them. During the evening, after the work day—and also, ironically, during the loud noise of a bombing raid—there was some freedom to talk loudly and move about, but during the day, quiet voices and movement were not only expected but imperative. On several occasions, Anne and her family had to sit absolutely still on chairs for several hours, when people were working directly beneath them. Anne talks about how this requisite quiet characterizes her whole existence on December 22, 1942, when she writes: "Just as if I didn't hear enough sh-sh during the day, for making 'too much' noise, my gentleman bedroom companion [Pfeffer] now repeatedly calls out sh to me at night, too. According to him, I am not even allowed to turn over" (b, 329–30). The silence oppresses Anne even at night, when she struggles to sleep on a bed that is too short for her and has been lengthened by chairs on which she rests her head.

The bodily sensations of smell and taste were also oppressed in the Secret Annex. Otto Frank was a spice merchant, and sometimes the dust generated from spices being ground would make life above the machinery unbearable: "We either can't breathe or else we keep sneezing and coughing, there is so much pepper being ground in the mills" (b, 339). Similarly, in spite of the best efforts of their helpers, the families' appetites were also restricted. On April 3, 1944, Anne writes:

> In the twenty-one months that we have spent here we have been through a good many "food cycles." . . . When I talk of "food cycles" I mean periods in which one has nothing else to eat but one particular dish or kind of vegetable. We had nothing but endive for a long time, day in, day out, endive with sand, endive without sand, stew with endive, boiled or *en casserole*; then it was spinach, and after that followed kohlrabi, salsify, cucumbers, tomatoes, sauerkraut, etc., etc.
>
> For instance, it's really disagreeable to eat a lot of sauerkraut for lunch and supper every day, but you do it if you're hungry. (584)

Hence, the bodily based desire for a variety of foods, or often just for food, was also silenced, since the inhabitants of the Secret Annex had no control over what or when they ate.

Worse was the prohibition against any kind of movement or physical feeling which Anne explains in her journals. On any given day she could not walk farther than a few dozen feet in any direction: the limited quarters restricted where and when she could move and what she could do with her body. Early on, she tried to do calisthenics, but had problems with her arms and legs coming out of joint, so she stopped. The fear of reprisals that policed such essential body sensations as movement extended to even more basic body functions such as defecating. The diary records many times when the WC was broken, or when visitors downstairs prevented its use, and even two occasions when fear of burglars in the lower levels of the building at night forced all members of the annex to hold their bladders and bowels while shivering in the attic for fear of being discovered.

But even more intense for Anne was the enforced lack of companionship. She writes of wanting to be held and touched, but her reality dictated that there was no one with whom she could pursue such a normal teenage relationship. Toward the end of the diary, when she and Peter Van Pels become confidants, their parents closely monitor the teenagers' physical contact. Ultimately, the conditions within the Secret Annex deny Anne all access to her physical body. To survive, she must deny all physical sensations, or as Foucault explains, "repression" of a feeling through "an injunction to silence" eventually becomes "an affirmation of [its] nonexistence" (4). In this Nazi-enforced sensory deprivation chamber, either all needs are denied Anne and the families or, in order to survive, they must deny those needs themselves. Additionally, Anne feels the guilt of a survivor for the few physical experiences she still has access to. After dreaming about a friend named Hanneli, Anne writes: "I saw her in front of me, clothed in rags, her face thin and worn. Her eyes were very big and she looked so sadly and reproachfully at me that I could read in her eyes: 'Oh Anne, why have you deserted me? Help, oh, help me, rescue me from this hell!'. . . I am not more virtuous than she; she, too, wanted what was right, why should I be chosen to live and she probably to die?" (b, 422). Not only are basic needs denied to Anne, but she is required to further deny her own physical sensations in order to live. She feels guilt for the slim bit of life that is allowed to her, for her bodily curiosity, and for the few moments of physical pleasure that she has left.

It is into this absolute and unequivocal denial of the body that Anne's sexual writings enter, providing a way for her to embrace and own her physical self and in some sense ensure her survival. In a situation where she must "renounce" herself, "not appear if [she does] not want to disappear," and exist "only at the cost of [her] nullification," the sexual passages carve out a small place of agency and bodily ownership for her, where some existence is possible without the price of total nullification. While resisting confessional disclosure and warding off the voyeuristic or intruding reader's judgment, Anne creates a safe body for herself: this creative process includes images, descriptions of bodily functions, and then a combination of the two, where she works with words to create her own images of a body—her body—for herself.

Resisting Silence and Rendering the Body Real

Anne's inclusions of photographs of herself throughout the journal begins to illustrate how she uses images to create some kind of bodily ownership. Although all of the photos were taken before the families went into hiding, and Anne is explicit that they are not entirely accurate representations of her at the moment she inserts them into her text, her repeated practice of including these photographs becomes a symbol of the kind of mirror the journal represents to her. She can look into the diary's pages and have herself (and her own development) reflected back, through both words and visual images. The journal becomes the mirror the outside world can no longer provide; it is a mirror she owns and controls. The power of this idea becomes all the more compelling when connected with her practice of cataloging her physical attributes from time to time (often in connection with inserting a photo)—"dimples in cheeks . . .

dimple in chin . . . white skin . . . straight nose"—that read as a poignant attempt to reaffirm her physical characteristics (177).

An entry from January 6, 1944, further illustrates her quest to provide images of her own body and to understand images of women's bodies in general. She explains: "I go into ecstasies every time I see the naked figure of a woman, such as Venus in the Springer History of Art, for example. It strikes me sometimes as so wonderful and exquisite that I have difficulty not letting the tears roll down my cheeks." In the same entry she confides a desire to touch, to put her hands on these images, and know that they are real: "Sometimes, when I lie in bed at night, I have a terrible desire to feel my breasts and to listen to the quiet rhythmic beat of my heart." Then she adds: "I remember one night when I slept with Jacque I could not contain myself, I was so curious to see her body, which she had always kept hidden from me and which I had never seen. I asked Jacque whether as a proof of our friendship we might feel one another's breasts. Jacque refused. I also had a terrible desire to kiss Jacque and that I did" (443). In this expression of desire to touch another woman's body lies Anne's desire to find, touch, and mirror her own body. Although she may have been exploring feelings of attraction for Jacque, Anne's desire to better understand her own body is inherent in her desire to see Jacque's. Her longing to feel her own heart and life beating within her own chest is implicit in her wish to touch Jacque's breasts; and her longing to own her changing body is bound to her action of kissing Jacque and her tears at the sight of the exquisite Venus figure. The photos, lists of physical attributes, and her desire to touch another young woman's body all work like a mirror, reflecting back to Anne her existence and her undeniable corporeality in the face of an outward injunction to disappear.

Just as images provide Anne with a mirror, her descriptions of bodily functions articulate the day-to-day reality of her physical existence. There are many references to Anne's menstruation—both early entries that record her eagerness for it to begin and curiosity about how it will happen, and then later details of actual menstrual periods. In fact, Anne chronicles the entire process of beginning to menstruate. Early in her diary she writes: "I'm so longing to have it [a menstrual period] too, then at least I'd be grown up" (268) and "I shall probably be having my period soon. I noticed that because I keep having a kind of sticky seed in my panties" (287). After a year and a half in the Secret Annex she reflects, "Each time I have a period (and that has only been three times) I have the feeling that in spite of all the pain, unpleasantness and nastiness I have a sweet secret" (442).

On one level, these entries reveal normal adolescent curiosity and Anne's desire to narrate the process of her changing body. However, given the body-silencing ever-present in the Secret Annex, and the practical problems menstruating would cause because "sanitary towels" and other products were not available (287), Anne's writing about menstruation seems to be about much more than just chronicling the process of coming of age. Anne hints at reasons for menstruation's heightened importance when she writes, "I hadn't had a period for over 2 months, but it finally started again on Sunday. Still, in spite of all the unpleasantness and bother, I'm glad it hasn't failed me any longer" (627). To be "failed" by her period was to be failed by her body, and to fear it had begun to heed the injunction to disappear. In those moments when her body performs its most corporeal functions, which ignore the edict to silence, Anne feels alive. Since it is difficult to deny the existence of a bleeding, menstruating body, it becomes the very metaphor for existence and survival in her writing.

But it is Anne's work to make words describe her own body—to bring it out of secrecy and darkness and into the light—that best demonstrates her effort to create a body for herself within a discursive space that she strategically controls. This happens through the way she articulates her inner most feelings, including sexual desire, and also in the descriptions throughout the journal that chart both what she is learning about her body and her efforts to render it real. Most of the journal's entries about sexual desire center around her relationship with Peter Van Pels, and a few are about another boy, also named Peter, whom Anne knew before she went into hiding. Peter Van Pels was a few years older than Anne, and during the last year of hiding, they became friends and then eventually became physically attracted to one another. Anne chronicles her desire and longing for Peter and also many of their encounters.

On January 6, 1944, she writes: "Once, when we spoke about sex, Daddy told me I couldn't possibly understand the longing yet, I always knew that I did understand it and now I understand it fully" (451). Several weeks later she explains, "I long for my Petel [her friend before going into hiding], I long for every boy, even for Peter—here. I want to shout at him: 'Oh say something to me, don't just smile all the time, touch me, so that I can again get that delicious feeling inside me" (483). Soon Peter does touch her, and Anne specifically recounts the details of both her feelings and their actions:

> He held me firmly against him; my left breast lay against his chest; already *my* heart began to beat, but we had not finished yet.
>
> He didn't rest until my head was on his shoulder and his against it. When I sat up again after about five minutes, he soon took my head in his hands and laid it against him once more. Oh, it was so lovely, I couldn't talk much, the joy was too great; he stroked my cheek and arm a bit awkwardly, played with my curls and our heads lay touching most of the time. . . . How

I suddenly made the right move, I don't know, but before we went downstairs he kissed me, through my hair, half on my left cheek, half on my ear; I tore downstairs without looking round, and am simply longing for today. (607–8)

Just as images and bodily functions provide Anne evidence that she exists, so do her encounters with Peter. Anne's desire for affection, touch, and sensual pleasure is a normal human characteristic, but within the body-silencing context of the Secret Annex, her desire becomes loaded with added meaning. When Peter touches Anne, he responds to her feelings and desire, hence validating her emotions. At the same time, he also acknowledges and affirms the existence of her body. This validation is especially pertinent given Anne's circumstances. Life in the Secret Annex demands that Anne not feel, not respond to physical stimulation. She must muffle sneezes, swallow screams, and hold her bowels, but her body *can* respond to Peter's caress. Hence, Anne's writing about their intimate moments and her response to them reads as a statement of "I exist. My body can respond to something." This detailed portrayal of her experiences with Peter introduces the specific descriptions Anne writes of her own body.

Owning Her Body and Defying Confessional Realities

The passages in the journal most vulnerable to being read as *confession* are detailed descriptions of her anatomy—Anne's efforts to render herself explicitly and specifically real. Significantly, these descriptions are also of the parts of her body that seem to have defied the injunctions to silence and nonexistence. On October 10, 1942, after five months in hiding, when Anne is thirteen years old, she writes: "My vagina is getting wider all the time, but I could also be imagining it. When I'm on the w.c. I sometimes look then I can see quite definitely that the urine comes out of a little hole in the vagina, but above it there is something else, there is a hole in that too, but I don't know what for" (276). Living out her teenage years in hiding, Anne had relatively few sources of information. Diary accounts reveal that her mother was reticent to talk about sexual matters, and Anne was left to glean what she could from books, tidbits of adult conversation, memories of schoolgirl conversations before they went into hiding, and her own observation. Hence, the diary becomes a literal mirror that she can look into and read her own body, providing her information and answering the questions she probably wishes she could have asked someone else. In some ways this parallels the normal developmental process of adolescence, but Anne's circumstance of being silenced—both by not being allowed to use a body and then by having no one to talk to about it—make her demands on the journal as an intimate mirror and audience all the more poignant.

The following description of her own genitalia reads as Anne's effort to make her body figuratively and literally speak to her. Written on March 24, 1944, this powerful passage of body articulation reveals a young girl very much trying to discover and own her womanness and to let her body exist:

> From the front when you stand up you can see nothing but hair, between your legs there are things like little cushions, soft, with hair on too, which press together when you stand up so that you can't see what's inside. When you sit down they divide and inside it looks very red and ugly and fleshy. At the very top, between the big outer lips there is a little fold of skin which turns out to be a kind of little bladder on closer inspection, that is the clitoris. Then come the small inner lips, they are also pressed against each other just like a little pleat. When they open, there is a fleshy little stump inside, no bigger than the top of my thumb. The top of it is porous, there are different little holes in it and that's where the urine comes out. The lower part looks as if it's nothing but skin, but that is where the vagina is. There are little folds of skin all over the place, you can hardly find it. The little hole underneath is so terribly small that I simply can't imagine how a man can get in there, let alone how a whole baby can get out. The hole is so small you can't even put your index finger in, not easily anyway. That's all it is and yet it plays such an important role! (567)

Within the body-writing context Anne includes this passage, the last seven words ring with multiple meanings. Her vagina has an important role with regard to menstruation and childbirth, but within the Secret Annex, it also serves the role of keeping her connected to her body and normal life cycles through monthly menstrual periods. Within the context of the journal it is a physical attribute made concrete through language, symbolizing to Anne that she is real, that she exists.

Anne's struggle to write-herself-real corresponds to the French feminist conception of writing-the-body. As the following examples will show, Anne was obsessed with words, with finding the right words—or the best possible words—to document her female bodily experience. Anne illustrates her frustration with not being able to find words in an entry where she and Peter talk about anatomy, using Boche, the warehouse cat, as a model. They argue about the German word *geschlechtsteile* and the Dutch word *geslachtsdeel*, both of which mean "genitals," trying to find more specific words for what they see. Anne finally asks, "How are you meant to know these words, most of the time you come across them by accident?" (467) This question holds her anger at not having access to words, an impediment that seems all the more severe in a reality where all she has are words.

Anne writes more about this difficult search for words when she explains that her mother will not tell her what her clitoris is for (566)—she has learned the word and wants to know its meaning—and when she complains that a particular text has illustrations of male sex organs because they are on the outside of the body, but fails to illustrate inner female organs, leaving the female figure both imageless and nameless or wordless (613). If the only way Anne can have a body is to write it, the limitations and entrapments of discourse become all the more obvious and problematic: she struggles to write a female body and life for herself against a linguistic reality that threatens to silence, and a confessional reality that threatens to entrap, her body.

Luce Irigaray (1991) has provided a theoretical framework through which to read this body-writing. Irigaray and other French feminist theorists explain that in a socially constructed reality where language is male-centered, created from man's phallogocentric connection to the word, a female construct of language and the world can only be created by women giving voice to their bodies:

> We must give her [woman] the right to pleasure, to *jouissance*, to passion, restore her right to speech, and sometimes to cries or anger. . . . We have to discover a language [*langage*] which does not replace the bodily encounter, as paternal language [*langue*] attempts to do, but which can go along with it, words which do not bar the corporeal, but which speak corporeal. . . .
>
> It is therefore desirable, for us, to speak within the amorous exchange. It is also good to speak while feeding a child. . . . It is also important to speak while caressing another body. Silence is all the more alive in that speech exists. (43–44)

By simultaneously challenging body silencing and confessional realities, Anne writes to render herself real, every time she expresses desire and gives expression to her sexual body. Each time Anne challenges the body-silencing of the Secret Annex with a passage about her body, while simultaneously refusing confessional disclosure, she also challenges the silence of female corporeal experience already implicit in language, while guarding her writing from the gaze of the censoring reader. Every time she writes about her body, bringing its needs, rhythms, and descriptions into her text, she is not only defying the call to silence and nullification in her actual world, but she is challenging the lack of a female corporeal language in her linguistic world as well. Her challenge of confessional realities becomes loaded as a way for Anne to preserve her life in a dangerous situation and as a creative link between a woman's word and the world of her body: Anne uses words to carve out survival not just for herself but for herself *as a woman*. These efforts to bring her female body into existence pressure every sexual passage to contain the experience of being female. The resistance against traditional confession is echoed in her struggle to make male-centered language enfold or signify her existence as a woman.

Finally, the connection between Anne Frank's work with language to write-her-body-real and *écriture féminine* begins to answer the specific criticisms that Michel Foucault lodged at the sexual confession earlier in this essay. Within Anne's journal, the power dynamics he claims divest speakers of authority are called into question: Anne is not concerned with pleasing or receiving approval from any outside audience. Instead, she is wrestling with words to make them enfold her experience of being a woman. This perceived lack of outside arbiter frees her to speak the unspeakable without fear of what might happen. Constructed as speaker and her own primary audience, she is the only person who must understand her text and feel empowered by it, and if this requires a movement away from male-centered norms of language and appropriate subject matter, she needs only answer to herself. In this way, the pursuit of "truth" Foucault is so quick to fault is replaced by the pursuit of the word, a kind of bodily based self-knowledge inscribed sometimes in detailed physical descriptions of the body, and sometimes in the resonant life experience of a single word, her signature "Anne" at the end of each diary entry. In her body-writing and work to find the right words, Anne resists literal, psychological, and linguistic edicts to silence, while simultaneously resisting confessional and linguistic traps that threaten to nullify her voice and existence.

Specific entries from Anne's journal illustrate the political awareness of her writing. The most telling of these are her references to anti-Semitism and sexism. This relationship between a woman's voice, her body, and politics is articulated in a passage in which Anne rebels against a history that treats "women as inferior to men": "Women suffer more pain, more illness and more misery than any war hero just from giving birth to children" (678). Her inclusion of "giving birth to children" illustrates the political potential of Anne's sexual writing. Connecting her detailed description of her vagina with its "important role" enables her to learn private as well as political realities about herself as a woman. Tied to her personal concern about "how a man can get in there, let alone how a whole baby can get out" is a larger political question about women as child-bearers and the respect Anne's own bodily experience tells her the act of giving birth to a child must merit.

Ironically, it is only Anne's tragic death that gave the world the gift of her most private, intimate writing. The message of this writing is dual: even as the personal and political body-articulation of the diary gives meaning to Anne's brutal death, it also shows the power of connected body-writing, suggesting altogether new, different, and inherently female ways of confronting confessional realities, and hinting at the bodily based training ground every strong-speaking woman must cover.

Postscript

As the winter of 1945 came to an end, a typhus epidemic swept through Bergen-Belsen, killing thousands of prisoners who were already severely weakened by hunger and exposure. Anne and Margot Frank were among those who died. In a painful reversal on the kind of meticulous attention to detail that marked Anne's living, the Dutch Red Cross was only able to estimate March 31 as the day of her death; other indications suggest that she may have died as much as two weeks earlier. The survival of Anne's diary can never compensate for the loss of her life, but the power of her bodily connected voice continues to resist the edict to silence, the injunction to disappear.

Notes

1. All quotes from Anne's diary refer to the original, unedited diary, labeled version *a* by the editors of *The Critical Edition*. Because some of the *a* manuscript was lost, several quotes are taken from version *b*— Anne's own revision. In these four instances, the *b* quotes are identified as such prior to the page number in parentheses after the quote.

2. In 1995, Doubleday issued another version of Anne Frank's diary, *Diary of a Young Girl: The Definitive Edition*, edited by Otto H. Frank and Mirjam Pressler. Marketed as an edition for readers rather than scholars, this version does not contain all of Anne's manuscript diary. It does, however, infuse the 1952 version of *Diary of a Young Girl* with new passages from Anne's diary brought to light by *The Critical Edition*.

3. For a general discussion of women's journals and confinement, see Franklin 1986, xix–xx.

4. Anne's own pseudonyms for these people are used in *Diary of a Young Girl*: Van Pels becomes "Van Daan" and Pfeffer's name is changed to "Dussel."

5. For a thorough discussion of the complexity of the term *speaking subject*, see Felski 1989, 51–85.

6. It is impossible to know what Anne would have chosen to do with the two versions of her diary had she survived the war. This study bases its analysis on the intentions suggested by the nature of Anne's existing revision. For a full discussion of Anne's revision, see Van Der Stroom 1989, 59–77.

2

Sexuality and Textuality Entwined: Sexual Proclamations in Women's Confessional Fiction in Québec

Lori Saint-Martin

While Anne Frank's desire for a safe space reflects her extraordinary situation, this desire is a predominant drive in women's sexual self-representations. Focusing on explicitly erotic writing in Québec, Lori Saint-Martin describes a continuum that ranges from "pulp" to esoteric literature, from heterosexual to lesbian eroticism, from confrontational to utopian perspectives on sexuality. Deliberately racy, savvy, provocative, and seductive, the erotic texts examined encourage voyeurism, but not to confirm the reader in expectations of a confessional truth: they lead the confessional reader into a labyrinth of confusion by blurring confessional boundaries through fictional strategies. In a traditionally Catholic and patriarchal framework, fictional distancing devices create a safe space for women to reclaim and proclaim their sexualities.

What is a woman's sexual confession? The question—like Freud's infamous "What does a woman want?"—can be heard in many ways. Most of the concerns it raises involve boundaries, whether generic or social. What formal and thematic features define the genre? How does confession differ from canonical autobiography on the one hand and fiction on the other? How have women internalized or defied taboos against their sexually explicit writing? And, in a deeper sense: what (and why) does a woman have to confess? What is it about her sexuality that links it almost inevitably to confession and, by implication, to shame?

The realm of the personal and sexual has always been literary for men (Saint Augustine, Rousseau, Michel Leiris, Henry Miller) and confessional for women (Colette, Erica Jong, Anaïs Nin editing out the references to sex in her *Journal*). Women attempting to write honestly about their sexuality, as they have begun to do only fairly recently, have had a difficult time of it. Despite patterns developed (not without struggle) by male writers, there has been no space and no language for women to write about sexuality. Even today, it remains more problematic for a woman to explore these issues than for a man, if only because readers tend to assume that the sexual experiences she describes necessarily happened to her.

In Québec, there are very few sexual confessions in the truest sense: a female subject writing a nonfiction work about her own sexuality and her emergence as a subject (Felski 1989, 113). Felski points out that there is a "strong Protestant element in the feminist preoccupation with subjectivity as truth," which may explain why the feminist confession is extremely popular in the United States and Germany but relatively rare in the Catholic and rhetorically conscious French tradition. The Québec tradition is similar to the French, which would explain why the longing for *truth* is less acute in Québec women's writing, why there is more playfulness, more blurring of generic boundaries, and less anxiety in their work. Women's writing about sexuality in Québec tends to emphasize the literary aspects of the body and of desire, their embodiment through writing, and the fact that without the act of writing, women's sexuality could not be known, shared with other women, socially and culturally inscribed. In the works I will be studying, I will explore how sexuality and textuality are inseparably entwined.

Contemporary Québec women's fiction raises some of the important issues linked to women's sexual confessions: the nature of confession, the links between women's sexuality and the confessional genre, the problems confronting women writing on sexuality. For readers unfamiliar with Québec, I will begin by briefly describing the social and cultural background. Subsequently, I will be claiming that the use of fiction—undercut by an implicit truth-claim in ways that will become clear—has made it possible for some women to explore their sexuality in the Québec context of a traditionally conservative and Catholic society. In other words, a hybrid genre has taken shape here: we might call it confessional fiction. It simultaneously invites a *literal* reading based on the name of the author (along lines described in Lejeune's concept of the "autobiographical contract" [1975]) and points to the self-consciously *fictional* nature of the work. This hybrid genre provides a *safe space* for women to explore their sexuality while both enabling and disrupting a reading of the text as autobiography (which could undermine the writer's claims to serious literary status). In this complex play on reality and fiction, the author is and is not the narrator-heroine; generic boundaries are both challenged and confirmed.

Three women writers' autobiographical stances have captured my attention. Anyone familiar with Québec writing will see my choice as iconoclastic: Nicole Brossard is the best known, most highly respected, and perhaps the most hermetic of Québec feminist writers and has consistently claimed she has no interest in writing about her own life; Anne Dandurand is a youngish writer of novels and short fiction that are often full of sex and violence and feature protagonists very like the writer herself; Lili Gulliver's erotic novels are closer to pulp than to literature. Such a choice is more or less the equivalent of studying Mary Daly, Erica Jong, and Danielle Steel in the same article. I am taking the risk because, in all three cases, I see comparable rhetorical strategies at work in order to both deploy and guard against confession.

Despite major differences I will return to later, these three authors have chosen similar stances. "Lili Gulliver" uses a pseudonym and writes a fictional autobiography. Anne Dandurand's 1990 *Un coeur qui craque* (literally, a heart that cracks) is described as a *journal imaginaire* (an imaginary diary).[1] In spite of her reluctance to see her work as autobiographical, Nicole Brossard's experimental writing does reveal a clear portrait of a lesbian feminist writer very much like Brossard herself. I will be reading these works as epitomizing the relationship between the "real" and the fictional confession, raising important questions about the genre itself and its conservative or radical aspects. Why do women writers today use some variation on the confessional mode? When they do so, do they play into the hands of those who hold a stereotypical view of all women's writing as "simply" autobiographical, or do they call that view into question by problematizing the very boundaries between life and fiction?

Women's Confessional Fiction in Québec

Until the 1960s, Québec society was a conservative one, particularly where women were concerned. Catholicism was the majority religion whose values permeated Québec society as a whole; the Roman Catholic Church also exercised control of key social sectors, including hospitals and education (nuns and priests were not massively replaced by lay personnel in those two areas until the 1960s). Married women were expected to bear a child almost yearly (while single women who became pregnant were submitted to severe social sanctions); even women who were warned by their doctors that another pregnancy might be fatal were advised by priests and advice columnists to fulfill their wifely duties and trust in the goodness of God. Nationalism and religion spoke as one on this issue; since the conquest of New France and the 1763 treaty handing over the colony to England, Francophone Catholics have seen their very existence as endangered. Women were essential to "la revanche des berceaux" (revenge by the cradle); large families were seen as a way of resisting assimilation by "les Anglais" (whether English-Canadian, British, or American). Despite the emphasis on reproductive sexuality—or perhaps because of it—sexual pleasure was, of course, taboo (the poet Hector de Saint-Denys-Garneau wrote that he wished his body ended at the waist), and sexual discourse even more so.

This, then, is the background out of which Québec women began writing. The 1970s saw the rise of feminist writing aimed specifically at creating a female language, ways of inscribing femininity in the text (Dupré, 1989; Gould, 1990). In some cases, the speaking subject inscribes lesbian sexuality, as Nicole Brossard has done since the 1970s. In the late 1980s and early 1990s, a number of women, including Lili Gulliver and Anne Dandurand, began writing specifically erotic, generally heterosexual texts. The works I will be studying have both a great deal in common with, and sharp variations from, the confessional mode of feminist writing as described by Rita Felski. To clarify the differences, I use the term *confessional fiction*. Again, this hybrid term points to the quite deliberate rhetorical play on reality and fiction that marks new women's writing from Québec. Felski's definition is a pragmatic one: "a type of autobiographical writing which signals its intentions to foreground the most personal and intimate details of the author's life" (1989, 87).[2] What I call confessional fiction is fiction which foregrounds the most personal and intimate details of the *female narrator's* life—a change which makes a world of difference. These fictional autobiographies create a distance between author and narrator; given taboos about expression of women's sexuality, that distance inscribes a kind of safe space that both protects the writer against a reductive autobiographical reading and allows her to go further under the cover of fiction than she could do without that cover.

At first glance, the term *confessional fiction* seems contradictory; we are too used to the idea of "true confessions," that is, a fairly straightforward, unproblematic relationship between the narrator-author, the text, and the female experience the text describes. The confessions Felski analyzes are particularly concerned with truth, sincerity, the exemplarity of their author's life as an embodiment of women's experience, and the unproblematic existence of some sort of direct access to the authentic self-expression of an authorial subject (97). But of course, "true confessions," to the extent that they are written down, immediately become fictions; there is no direct, unmediated access to personal reality or to the past. In fact, the expression "true confessions" is either a redundancy or a logical impossibility, depending on one's point of view. Confessional fiction merely plays explicitly and self-consciously on the shifting boundary between reality and fiction that "pure" confession struggles to present as unproblematic.

The term *confessional fiction* points to the double nature of this writing, both intimate and rhetorically sophisticated. Like the texts Felski describes, Québec confessional fiction deals with "the most intimate and often traumatic details" of a woman's life (88)—although that woman is narrator-character rather than author—and, in some cases, such fiction draws political conclusions from personal experience. All three writers created some form of implied female reader(s), even a female reading community rhetorically encoded in the text (99). Another obvious parallel is the use of the first-person narrative to present intimate personal experience. A story told in the third person—whether autobiography or fiction—could never be seen as a confession: the female writing "I" (and the female eye) are essential here. These are narratives of sexuality, love, and writing, writing being the key element (I will return to this point).

Despite similarities, however, the fictional element of confessional fiction means major differences between these works and Felski's model. Québec confessional fiction does not downplay the formal specificity of textual communication in order to emphasize its "referential and denotative dimension," as feminist confessions tend to do (88), or avoid literary language in order to foster intimacy between author and reader (101). On the contrary, it is self-consciously literary, closer to the formal characteristics of literary autobiographies (Simone de Beauvoir, Lillian Hellman, Nathalie Sarraute, Christa Wolf, etc.). It often deploys the irony, indeterminacy, and linguistic play that feminist confessions tend to avoid (100).[3] I would argue that these self-consciously literary elements do not block reader identification but situate it on another level, on the level of *writing* rather than on the level of *experience*. Rather than simply increasing distance between author and reader, they create a literary space where women's sexuality and women's experience can be inscribed. In the place of a simple truth claim, we have a work of fiction clearly identified as such, but presented as an autobiography *at the same time*. Of course, this kind of play is not unique to Québec; it must be read in the context of the trend, common to much current fiction of many nationalities, toward a blurring of the distinction between fiction and autobiography. Secondly, within the Québec context, it may also be linked to the movement toward "écriture au féminin" (i.e., self-consciously gender-marked women's writing), as in the case of Nicole Brossard. Even women writers who do not practice this type of writing have often been deeply influenced by it.[4] When these women write about sexuality, indeterminacy and playfulness are also part of a defensive formal strategy, a way of putting some distance between writer and character without surrendering the enormous political and rhetorical power of the truth claim.

As a hybrid genre, confessional fiction becomes a way of writing about a dangerous subject while protecting oneself as a woman and as a writer.[5] Major traits of confessional fiction are thus to be found on the level both of content (the intimate adventures of a female subject addressing herself to a female reading community) and of rhetoric (playfulness, self-consciousness, indeterminacy). Despite their similarities, the three authors I focus on here are highly individual. I will be discussing each in turn to show both similarities and differences in their respective rhetorical stances and levels of political awareness.

Lili Gulliver: "Fictional, Alas!"

Lili Gulliver's erotic writing has sold well in Québec despite harsh reviews. From a literary standpoint, her work has little merit;[6] it is poorly written, awash in dreadful puns—more puns than sex—and quite antierotic. She writes, for example, that after a session of group masturbation, there was "sperm everywhere, enough for a plain yogurt footbath" (plein de sperme partout, de quoi prendre un bain de pieds au yogourt nature [Gulliver 1990, 81]).[7] What is interesting about her work, though, is the self-conscious way it plays on the fine line between reality and fiction, autobiography and novel, creating a safe discursive space for articulating female desire.

Like the author of *Histoire d'O*, the creator of *l'Univers Gulliver* chose a pseudonym; unlike "Pauline Réage," however, she has revealed her real name (Diane Boissonneault) and appeared in the media. But within the space of the novel, Lili Gulliver is both author and subject. It is as if "O" were also the author of *Histoire d'O*. Gulliver constantly plays reality and fiction against each other. Like a work of nonfiction, her novel begins with acknowledgments to all the friends who helped her along the way. But their names are playful ones: Jo Ravioli, Kosta Feta, Bruno Meringue, Dieter Frankfurt, Mark Goodcooking, Trévor Butter (7). Their status is somewhere between reality and fiction: their names mark them as fictional, yet, like people in real-life acknowledgments, they play no role in the novel. In addition, the novel begins with a preface and ends with a conclusion by real people claiming to have met Lily Gulliver; the author of the afterword, Dany Laferrière (who wrote the controversial *Comment faire l'amour avec un Nègre sans se fatiguer*), also appears in the novel, flirting with one of Lili's friends in a bar.

This play with reality is further complicated by an ingenious reworking of the generic boundary: "This is a novel, any resemblance to reality is purely fictional, alas!" (Ceci est un roman, toute ressemblance avec la réalité est purement fictive, hélas! [11]). The truth claim implicit in the fact that Lili Gulliver is both author and first-person narrator is explicitly denied here, turned inside out: this is not an autobiography, as Lejeune's autobiographical contract would have it,[8] but a novel. The conventional disclaimer about any resemblance to reality being purely coincidental becomes a playful contrast between reality and fiction. The wish-fulfillment of the last word (the regretful sigh of "alas!") adds a final twist, as the neutral disclaimer is personalized. *L'Univers Gulliver* thus stands both as an autobiography, because author and protagonist are one and the same, and as a novel, because of the disclaimer. Before the novel even begins, the generic distinction is ingeniously problematized.

Lili Gulliver has placed herself in the curious discursive position of writing a true novel about herself. What is more, the novel is so delightful she only wishes it could "really" be true ("alas"). This kind of playful questioning of the line between reality and fiction is typical of women's writing about sexuality in Québec.[9] Again, it is part of a discursive strategy that permits the writer to both protect herself and put herself forward, advancing under the cover of fiction. Similarly, in interviews, Diane Boissonneault has said that Lili is a heroine and a model for her: "There's something reckless about her I like very much. I try to be as much like her as I can" (Il y a chez elle quelque chose d'irréfléchi qui me plaît beaucoup. J'essaie le plus possible de lui ressembler [Germain 1991, 90]). This is an interesting approach to the relationship between fiction and reality: instead of fiction resembling life, life strives to re-create itself along fictional lines.

What is disappointing is how little Lili Gulliver does with the clever framework she sets up (we will see how Anne Dandurand uses hers to much better effect).[10] Despite her claims to outrageousness (she plans to travel around the world—hence her surname—and write a guide to lovers from different countries, like a restaurant guide with cocks instead of stars), Lili is quite traditional. She feels betrayed when her first Parisian lover tells her afterwards that he is married (40). When another lover asks her to be faithful to him, she is thrilled: "This sudden possessiveness makes me shiver with pleasure" (Cet accès de propriété m'arrache un frisson de plaisir [69]). She is a tease and a closet romantic. When she is offered the chance to live out her ultimate sexual fantasy, she cannot think of anything:

> "Well then, what turns you on?"
> "Good question! I don't really know. The missionary position in a soft bed with a super affectionate lover? No! That's not a fantasy, it's common."

> 'Bien dis donc, c'est quoi ton truc?' Bonne question! Je ne sais pas trop. La position du missionnaire dans un bon lit avec un amant super affectueux? Mais non! C'est pas du fantasme, c'est commun (79).

She never does answer the question.[11] Rather, as the text explicitly recognizes, *L'univers Gulliver* is like a traditional Harlequin romance with a bit of sex added. The only idea the novel defends (women should be able to choose their sexual partners freely) is hardly new or radical; it merely echoes Erica Jong's famous "zipless fuck." Relationships between men and women have not changed much. Lili and her friends agree that the ideal man should make one feel like a princess (101); he should be tender, passionate, and faithful, slim and athletic, willing to foot the bill in expensive restaurants yet also do half the housework (28). Certainly a woman who states complacently that men "are never more than grown-up children" (les hommes ne sont jamais que de grands gamins [92]) yet is fascinated by their power, recalling "his smile, his eyes shining with a dangerous little spark, his charisma or his Machiavellian magnetism" (son sourire, ses yeux brillant d'une redoutable petite étincelle, son charisme ou son magnétisme machiavélique [94]),[12] has little ambition to revolutionize sexual politics and no desire to think through her own contradictions and desires. In Paris, Lili is surrounded by more indiscriminate females who make her look moderate by comparison. And her closet romanticism—"as if my clit were hooked up to my heart" ([comme si j'avais le clito branché sur le coeur [81])—reiterates a stereotype of receptive female sexuality while encouraging female readers to identify with her.

Playing less on sexual fantasies than on dreams of intimacy and romance, the Harlequin-type references are calculated to appeal to a broad base of women readers. Despite promises, there is little here of a woman's authentic sexual desire. What drives the novel is a fantasy of female power through manipulation of male sexual desire.[13] Lili sometimes goes to orgies just to watch and enjoys awakening men's desire only to turn away from it. The cover illustration is revealing: it shows a sidewalk café in Paris where all the customers and all the passers-by are men. In the centre, a single voluptuous female figure in a halter top and a tight miniskirt is the focus of all their gazes. What a fantasy. Each woman is unique and all men desire her, long for her and her alone. As the father once loved his daughter, perhaps (Coward 1984, 196).

How then does *L'univers Gulliver* relate to women's *feminist* confessions? Despite rivalry with some women, Lili's text does explicitly enact within the text a community of female readers. Here, the female reading community is not only addressed but actually portrayed within the novel. Lili has four female friends—Coucoune, Mari-loup, Miss Miou, and Lolo reine (Queen Lolo)—with whom she corresponds during her travels. They all see her as a kind of spiritual leader, and their stories of their affairs, told through letters included in the novel, complete and interact with hers. So within the text, both a female interpretative community (the novel we are reading is the sum of the stories Lili sent to her friends) and a female writing community have been inscribed. In addition, Lili's friends enact a reading and interpretation of her letters, reciting them out loud and trying unsuccessfully to imitate her voice (83). Rather than raising political

or social issues or challenging accepted forms of writing, Lili Gulliver relies on female friendship both to complete her work and to confirm her
status as the unique voice, the queen of sex and story.

Even in this relatively innocuous and nonliterary work, then, the female narrator insists on the inscription of desire *in writing*, particularly
through written exchanges between herself and her female friends. There
is a rather funny scene where Lili meets with potential publishers of her
"Guide Gulliver" and leaves them salivating with desire both for her and
for her words. Even here, women's sexuality is an effect of discourse.

Anne Dandurand: An "Imaginary Diary"

Un coeur qui craque is a short novel with a rather sensationalist title in
the confessional mode. It is an open-ended, day-to-day journal form written in the present tense to reinforce the link to lived experience. Yet it also
makes extensive use of self-consciously literary devices. Where Lili Gulliver
relied on her double status as (real) author and (fictional) character, Anne
Dandurand creates a double literary form, both referring to lived experience and calling it into question. The result is a complex play that blurs
the distinction between truth and invention, confession and fiction.

Its narrator closely resembles the author (or at least her public persona).
Like Anne Dandurand, she is in her late thirties, a former actress who currently ekes out a living by writing; she writes with fingerless gloves on because she is on welfare and can't afford to heat her apartment; she smokes
constantly, cries when she watches the TV news, wears extravagant cos-
tumes, has a dozen boxes filled with illegible manuscripts she can't bear to
part with, etc.

To people in the know, hers is clearly a roman à clefs. At least two Québec
men of letters have published disclaimers. One, a journalist named Jean
Barbe (*barbe* means "beard" in French) has given the "true" version of events
transposed in the novel:

> Now take the young journalist, Pierre-Marie Moustache
> (Moustache, really!), she allegedly met at a meeting of "Les
> fous du livre" (not true, it was "Les gens du livre"). It seems
> they shared a meal at a restaurant called l'Européen (not true,
> it was the Continental). And she imagines, in the course of one
> chapter, hot sex in the bathroom of a train bound for
> Ascheberg (Germany), during which she finally manages to
> take off his glasses, and then all the rest (all right, I do wear
> glasses, but I've never been to Germany).
>
> Ou cet autre, là le jeune journaliste appelé Pierre-Marie Mous-
> tache (Moustache, vraiment!), elle l'aurait rencontré à la réunion

des Fous du livre (c'est pas vrai, c'était les Gens du livre). Elle aurait partagé avec lui un repas au restaurant l'Européen (c'est pas vrai, c'était le Continental). Et elle imagine, l'espace d'un chapitre, une baise torride dans les toilettes d'un train à destination d'Ascheberg (Allemagne), baise au cours de laquelle elle réussit enfin à lui enlever ses lunettes, et tout le reste (d'accord, je porte des lunettes, mais je ne suis jamais allé en Allemagne). (Barbe 1991, 12)

Yet Dandurand insists that *Un coeur qui craque* is not autobiographical: "Except for the story of my cat, which is real, the rest is vastly exaggerated, and in any case my heroine is a liar" (sauf l'histoire de mon chat qui est réelle, le reste étant grossièrement exagéré, d'ailleurs mon héroïne est une menteuse [Roy 1990, 30]). "My heroine is a liar" (though some passages make me wish she were telling the truth): is this another variation on Lili Gulliver's "alas!" as a way of maintaining control of her fiction?

Dandurand is herself a paradoxical character. She insists she is a feminist and is bringing a female voice to erotic writing, yet she appeared nude for an interview on a popular TV show. ("There's nothing I wouldn't do to make my work better known," she later said.) The confusion is deliberate; I would suggest that the whole point of the novel is precisely the blurring of the fine line between autobiography and fiction. It is true, as Dandurand has pointed out, that women are always suspected of describing their own lives when they write erotica:

A woman who writes erotica is typecast as a tramp, whereas with a man, people don't automatically assume he has experienced everything he writes about. If I had realized that when I was starting out, I would have used a pseudonym. People make a lot of assumptions about me and it is very hard to live with.

Une femme qui écrit de la littérature érotique a l'image d'une salope, alors que pour un homme, on ne sous-entend pas automatiquement qu'il a vécu tout ce qu'il écrit. Si j'avais compris ça lorsque j'ai commencé, j'aurais pris un pseudonyme. On présume beaucoup de choses à mon égard et c'est lourd à porter. (Presse canadienne 1991)

On the other hand, Dandurand quite deliberately invites an autobiographical reading by multiplying parallels between herself and her character instead of creating someone very unlike herself. You can't have it both ways—or can you? The novel's subtitle, *Journal imaginaire*, suggests that you can. Dandurand has found an ingenious way of playing both sides against the middle. The diary form makes it possible to introduce the

concerns of daily life and the process of a changing self while commenting on current events. The word *imaginary* points up an attempt to avoid
the banality of a strict transcription of everyday life by adding fantastic
and fantasy elements and by playing with self-referentiality in various
ways I will discuss later. The very subgenre Dandurand uses confirms the
hybrid nature of confessional fiction and its literary and rhetorical power.

In interviews, Dandurand has discussed the passage from real to fictional diary:

> I have a diary near my bed, a diary I lug around with me when
> I travel, and another on disk, with short scattered passages in
> code. The diary on disk expands. Not only do I pour out my
> heart to it, but fiction starts to mingle in. . . . There are frag-
> ments of poems. . . . It's soppy, ridiculous. . . . But it does me
> good. So I look at it all, what is fictional and what is real, I
> wonder what I could "fictionalize" further, what I could write
> to get myself excited about my own reality. What I could do
> to transform my basically boring reality.

> Moi j'ai un journal, près de mon lit, un journal que je traîne
> avec moi en voyage, et un autre, sur disquette, constitué de
> petits bouts disséminés, codés. Le journal sur disquette s'étend.
> Non seulement j'y vide mon coeur, mais la fiction commence
> à s'y mêler. . . . Il y a des petits bouts de poèmes. . . . C'est
> tata, dérisoire. . . . Mais ça fait du bien. Alors je regarde tout
> ça, ce qui est réel et ce qui est fictif, je me demande ce que je
> pourrais 'fictionnaliser' encore, ce que je pourrais écrire pour
> me faire tripper sur ma propre réalité. Ce que je pourrais faire
> pour métamorphoser un réel somme toute assez ennuyant.
> (Barbe 1991, 12)

This passage is worth a closer look. The real diary on paper, with its emphasis on the body ("near the bed"), coexists with a second "real" diary
which is already slipping toward fiction ("in code"). Gradually the "code"
diary expands in size and becomes the more important one. Writing as
therapy ("I pour out my heart"; "it does me good") moves gradually toward writing as rewriting reality, magnifying it while still remaining
embroiled (or entwined) in it ("to get myself excited about my own reality"). Personal experience is heightened (although not erased) by adding
new elements ("fictionalizing") and by experimenting with language. Although Dandurand does not say so, presumably irony replaces "soppi-
ness." As in confession, the primary concern is with the self and its development; but here, fictionalizing adds aesthetic distance. Interestingly
enough, the narrator of *Un coeur qui craque* follows exactly the same pro-

cedure: "Where is my truth? In the illegible and whining scrawl of my private journal from which, a few times a year, the aromatic sapphire of a short phrase emerges? Or here, in the patient labour of stringing together tiny word pearls? Does my truth need to choose between sapphires and pearls?" (Où est ma vérité: dans le gribouillis illisible et plaignard de mon journal intime, d'où émerge quelques fois par année l'odorant saphir d'une courte phrase? Ou ici, où je besogne patiemment à enfiler les minuscules perles de mots? Ma vérité a-t-elle besoin de choisir entre les saphirs et les perles? [Dandurand 1990, 16]).[14] For both author and narrator, confessional fiction transforms real life while remaining explicitly anchored in it (there is no need to choose between sapphires and pearls). Again, one of the major differences here is in tone: the diary "whines," whereas the novel is wry, ironic, comical, passionate but detached. Dandurand certainly avoids the stereotype of confessional writing as "lachrymose and self-indulgent" (Felski 1989, 118).

Various literary devices highlight the fictional nature of the diary, disrupting the autobiographical reading that the text simultaneously invites us to perform. The narrator refers to her friends both as real people and as her characters (75).[15] Her cat is called "Chapter Two." Unlike the straightforward diary Felski describes, Dandurand's is not a pure one. It includes fantasies, flashbacks, dreams, and constant references to itself as a literary artefact: "Still in my dream, I fell asleep with the guy from page 10" (toujours dans mon rêve, je m'endormais avec le garçon de la page 10 [31]). In addition, the narrator plays on the inevitable gap between real time and fictional time: "All you do is turn a page, and the universe, including my skinny little self, has grown three weeks older, oh the magic of literature" (Vous n'avez que tourné une page, et l'univers, y compris ma personne maigrichonne, a vieilli de trois semaines, ô magie de la littérature [41]). The bulk of the diary covers about a year; in a rather startling formal break with the rest, the final entry, written six years later, sums up the events of the interim period interspersed with extensive bracketed passages in the writing present.[16] At one point, the narrator writes: "I know [what's the matter]: I'm somewhere around page 100 of my manuscript, and anyone who writes will confirm that page 100 is a crest, to climb up to, or throw yourself off of, or smash against" (Je sais ce que j'ai: je suis aux alentours de la page 100, et tous ceux et celles qui écrivent vous le confirmeront, la page 100, c'est une arête, soit à grimper, soit à se jeter du haut de, soit à s'étouffer avec [108]).[17] The double nature of the "imaginary diary" is once again highlighted here: the narrator claims to be writing events down in the order in which they happen (as in a real diary), but acts at the same time as if she were creating a work of fiction (nobody counts the pages of a diary and gets discouraged). A similar play occurs when the narrator claims she lied about a just-related event: "Excuse me: I have not only been making things up, I've been telling outright lies from the second half of page 93" (Pardonnez-moi: non seulement j'invente, mais en plus je vous ai menti pendant la seconde moitié de la page 93 [97]). She often addresses the reader directly in this way, not so much to engage sympathy or encourage reader identification as to play up the self-consciously literary nature of her writing; in this case, she then proceeds to tell the same event all over again the way it "really" happened, effectively destabilizing both textual versions and even the idea that it is possible to represent actual events.

Dandurand has written, "The best erotic literature is also metaphysical, in that it touches on all moral aspects of life" (La meilleure littérature érotique est aussi métaphysique, car elle touche à tous les aspects moraux de la vie [Presse canadienne 1991]). In her novel, public and private life merge. The narrator's suffering is linked to others' pain: "poverty, pollution, the bombs, torture everywhere in the world, Palestine, South Africa, my sore throat, sore soul, sore being" (la pauvreté, la pollution, les bombes, les tortures à travers le monde, la Palestine, l'Afrique du Sud, mon mal de gorge, d'âme, d'être [111]). Her solution is love:[18] she later adopts a girl who was sexually abused by her father, uncle, and brother when she was seven years old, another who went through seventeen foster homes after her mother abandoned her, another whose father beat her and then killed her mother and himself, and so on. All eventually recover under her loving care. Both intimate and political, true and not true, autobiographical and rhetorically sophisticated, *Un coeur qui craque* recalls those optical illusions which are simultaneously two wine glasses and a woman's profile. It constantly poses as both real and not real, with each term reinforcing the other rather than undermining it. The more it is confessional, the more it is fictional, and vice versa. An endless spiral from one to the other: confessional fiction at its best.

Nicole Brossard: "Between the Lines"

It may seem strange, almost heretical, to speak of Nicole Brossard in relation to sexual confessions.[19] Unlike Anne Dandurand's work, which is funny, reader-friendly, and accessible despite its various forms of textual play,[20] Nicole Brossard's experimental lesbian feminist writing is deliberately hermetic. (She could perhaps best be compared to Hélène Cixous, who taught in Québec in 1972–73 and influenced many Québec writers, or to Mary Daly.) Although her writing is (among other things) a celebration of lesbian sexuality, its abstraction and complex textual play are light-years away from the standard confessional mode. She has repeatedly declared that her own life is not the impetus behind her writing. Still, in the sense that all of Brossard's work since 1974 is a direct textual consequence of her lesbian sexuality and given the importance she attaches to motherhood and sexuality as crucial for the direction her writing has taken, I would argue that it presents a confessional intervention.

"I have often said that I don't write in order to express myself but that I write to understand reality, the way we process reality into fiction, the way we process feeling, emotion and sensation into ideas and landscapes of thought," Brossard writes (1993, 107). According to this statement, she concentrates on women's reality in the act of becoming fiction, as it is transformed into ideas and into written words. The real-life events of autobiography or confession therefore become elements in a more global process of working toward a practice of writing in the feminine. Yet their importance is central throughout: many of Brossard's works are above all a celebration of lesbian sexuality and writing, deeply anchored in the personal and yet transcending it. The paradox is, in my opinion, symptomatic of confessional fiction. Brossard has in fact written, "I don't like to describe my life, even between the lines" (je n'aime pas faire état de ma vie, même entre les lignes [Brossard 1984, 15]). But this statement appeared, of all places, in a published diary.

Since 1974, all her work has been explicitly written for women and creates a feminist interpretative community through the use of a clearly female "we" and the detailed inscription of the act of reading and writing in the text. Certainly women have been her most appreciative audience[21] and female academics—including a number of Americans and English-Canadians—have been instrumental in giving her prominence within the literary circles of Québec. Two works are emblematic of Brossard's autobiographical stance: her *Journal intime (Diary)* and the novel *Picture Theory.*

Brossard's *Diary* was commissioned by French CBC radio as part of a series; in it, she states that she had never before kept a formal diary. Even in the published work, she chooses a form which, like the second type of confessional form Felski describes (in contrast to the simple day-to-day diary), incorporates other genres (poems and nonfiction meditations in Brossard's case) and is "episodic and fragmented, not chronological and linear" (Felski 1989, 99). Some entries are undated, others bear dates ten or fifteen years past, usually during trips Brossard has taken. Brossard plays with time to show how real life is shaped (or, in her term, processed) into fiction. For example, her entry for February 4, 1983, begins: "I moved the date of my diary up one day to imagine what it would feel like to think I'm writing tomorrow" (J'ai déphasé d'un jour la date de mon journal afin d'imaginer la sensation que cela pourrait me procurer de penser que j'écris demain [Brossard 1984, 25]). The dates themselves are misleading; if, as she says, she has never kept a diary, then an entry dated Athens, June 20, 1973, was presumably written in 1984. The apparently straightforward idea of the writing present is challenged. At one point, Brossard writes: "I must be careful not to mix up my notebooks, the ones where I exist and the ones I write in" (Je dois faire attention de ne pas confondre mes cahiers, ceux où j'existe et ceux dans lequel j'écris [Brossard 1984, 52]). Like Dandurand's double diary, Brossard's two types of notebooks point to the fact that existence is always already fiction; it takes place within language and can only be captured in language. Even the subtitle of her *Diary*, "Or, so here is a manuscript" (Ou voilà donc un manuscrit), plays up the fictional nature of the enterprise, the dimension of writing as opposed to the dimension of reality.

Similarly, at the end of *Picture Theory*, the writer-protagonist M.V. (the phonetic resemblance to N.B. is worth noting) attempts actually to create a "real" woman, a hologram which will be both physical and abstract, body and text, "perfectly readable" (184). The hologram of the female lover points to a recurring paradox in Brossard's work: the opposition between "fiction" and "reality" (Saint-Martin 1989). Both words can bear negative or positive connotations, depending on whether they are female- or male-identified. Brossard writes that "reality has been for most women a fiction, that is the fruit of an imagination which is not their own" (75) but was invented by men (TV news, pornography, war), while women's reality (motherhood, sexuality, sexual violence) has been perceived as fiction, i.e., as unreal or unimportant (La réalité a été pour la plupart des femmes une fiction, c'est-à-dire le fruit d'une imagination qui n'est pas la leur [Brossard 1985, 53]). Since "the experience inflicted on women's bodies urges toward reality" (82) (l'expérience infligée au corps des femmes incite à la réalité [Brossard 1980a, 90]), radical women's fictions need not only to denounce but also to demystify patriarchal "reality," revealing it to be a fabrication, and then create ways of inscribing women in language, thereby changing their lives by making their experience visible. Women's texts will thus have revolutionary potential:[22] "Reality is an apparent certainty which the textual real undoes" (La réalité est une apparente certitude que le réel textuel déjoue [Brossard 1984, 69]). The woman-hologram, the ultimate figure of both reality and fiction, marks the simultaneous emergence of the feminine in life and in writing.

In Karen Gould's phrase, Brossard offers us a look "at how a particular woman's emotional awakening and ecstatic sexual discovery become, of necessity, the generative sources for her own literary exploration, the seeds of a new sexual-textual identity" (Gould 1990, 94). Brossard's coded hermetic writing[23] offers an antidote to the personal and the confessional; at the same time, it is a way of letting personal elements shape and radiate throughout the works without tainting them with the confessional label. By insisting on the links between body and writing—"words gather around the clitoris" (les mots affluent autour du clitoris

[Brossard 1980b, 114])—rather than on a direct representation of reality, Brossard both avoids and integrates the personal, resists and rewrites the confessional. While anchored in the personal and the sexual, her writing carries them into the realm of feminist utopia.

"I have no other subject than what gives volume to the woman-subject I am" (Je n'ai d'autre sujet que ce qui donne du volume à la femme-sujet que je suis [Brossard 1982b, 31]). It seems clear that her writing incorporates, if not the details and anecdotes of her life, then the shape of that life and more particularly its passage into language. Ultimately, the links Brossard establishes between sexuality and writing bring the confession fully into the literary domain while still retaining its political power, at least for feminist readers concerned with avant-garde textuality. Within the safe space of a feminist context of reception, her celebration of lesbian sexuality plays on the shifting border between confession and fiction.

Sexuality and Textuality Entwined

Having explored three writers' stances vis-à-vis sexual confessions, I would like to return to some generic and theoretical issues. The term *confession* is a problematic one. I would prefer to speak of *sexual proclamations*, at least in the context of modern confessional fiction. This term is preferable both because it eliminates the under-the-table sense of shame that the word *confessions* inevitably calls up,[24] and because it emphasizes the declarative, even performative nature of women's sexuality *as brought into being through writing*. This is particularly true in the case of authors like Nicole Brossard, whose work turns precisely on the establishment of a lesbian identity through writing, but in all three cases, the feelings of shame traditionally related to women's sexuality would seem to be a thing of the past. Women no longer confess; they proclaim.

Just how radical is this writing? Following Foucault, Rosalind Coward has pointed out that dealing explicitly with sex is not, in and of itself, a sign of a move from repression to freedom: "Even the most apparently open and explicit detailing of sex can be an expression of sex in a way which means it is structured by very definite social movements and relates to the structures of power in society at large" (Coward 1984, 183). Certainly Lili Gulliver has no interest in changing existing power relations, or even in understanding them: all she wants is a passionate lover who will also bring her breakfast in bed. Her vision of sexuality entirely eliminates the dimension of danger: "When I think there are girls who see men as wild beasts waiting to devour them . . . I see them as little cabbages coming to be picked" (Quand je pense qu'il y a des filles qui voient les hommes comme des bêtes féroces prêtes à les dévorer . . . moi, je les vois plutôt comme des petits choux qui vont se faire cueillir [Gulliver

1990, 8]).[25] Given power relations between the sexes, any view of sexuality that does not consider both "pleasure and danger" (Vance 1984) is a dangerously naive one.

In contrast, Anne Dandurand deals with a number of political and social issues, including sexual abuse, abortion, poverty, and the social role of the writer. Both erotic and literary, tender and violent, her writing opens up a new space that women have not traditionally occupied. Nicole Brossard's contrast between women's and men's reality and her emphasis on the real and symbolic violence of patriarchy place the problem on a political and theoretical level. Brossard's writing is less liable than Dandurand's to be typecast as women's confession and therefore trivial; however, Dandurand's more accessible work can reach larger audiences than Brossard's. Certainly the work of both writers, to varying degrees, "uncovers the political dimensions of personal experience, confronts the contradictions of existing gender roles, and inspires an important sense of female identification and solidarity," as good confessional writing does (Felski 1989, 86), while Lili Gulliver's remains shallow and narcissistic because "sexual experience has been represented as an end in itself, as if other social decisions and work experiences didn't affect it" (Coward 1984, 184). Dandurand and Brossard move from individualism toward a conception of communal identity defined through women's shared sexual experiences, both positive and negative (pleasure and fantasy, but also rape, abortion, torture). But because of the fictional nature of their work, they also insist on the creation of this communal identity *through the act of writing*, which thus becomes a political act.

In various ways, these three writers create a stance that both confirms and denies the confessional nature of their work: Lili Gulliver through the use of a pseudonym to create a fictional autobiography, Dandurand through the "imaginary diary," and Brossard through the play between women's and men's "reality" and "fiction." Gulliver's vision is essentially traditional; Dandurand's is heterosexual and confrontational (von Flotow 1992, 110); and Brossard's is lesbian and utopian (Saint-Martin 1986, 104). Yet all three play on the borders between truth and fiction, distance and proximity in order to articulate female desire through writing. Playful, self-consciously rhetorical, both/and rather than either/or, they work toward the creation of safe spaces for women to write—and live—in.

Notes

1. The subtitle does not appear in the English translation. I have analyzed only the original French version of all works studied here.

2. Unless otherwise stated, all parenthetical references in this section will be to Felski's text.

3. This distinction between truth and fiction is sometimes blurred in feminist confessions as well, as Felski points out, but generally, the emphasis is on direct and honest depiction of past experience in order to unearth the authentic self. I would argue with Felski (97) that there is a sort of confessional continuum, with confessional fiction at one end and "true" confession, with its "explicit rejection of distance, of aesthetic criteria, of fiction, in favour of direct truth and immediate access to experience" at the other.

4. Throughout, I assume that the differences between Brossard's radical feminist writing and "metafeminist" writing like Dandurand's (Saint-Martin 1992) are not as significant as they may seem; metafeminist writing is an outgrowth and a new development of radical feminist writing in Québec.

5. To the extent that a woman writing about sexuality wants to be taken seriously as a writer, she makes greater use of rhetorical devices of all sorts. Lili Gulliver does not have serious literary pretensions, but Anne Dandurand and Nicole Brossard do. and have received critical recognition.

6. It is to be distinguished, though, from pulp pornography: it was brought out by a serious publisher and reviewed by the literary establishment (although it received much more attention in the tabloids than in the serious press), the author gave magazine interviews, and so on.

7. Unless otherwise stated, all parenthetical references in this section will be to Gulliver's text.

8. According to Lejeune (1975), we are dealing with an autobiography whenever the author's name on the cover and the protagonist's name within the work are one and the same. Otherwise, a work is fiction. Lejeune has reworked this concept, but it remains useful here.

9. In a short story called "Montréal moite," Anne Dandurand's narrator relates a long erotic encounter and then says that almost none of it is true. She only imagined it to please her lover (Dandurand 1987, 69–71).

10. It may be that once she had created the safe space I referred to earlier—which she did at the very outset of the text—she lost interest in the rhetorical process.

11. This refusal to answer could also be seen as a form of resistance to male probing into women's sexuality, a refusal to answer Freud's (and Lacan's) question about what a woman wants.

12. This description and others are surely inspired by romantic fiction.

13. Again, the parallel with romantic fiction is revealing.

14. Unless otherwise stated, all parenthetical references in this section will be to Dandurand's 1990 French text.

15. In addition, all the women are named after flowers, highlighting the fact that they are an artifice of language.

16. In a rather implausible attempt at a happy ending, Dandurand gives

her narrator a passionate and tender lover as well as various foster daughters, but we are informed she has not written for six years, since the first little girl arrived (difficult to believe, since she constantly insisted on how vital writing was to her), and is only now beginning again.

17. Von Flotow's translation reads, "I know what I have," an erroneously literal translation of the idiom.

18. In a short story, "Le corps des saisons" (1991), Dandurand presents Eros—the life force—exemplified as a couple making love, as an antidote to world violence.

19. Although much of Brossard's work predates that of Dandurand and Gulliver, I have chosen to turn to it last because it lends itself the least obviously to being read as a sexual confession.

20. Another important difference is that Brossard's work contains little or no self-directed irony; what little there is is aimed at patriarchy.

21. Because of its experimental nature, Brossard's work is not accessible to all. Although she has won many literary prizes, her writing has been criticized as elitist and overly abstract. She is best known and most widely read within the scholarly feminist community.

22. Felski (1989) has shown some of the limitations of avant-garde writing, questioning its claims to political radicalism. However, many feminists in Québec and elsewhere have found writing like Nicole Brossard's stimulating and energizing. I would agree with Felski, however, that it is important that one type of feminist writing does not become enshrined as the norm, to the exclusion of other practices.

23. Because of my subject matter, I have drawn mainly on straightforward expository passages; the quotations used here do not give a true picture of Brossard's experimental linguistic practice.

24. Felski does acknowledge the negative connotations that the word *confession* carries; however, she merely states she does not subscribe to them. I feel that the term itself needs rethinking.

25. *Chou* means "cabbage" and is also an affectionate diminutive like "honey" or "sweetie."

3

Parading Sexuality: Modernist Life Writing and Popular Confession

Irene Gammel

If disguise and self-protection describe one end of a spectrum, the other end describes women openly confronting their audiences with their sexual self-representations, using shock, comedy, and parody as effective tools to demand their sexual rights in public and to poke fun at traditional confessional modalities. Some of these daring diarists were, however, effectively silenced after making an ephemeral splash. Focusing on cosmopolitan German women who demanded their rights during the twenties, the essay below investigates the relationship between female sexual expressions that are marketed as popular female "confessions" and those playful and experimental self-disclosures that were denied publication.

The public disclosure of an intimate life story is a form of exhibitionism, and it is perhaps significant that some of the women who historically disclosed their sexuality made their money as performance artists, freely exhibiting their bodies in public. Some were well known, like Kiki de Montparnasse in France, who made her name as a model before writing her popular memoirs in 1929. Others joined the familiar history of forgotten women. In Berlin, Paris, and Greenwich Village, Baroness Elsa von Freytag-Loringhoven drew attention to herself with outrageous and nude performances among the avant-garde of the twenties, while also inscribing an unconventional life of promiscuity into her autobiography. While Kiki's art was a commercial success, Baroness Elsa descended into the realm of obscurity after her short-lived success in Greenwich Village. Her fate is similar to that of Helen Hessel, whose goal it was to invent new pleasures for women by writing a collaborative sexual diary with her lover.

47

Hessel's diaries were denied publication, but her sexual life story entered cultural history in appropriated form, in François Truffaut's 1961 cult film, *Jules and Jim.*

By focusing on women who used their self-representations to claim their sexual rights, I will demonstrate that many of the forgotten sexual diarists did more than just *confess:* they strategically used and abused traditional confession, turning its conventions upside down and inside out in order to voice critiques against sexual norms and traditional forms of female sexual self-representations. Determined to push against the boundaries of popular confession, which regulated the expressions of female sexuality, the experimental diarists used comedy, masquerades, and linguistic code-switching as their critical tools. Not surprisingly, Regina Barreca's characterization of feminist humor as a "comedy paired with anger" (1988, 5) is illustrated in female sexual self-representations in the early twentieth century, with women using humor to frame confrontational positions and explicit demands for change. Through parody and ridicule, the experimental self-representations that are my focus strategically disrupt and challenge "normalized" assumptions about sexuality as they are codified in sexology, including its popular outlets (sex manuals, text books, magazines), and in erotic writings (traditional sexual confessions for both men and women).

Baroness Elsa (1874–1927) and Helen Hessel (1886–1982) will serve as case studies to illustrate women's strategic pushing against the boundaries of popular confession. With her funky and outrageous Dada art, Elsa inscribed her sexual demands on her own body and became a living icon for feminists in Greenwich Village. Rebelling against the compliant femininity of traditional erotic confessions, Helen was Elsa's equal in poking fun at confessional conventions. After discussing Helen and Elsa's use of parody in their challenge of the popular modes of sexual self-representation, I will shift my attention to more recent popular confessions in Germany and investigate the use of feminist comedy in Svende Merian's 1980 confessional best-seller, a work whose popularity continues.

The Sexual Confession as Best-Seller

Two examples will help to illustrate the emergence and institutionalization of the female sexual confession as a best-selling genre in the early twentieth century. The first, Margarete Böhme's *Tagebuch einer Verlorenen* (Diary of a lost woman, 1905), follows Thymian Gotteball from her seduction by her father's assistant at age fifteen to her death as a prostitute. Linked to the cosmopolitan centers, mostly in Berlin, Böhme develops the plot of the "good bad girl" whose premature death acts as a convenient ending that preempts her moral and physical disintegration. It was so popular in Germany that it was turned into a movie by G. W.

Pabst in 1929, starring American actress Louise Brooks. Its commercial success signals the high marketability and popularity of the genre from the fin de siècle on, while placing the female sexual confession firmly into a "low" popular culture rather than into "serious" literature.[1]

Given the proliferation of women's sexual life stories in popular culture, it has to be remembered that the telling of "authentic" lives is often as much constructed as fictional narratives, if only to the extent that the women who produce them draw on a pool of prescribed conventions. German waitress Mieze Biedenbach, for example, was encouraged by a literary friend to write her memoirs like Böhme's *Tagebuch* (Maynes 1989, 113); in other words, she was to craft her book along the conventions of the female confession in order to ensure its marketability. Indeed, as Hanne Kulessa (1989) notes, Böhme's book was followed by a wave of imitations, suggesting that the female confession's popularity stimulated other women—many of them working women—to articulate their sexualities in similar terms. This is all the more significant as Böhme's *Tagebuch* is in all likelihood fictional (although the author makes a deliberate effort to present it as her deceased friend's authentic diary notes, overtly assuming the function of an editor who intervenes only in italics and footnotes, thus blurring the boundaries between confession and fiction in a way similar to the one theorized by Lori Saint-Martin in this collection).

Published in France, *Kiki's Memoirs* (Prin 1930) further illustrate the confessional conventions surrounding women's sexual self-representations. The star model and lover of American photographer Man Ray, Kiki de Montparnasse (alias Alice Prin) inscribed the rapidly changing sexual mores into one of the fastest growing visual art forms of the twenties— photography. She advocated the open sexuality that we have come to associate with the flapper: provocative, yet pleasing; assertive, yet never confronting the male gaze. Through her public disclosures, Kiki embodied sexual change.

During a period when the representation of sexuality in (male) fiction risked being censored as pornography (as the examples of D. H. Lawrence or Theodore Dreiser illustrate), female sexual truth—that is, truth authenticated by a female body behind the text—became an accepted feature of cultural expression. From the turn of the century on, women's "true" confessions were so popular that they quickly rivaled the "serious" literature produced by men, particularly naturalist fiction, which also claimed to present a documentary truth on issues of sexuality (Gammel 1994). Besides the commercial principle behind the proliferation of women's sexual stories, it was the scientific realms of sexology, as well as psychoanalysis, that authorized, even encouraged, the production of female "confessions" in order to "lift the veil of mystery" surrounding female sexuality. Viennese psychiatrist Wilhelm Stekel, for instance, wrote in his book *Frigidity in Woman* that the "scientific significance of this confession is very great" and that the female confession gives the male scientist insight into what the woman wants (1943, 67).

While official and popular sexological authorities prompted women to confess, feminists intervened to negotiate their self-representations by challenging traditional confessional politics. In the first three decades of the century, feminists in Europe and North America reclaimed their sexuality frequently outside the institution of marriage, often articulating a reverse female philosophy of promiscuity in their life writing. These changes are echoed in the writings of women from Franziska zu Reventlow and Lou Andreas Salomé in Germany to Djuna Barnes and Peggy Guggenheim in the United States. It is within the context of these different ideological claims and gender positions that we need to investigate women's sexual self-representations in the twenties.

The reception of Kiki's autobiography in the popular media and its subsequent co-optation, for instance, speak volumes. The work was enthusiastically embraced by the male press. Moreover, the English translation, first published in 1930, is framed by three introductions, each written by a man and each celebrating not so much Kiki's text but Kiki—the authenticating female body behind the text. Putting his literary weight behind the French model, Ernest Hemingway writes, "Kiki now looks like a monument to herself" (9); then the English translator explains that "the problem is not to translate Kiki's text, but to translate Kiki. . . . To be able to do this one must have the feel of Kiki" (20); and finally, the publisher claims ownership in the project: "It was from me that Kiki received the first suggestion to write them. For over two years I continued urging her to buckle down to the job" (24). Imposing their own stamp, the *men* are the ones who select Kiki's voice to function as *their* representative woman's voice of an era known for its significant proliferation of discourses of women's sexual and legal rights.

It is within such politically strategic male framing and appropriation of the female voice that we need to examine other, perhaps more daring and experimental, sexual life stories in the twenties. While Kiki was elevated by males as a female symbol of the twenties, and while Böhme's "confession" was further popularized in a successful movie, other—more overtly militant—versions of female sexual lives including those of Elsa von Freytag-Loringhoven and Helen Hessel, were relegated to the substrata of what Michel Foucault (1980) has called the "suppressed knowledges"; neatly cataloged and boxed, their manuscripts remained submerged for several decades in the academic vaults of rare book archives. Rediscovered fifty years later, Elsa's memoirs have been published under the title of *Baroness Elsa* (1992), while Hessel's sexual diaries appeared in the French translation as *Journal d'Helen* (1991).[2] Indeed, recent years have witnessed a search for and reclamation of women's "authentic" voices, which has led to a surge in publication of "lost" texts, in which women use and abuse the popular confessional mode. In light of this rather belated acknowledgment, we must now question why, given the female sexual confession's high marketability from the turn of the century on, Elsa's and Hessel's sexual life stories were not embraced by publishers, as Kiki's and Böhme's texts were. In other words, what is the relationship between the best-selling and the "silenced" sexual confession? Is the unpublished text, perhaps, more radical in its demand for social change? Is it more subversive in its challenge of confessional modalities? I will now focus on two such interventions, examining how Baroness Elsa and Helen Hessel push against the boundaries that wish to frame and contain the female voice.

Confessional Masquerades: Baroness Elsa and Helen Hessel

As an avant-garde artist in Greenwich Village, Baroness Elsa von Freytag-Loringhoven attracted the attention not only of the Village bohemians and of American modernists (e.g., William Carlos Williams, 1967) but, more importantly, of feminists. Margaret Anderson (1930), Jane Heap, photographer Berenice Abbott, writer Djuna Barnes, art collector Peggy Guggenheim—they all recognized their own desire for sexual experimentation in the German-born baroness's street performances and recognized her as a feminist icon, an icon into which they projected their own desires for breaking sexual and artistic boundaries. Some helped her financially, some provided a venue for her provocative art performances, and they all embraced her as an artist, an acknowledgement denied Elsa by many males.

Using confrontation and scandal as tools to push against the boundaries regulating sexual self-representations, Elsa ruthlessly dismantled the pleasing sexuality popularized through Kiki's photographs and memoirs. In her nonverbal "body intrusions," for instance, she ridiculed the confessional exposure of the flesh; her sexualized body intrudes into the public frame, as in the following scene when Elsa poses for painter George Biddle: "With a royal gesture she swept apart the fold of a scarlet raincoat. She stood before me quite naked—or nearly so. Over the nipples of her breasts were two tin tomato cans, fastened with a green string about her back. Between the tomato cans hung a very small bird-cage and within it a crestfallen canary" (Biddle 1939, 137).

Offered as it was for the painter's judgmental eye, Elsa turns her body into a parodic vehicle of confession. Deliberately avoiding the traditional theater context, which allows for conventional veils and distances, her sexualized body intrudes into everyday and workaday surroundings—the studio of a painter (Biddle 1939), the offices of the *Little Review* (Anderson 1930), and the street (Williams 1967)—settings in which she exposes her body in defamiliarized forms, always creating effects of humor and scandal. While the nudity of her body may attract a voyeuristic interest, Elsa deflates the potential eroticism of her performances through humorous costuming: vegetables adorn her body; stamps decorate her painted face; her hair is shaved and head lacquered in a striking color (Anderson 1930). The sudden unexpectedness of her public disrobing puts her spectators at a distance and puts her in control.

Similarly, in her sexual autobiography written in 1924 and 1925 in Berlin, Elsa did more than simply confess.[3] The autobiography allowed her to theatricalize her personal and intimate life: her sexual infatuations with Marcel Duchamps and William Carlos Williams (1992, 85); her experiences with orgasmic satisfaction, or lack thereof ("I wanted something that is called 'orgasm'" 77); and the status of coitus as a sexual stimulus ("as much as I liked sex intercourse . . . I was in truth searching for my counterpart" 46). But despite the explicitness of her personal revelations, Elsa effectively resisted confessional readings through use of parody, distances, and provocative excess. She significantly begins her personal disclosures with a gesture that signals distance, not voyeuristic titillation, as when she writes early in her text: "[T]he clap and later syphilis I took like a Trojan battle. [They were] blood of dragon—love—turning one immune from injury" (46). Elsa's writing of sexuality is deliberately provocative and outrageous, designed to keep the reader at a distance.

Presented in a tone of satire and parody, Elsa's autobiography does more than ridicule the sexual self-seriousness of her male partners. It is the authoritative male claim to speak for women that Elsa calls into question. In her study on sexuality in Weimar Germany, Atina Grossmann (1983) has illustrated that German sex reformers of the twenties not only put the sole responsibility for female pleasure on the male but also "treated the body as a machine that could be trained to perform more efficiently and pleasurably. The goal was to produce a better product, be it a healthy child or a mutual orgasm" (164). If anything, Elsa ridicules the discourse of sexual techniques and teleology so important in contemporary male diaries and sexological accounts. Showing how her lover Felix turned the female orgasm into a male project and goal, Elsa makes fun of her former "sex sun," by exposing how much he kept her at a distance; he was "lacking playfulness in sex" and "was too much business mechanic," so that despite his "purposeful potency," there always remained "a barrier" (90–91).

By calling into question male sexual authority, Elsa is much more daring than Kiki. One example will suffice to illustrate the striking ideological difference between the two self-representational models. If in male erotic writings, the woman's sexual initiation is conventionally embedded in a language of male conquest, attack, assault, and siege and assigned a key role,[4] Kiki's play appears to cater to traditional expectations. In a chapter entitled "The Initiation That Failed to Come Off," Kiki describes her sexual experiences with a much older man, experiences that leave her "still a virgin, alas" (Prin 1930, 85). The next experience with a younger lover describes another failed initiation, this time, however, dressed in a language of female sadomasochism: "I screamed and suffered," she writes, only to note with regret, "At the end of a month's time, I was still a half-virgin" (89). While the reader is invited to read in these passages Kiki's parody of male sexual conquest, the sequence also shares much with a pornographic male fantasy, as Kiki caters to the age-old male desire for the virginal woman on whose body can be practiced everything from seduction to rape.

In comparison with Kiki's, Elsa's challenge goes deeper. She deliberately relegates her sexual initiation into the gaps of her autobiography, subverting the conventions of a whole tradition of male writing by omitting the supposedly all-important "primal" scene. Deconstructing virginity as a male-constructed "freak," Elsa deliberately refuses to cater to it: in a narrative saturated with sexual episodes, she does not describe her "loss of virginity." Her deliberate gap inscribes her ideological critique, as it reveals virginity as a discursive locus of male power. "To adore virginity as essential property . . . is the most flagrant illogic possible" (83), she writes, polemically exposing this "sentimental" adherence to virginity as a male defensive strategy directed against the sexually free woman. Consistently, Elsa's satire targets the misogynistic obsessions of her lovers—August Endell, Karl Wolfskehl, and F. P. Greve—all established artists by the time she wrote her autobiography.

While Kiki's limitations are, perhaps, best symbolized by the simplicity of her confessional style, Elsa's radicalism is encoded in her linguistic shifts and challenges. Using modernist techniques, her writing includes syntactical breaks, shifts in time, rich imagery, and lyrical passages, as well as neologisms, as when she insist on her "sexrights" or publicly claims her right to female "sexsatisfaction." Moreover, writing in an asylum in Berlin, Elsa used English, her second language, to reconnect with the group of cosmopolitan feminists who had applauded her street performances in Greenwich Village. Her memoirs were addressed to Djuna Barnes, who subsequently prepared a typescript and tried to get it published. It was the women who remembered Elsa as a role-model and an icon, as she became the living embodiment of avant-garde experimentation with female sexual self-representation. If her cosmopolitan spirit symbolized her dismantling of codes and boundaries, her confrontational spirit also called attention to the ideological seriousness with which these discursive battles were fought.

Like Elsa, my second example, Helen Hessel, was committed to modernist experimentation in her sexual self-representations. Describing a ménage à trois with a Jewish husband and a French lover in Hohenschäftlarn near Munich, Helen wrote her diaries in three languages, combining French (the language of her longtime lover, writer and art collector Henri-Pierre Roché), German (her mother tongue), and English. This uncompromising mixture is crucial in that it has less to do with a polite masking of sexually explicit material than with a crossing of boundaries of cultural and gender roles. Helen's multilingualism, like Elsa's bilingualism, encodes her flexibility in inhabiting new sexual (and cultural) positions, defying the limitations of one prescribed script. Just as for Elsa, sexual "success" lay somewhere beyond the realm of Felix's (and the sex reformers') cerebral sex, for Helen, sexual satisfaction consists in "spending herself in all directions" (Me dépenser dans toutes les directions) (1991, 48),[5] a concept that anticipates Luce Irigaray's evocation of the nonessentialist plurality of female sexual pleasure (1985). Consistently switching codes represents a linguistic and cultural versatility, permitting her to traverse boundaries of sexual discourse and genre.

Helen's diaries detail her stormy 1920–21 love affair with Henri-Pierre Roché. Helen wrote the diaries to be read and revised by Roché as a testimony to their unconventional love affair. About six months into the project, however, she told Roché in a private letter (dated January 6, 1921): "My journal is turning into autobiography; it has very little to do with you" (Hessel 1991, 526). If Helen's project was "to invent new pleasure" (31) and "to create love without tradition, without mechanics, to move beyond easy contentment" (241), her strategies included comic excess and parodic provocation: "I know that this is *faire l'amour*," she writes. "It's pretty— but it does not make use of all my strengths. It's like bathing in a lake; where is the roaring sea that I can do battle with?" (49). Helen identified with Penthesilea, the warrior queen and title heroine in Heinrich von Kleist's play. In Kleist's adaptation of the Homeric myth, the Amazon's love-hate relationship with Achilles eventually leads her to dismember him. Like Kleist's Penthesilea, Helen initiates the contact with her male lover with a deliberate provocation: "If you are an enemy, I challenge you to a fight," she writes in a letter dated October 3, 1919 (1991, 483).

If naively truthful narratives of self can easily lead to entrapments, Sidonie Smith has provided a taxonomy to show how, through mime and parody, the female autobiographer can successfully resist some of the imprisoning snares. As Smith shows, the woman can parody "the text of man," and by overdoing their masculine role, "expose it as fraudulent, as a fiction, as a kind of 'narcissistic phallocentrism'" (1990, 159). Hessel, like Elsa, appropriates for her sexual self-representations typically masculine positions, explicitly rejecting the role of "woman." As Hessel writes: "I have never accepted playing the role of woman. A weak animal that

needs protection is ashamed and dependent" (1991, 517). While her journals do not exclude problematic instances of female self-hatred, she more
specifically rejects the "feminine" confessional script with its emphasis
on a passively seductive sexuality. Deliberately vacating the "female" position, Helen appropriates for herself the male sexual position, encoding
activity, promiscuity, and aggression into her self-representations—albeit
with significant parodic differences.

In her journals, she includes passages termed *visions* and *rêves*, creating new experimental spaces for the expression of female sexual fantasies and desires. Her favorite fantasy, significantly, is that of a sexual role
reversal in which she appropriates for herself the male obsession with penetration. Using German, she desires "to penetrate [her lover], like lightning
entering the mountains, the water, the tree, the earth." At the same time,
she strategically turns her dramatic image into comedy by deflating it,
adding that her penetration will be more like "a coin entering a slot."
Deliberately parodying the male genre, she turns its conventions inside
out and upside down, ab/using many of its key conventions in the spirit
of feminist comedy. Her utopian *vision* ends in French with her desire
"to be upright in him" (être debout en lui). Inhabiting the other space
(en lui), and yet remain herself (debout), she is determined not to lose herself in the other, and she strategically maintains some of her boundaries,
even while crossing them (51).

And yet, despite Helen's parodic challenges, the complex reception history of her life shows the limits of Helen's experimental diaries. Since
Helen wrote her journals as part of a collaborative, multivoiced love story
set in the Isartal, of which Roché was to write the final version, her lover
and her husband were the first readers. Simultaneously fascinated and
threatened by Helen's writing, the men read the diaries as a kind of male
erotica, and they were both inspired to write their own versions of the
events. Much more conventional in his conceptualization of sexuality,
Roché's private diaries (1990),[6] for instance, reveal his desire to withdraw
as a lover from Helen, as he complains about "her lies" (279), her "po-
lygamy" (268), and "her desire for destruction" (408). His growing distance, however, did not keep him from recycling her voice in his autobiographical novel. As a result, Hessel's sexual experimentation in life
writing has entered the cultural text in mediated form: Henri-Pierre Roché's
novel *Jules and Jim* (1953), and François Truffaut's film by the same name
(1961), based, in turn, on Roché's diaries and absorbing Helen's Amazo-
nian sexuality and modernist experimentations into a cycle of confessional readings.

In the hands of a French writer and filmmaker, the multilingual Helen
underwent a significant metamorphosis into largely monolingual Cathérine
(played with sensual bravado by Jeanne Moreau). A muse for male art-

ists, the only creative expression allowed Cathérine in the film is the key song with its telling refrain, "Je suis une femme fatale." Similarly, Helen's celebration of "life as it flows" (la vie qui se forme toujours coulante) (Hessel 1991, 533) is translated in the film's song as *le tourbillon de la vie*, realigning Helen with the destructive feminized whirlpool of Greek mythology. Even as the film pays homage to Helen's unconventional playfulness, role reversals, and activity, it superimposes a frame on her parodic voice.

In a final twist of the real-life events, Cathérine purposefully and triumphantly speeds her car into a river, confirming the femme fatale motif of the key song by killing her lover and herself. In real life, Helen survived both lover and husband, and she broke all ties with Roché after he had secretly married another woman. Helen, in fact, supported her family through her journalistic writing, after her Jewish husband lost his prestigious position with the arrival of the Nazis in Germany. The reduction of the cosmopolitan Helen to *one* culture (the French culture of her lover Roché) mirrors the historical containment of Helen's experimentation.

From a feminist point of view, the history of recuperation outlined above draws attention to the female concerns that have remained silenced over decades. In the eighties and nineties, formerly silenced sexual motifs have become part of mainstream culture and may even function as popular entertainment. Indeed, the notion of *unexpurgated* diaries has become a convenient marketing feature, suggestive as it is of repressed and censored sexual material that is finally unveiled. If the late-twentieth-century proliferation of women's contesting sexual voices in popular media is reflective of a new feminist era, it also raises questions about the continued, if not to say growing, commercialization of the confessional practice. Is this practice successful precisely because in it "man" frequently continues to be the focal point and obsession of female thinking, writing, and reading? Should we interpret the continued popular success of confessional texts as a suspicious signal for the genre's lack of transformative power, as some feminists suggest? Or conversely, to what extent can the genre's popular success be explained by the fact that it helps middle-class women resist sexist strategies in their everyday lives? To answer some of these questions, I will now turn to an eighties autobiographical best-seller, Svende Merian's *The Death of the Fairy-Tale Prince* (Der Tod des Märchenprinzen), which I would like to discuss as part of a spectrum reaching from the compliance of Kiki to Baroness Elsa and Helen Hessel's demands for their rights.

Sexual Emancipation: Death of the Fairy-Tale Prince

Like her experimental predecessors in the twenties, Svende Merian,[7] a student of literature at Hamburg University during the late seventies, turns her personal history into feminist comedy. Tracing the painful breakup of a romantic and sexual friendship, Merian turns complaint and anger into feminist satire. Many of the episodes she describes are innocuous in their dailiness, but are turned into poignant moments of feminist epiphany and comedy. "Do you take the pill?" (29),[8] she asks her lover Arne during their first sexual intimacies, thus parodically reversing a gender-stereotypical formula to signal her disappointment with a self-proclaimed progressive male who conveniently ignores that contraception should be a shared responsibility. Her comic act disrupts the carefully developed romantic scenario and turns her formerly idealized lover into the butt of a feminist joke.

In another scene, she provocatively claims, "I don't want an orgasm" (81), thus dramatically enacting her rejection *not* of sexual *jouissance* but of the male scripted version of female pleasure, one that is quantifiable in numbers of orgasms. Parodically reversing pop-sexology's pet slogan, she provides a plethora of examples that illustrate how easily her orgasms are (mis)interpreted by her lovers as a signifier for her sexual fulfillment when, in fact, they often leave her with the feeling that she has allowed her body to be turned into a site for the inscription of male skills and techniques. Merian's punch line strategically calls into question the unquestioned teleological goal of popular sexual scripts, as it echoes a critique voiced several decades earlier by Elsa von Freytag-Loringhoven and Helen Hessel.

Yet, despite Merian's commitment to feminist comedy and despite the fact that her work continues to sell well in the nineties, academic feminists have reacted negatively to Merian's work. One reason for the lack of feminist support can be found in the general devaluation of popular culture within the category of *Trivialliteratur*.[9] A more important reason can be found in the machinery of confessional readings that have been applied to Merian's work in the popular media, which may have led feminists to argue that the work has no serious transformative impact.[10] Indeed, Merian's text has become an easy target for commercial recuperation, one that brings to mind the male recolonization of Kiki's memoirs in the late twenties. After its initial success, Merian's work was reviewed in the popular media and reprinted by Rowohlt, a mainstream publisher. Packaged for reception by a mass audience, the book featured a blurb on the back cover with a classical confessional frame: the prospective buyer reads that Merian leaves feminism behind her after the day's work is done. This antifeminist slant is a convenient (mis)reading, as it clearly caters to Germany's middle-class discomfort with the term *feminism*.

If this recuperation calls into question the narrative's feminist agenda, I would caution feminist readers that a simple dismissal of Merian's text is not necessarily the most effective strategy of counteracting the seductive power of confessional readings in popular media.[11] Since any (resisting) discourse is vulnerable to recuperation, as Michel Foucault has demonstrated (1978), I would like to propose a reappropriative reading strategy, a model of *feminist contextual reading*, which refrains from blaming the writer. Instead, contextual reading situates Merian's feminist satire back into the context of German activist women whose personal disclosures strategically challenged conventional sexual politics: in the seventies, 374 women disclosed in a popular magazine that they had had an abortion to stage their demand for a change of Germany's restrictive abortion laws (cf. Altbach et al. 1984, 102–4); German journalist Alice Schwarzer dismantled the myth of sexual liberation by presenting her interviews with women in her influential text, *Der kleine Unterschied* (1992). She popularized her radical feminism and lesbianism in her magazine *Emma*; spectacular court cases launched by Schwarzer and others intruded powerfully into the dailiness of sexual politics.

Recontextualized and seen from a new vantage point, Merian's feminism does more than just occupy a place at "the wailing wall of patriarchal evil," as Keitel put it in her critique (1983, 450).[12] Indeed, Merian's confessional voice, which mourns the loss of her fairy-tale prince, is effectively parodied and dismantled from within the text. For Merian, slang, irreverent neologisms, and use of sociolects in her personal writing do not merely serve as signifiers of truthful authenticity. They also present a deliberately "low" popular form of writing that allows the writer to poke holes into established discourses and frames. The feminist comedy in Merian's text hinges on the second, parodical, critical voice, which consistently pokes holes into accepted scripts—scripts that she admits to having internalized. Determined to leave the victim position behind, the mature—writing—self assumes a critical voice: she adopts an activist agenda by writing her feminist comedy, using her younger self as well as her male partners as a target. Through her personal history, Merian turns her encounters with sexual misogyny into feminist humor and, in popularized form, pays homage to a tradition of feminist activism in Germany.

Merian's jokes are designed to appeal to a readership of women. Like Elsa, she demonstrates that if women claim their right to (what Elsa termed) "sexsatisfaction," then the (hetero)sexual act turns into a field of debate, discussion, separateness, and difference—a point enacted by Merian with all the more force as she contrasts this realization with her own romantic desire for union. Indeed, the word *Auseinandersetzung*, carrying the appropriate double meaning of (1) "conflict" and (2) "coming to terms with," is a key concept in her text. Analyzing women's autobiographies in France, Nancy Miller (1988) has suggested that the female self in autobiographies can be seen as public theater, as a thesis drama that includes defense, illustration, and an advocacy of minority rights. With her personal story, Merian, like Elsa, puts a former lover on trial, continually exposing his behavior to "witnesses" who act alternately as judges, mediators, and jury, engaged in a hermeneutical task of deciphering which of his acts are misogynistic and exploitative.

Just as Elsa, after her love had been spurned, publicly read William Carlos Williams's private letters to her in order to expose "the case of the American man" (Anderson 1930, 210), so Merian eventually sprays in purple paint on the window of her ex-lover's apartment, "Here too lives a woman hater." The book cover shows a photograph of Arne's window with flower pots behind Merian's huge purple inscription. The carnivalesque publicizing of her accusation draws attention to "normalized" misogyny that thrives behind the facade of innocent flower pots; the carefully written text, the choice of purple paint, and the incongruity of text and context give the "denunciation" an inevitably comic twist and turn it into satiric provocation. This comic performance act, though confrontational, opens the dialogue (Arne, after all, answers with a visit and eventually with his own confessional book). The act takes a political twist, becomes public feminist comedy, a street performance, with domestic conflict "outed" in public satire.

Conclusion: "Confronting Men with Their Illogic"

The confessional intervention should be seen not as a tool to reach an illusory sense of liberation but rather as a genre that allows women to disrupt and caricature normalized conceptions of sexuality. As case studies, Merian, Helen, and Elsa's interventions show that the genre lends itself to parodic play and subversive gambits. Indeed, the female confessional intervention always implies a staging—a theatricalization and performance—of female sexuality, in which women are allowed to tell their side of the story, replaying the sex roles that exploit them, but always replaying them with a significant twist, often with a deliberate excess that highlights the inherent mechanism of subjugation and fills the reader with unease. The reception and the debating voices surrounding the publication of Merian's book exemplify the subversive quality of the narrative.

This is not to say, however, that the genre is without its problems or complicities, as Elsa explicitly notes. Despite her status as a transgressive and outrageous figure, Elsa seems to speak for many other women when she characterizes herself as neither a "traditional woman" nor a "successfully liberated" one. She places herself, appropriately, into a third transitional category of women, those who become inevitably victimized by society's misogynistic norms, even as they try to challenge them. In the persona of the female sexual warrior, she stages her feminist critiques through her own body: "Ill-starred women like me—of European origin— are sexscience's tools to make men confront their illogic" (115). Confronting men with their "illogic" through her body and voice, Elsa insists that "true quality in a woman cannot be bullied and bluffed" (121). By the end of her life, however, Elsa is also forced to admit that the men she loved were incapable of granting "a woman her right to personality—as was [her] father" (121). And, as readers, we are forced to recognize the circularity of Elsa's life, as we are forced to admit that a woman's voice of accusation can easily be buried and silenced, while those "accused" are allowed to occupy the places of power in cultural history.

Finally, the sexual autobiographers discussed in this essay exploit the shock value of a daring personal revelation to capture the limelight and to stage their accusation. If such exhibitionist performance is inevitably implicated in the power structures in place, the narrative's qualities of caricature, excess, and outrage frequently succeed in unsettling the reader. The reader is ultimately left with questions, not with ease and comfort. Confessional interventions stimulate debate, forcing the reader to acknowledge the reality of normalized sexual misogyny which does not simply disappear with good intentions: what is needed is *aktive Auseinandersetzung*—that is, dialogue, debate, and oppositional discourses both within oneself and with others.

Notes

1. Although the nineteenth century produced such important works as Wanda von Sacher-Masoch's *Confessions of My Life*, Judy Simons (1990) has noted in her study on women's diaries that the female confession "did not come fully into fashion until the twentieth century, [after] the psychoanalytic revolution" (6). Similarly, Mary Jo Maynes's study on "Gender and Narrative Form in French and German Working-Class Autobiographies" (1989) confirms that authentic women's stories were a hot commodity at the turn of the century.

2. It should be added here that the life stories of these women were used by the writers' male lovers. For a detailed discussion of the appropriation of Elsa's personal life writing, see Irene Gammel (1993, 1995).

3. Elsa wrote parts of the autobiography in an asylum; it was stimulated by Djuna Barnes's request for a biographical sketch to accompany the proposed publication of Elsa's poetry. Barnes carefully prepared a typescript of Elsa's memoirs, and for at least a decade, she was preoccupied with publishing it. The manuscript is housed in the Rare Book Archives of the University of Maryland.

4. Cf. Simone de Beauvoir's chapter on "Sexual Initiation" in *The Second Sex* (1989).

5. All translations from the French text are mine. Italicized passages belong to the editor of Hessel's journal and mark Helen's switch from French into another language, generally into German.

6. Following the conventions of the male sexual diary (cf. Spender 1980,

118–21), Roché writes himself as a conquering Don Juan figure; catalogs of women and of sexual techniques characterize his writing.

7. Although the name is a pseudonym, the author relates the experiences of her own life.

8. This translation and all subsequent ones are mine.

9. Evelyne Keitel (1983), for instance, has introduced the highly useful concept of *Verständigungstexte* to describe works that initiate dynamic processes of reception such as group discussions, which had started to flourish in the 1970s subculture. Keitel distinguishes between genuine (echte) and trivial Verständigungstexte, a distinction rendered complex by the fact that much of women's literature has historically been rejected with the help of the term *trivial*. Trivial texts confirm the reader's expectations and norms, Keitel argues, and she applies this term in passing to Merian's *Märchenprinz*.

10. For readings that range from cautionary acceptance to polemical rejection, see Felski (1989); Weigel (1984); Keitel (1983); Kolkenbrock-Netz and Schuller (1982). The work has been criticized for confirming rather than transforming hierarchically structured gender relationships of power (Kolkenbrock-Netz and Schuller 1982), for being part of "a problematic trend in contemporary West German literature" that often conflates women's literature with confessional texts (Weigel 1984, 82). Merian's is only one of many works that have been dismissed as confessional by feminists. Verena Stefan's 1975 poetic coming-out story, *Häutungen*, was polemically dismissed, with feminists arguing that hers is not an effective way of overcoming speechlessness (Goettle, 1989).

11. Given the sharp feminist criticism and dismissal that Merian's work has encountered in Germany and elsewhere, perhaps readers should not be surprised that Merian's most recent work (1994), a novel written after a long period of creative silence, has lost much of what made the first book a success and a good read: its feminist energy, its demands for female solidarity, and its hopes for changes through female activism.

12. My translation. Merian's project is also a popularized form of the consciousness-raising activity undertaken by a collective of German women in what they call *Erinnerungsarbeit* (memory work) (Haug et al. 1987). In order to uncover the process of sexualization their bodies had undergone in the course of socialization, these women decided to write down memories connected with the sexualization of their bodies—stories about their legs, hair, stomach, height, etc. These memories in turn were read by all members of the collective and analyzed and critiqued (16). The project of "liberation" thus does not consist in passively confessing sexual memories but in actively recontextualizing them, conceptualizing a new language that will initiate change.

Part Two

Sexual Trauma and Confessional Modalities

In increasing numbers, women give public testimony of childhood sexual abuse, incest, rape, and sexual harassment. In popular media, personal accounts of sexual trauma have become a stock topic for news shows, television talk shows, self-help books, magazines, and personal memoirs. Disclosing the sexual abuse she has suffered is often the first step in breaking the vicious circle that characterizes the survivor's life. For most women concerned, however, the task of putting sexual trauma into words is an extremely difficult one. Women struggle with finding an appropriate language with which to express their experiences, to talk about the abuse in a way that does not involve a second—a linguistic—rape. Women disclosing experiences of abuse have been victimized by the existing, often traditional and powerful, confessional modalities. While personal disclosures are frequently subject to doubt and reinterpretation, survivors have cautioned that more talk does not necessarily create more change. The essays in this segment investigate a range of confessional modalities that frame the articulation of sexual trauma and frequently contain the survivor's demands for change. More importantly, however, part two is concerned with investigating creative and strategic ways that allow women to challenge and transcend traditional confessional modalities in their voicing of sexual trauma. Since sexual trauma has been translated through a variety of confessional modalities, the essays in this section mirror and sample that diversity; they investigate disclosures in poetry and self-help books, before moving on to expressions of sexual trauma in performance art and political hearings.

4

"Mi rage": The Confessional Politics of Canadian Survivor Poetry

Nathalie Cooke

In recent years, poets and writers have produced exceptionally powerful strategies that help women deal with experiences of sexual trauma. Poeticizing experiences of sexual trauma does not involve a sanitizing of the experience but presents a strategic way of exiting the victim role. Aesthetic distancing devices help the survivor deal with a memory that appears too threatening and traumatic to be faced without mediation. The survivor creatively transforms her identity and role in and through the process of writing. The poet inscribes rage into her poetic disclosure, not shame; the survivor poem exorcises the power of the traditional confessional reader who passes judgment; reader sympathy is the strategic centerpiece of the survivor poem.

In the past few years, a number of Canadian women have used poetry to explore personal encounters with sexual violence, and readers have stilled to powerful and courageous disclosures of rape or abuse. Not only is their subject matter painful, but for a critic to open a discussion of their form is to risk a failure of respect for poetry which has objectives that reach far beyond the aesthetic. Still, these disclosures demand serious critical attention, as they are an important part of Canada's recent drive to "break the silence" surrounding sexual abuse. Of course, the appearance of such poetic disclosures is paralleled by women's growing awareness of the need to speak out about violence against women, as evidenced by the appearance of related topics in all aspects of contemporary culture: art, film, television, newspapers and magazines.[1]

At the same time, "breaking the silence" comes at a high cost. As Linda

Alcoff and Laura Gray (1993) point out, the sensationalization of survivor discourse in both "fictional" and "journalistic" formats (such as television talk shows) renders the survivors "dependent upon expert advice and help" rather than empowering them and acknowledging their authority in matters of their own personal experience (262–63). Perhaps even more important, while on the witness stand, female victims find themselves reliving the horror of rape and abuse; and the publicity such events entail risks turning "the victim" into "the accused," as the Hollywood movie of that title makes painfully explicit.

In Canada we have seen courts banning media coverage to spare victims. Anonymity, it is hoped, protects the victim as she articulates a painful disclosure in a forum over which she has little control. Ironically, then, at a time when Canada feels pressure to air its concerns about society's ills in the hope of correcting them, many details of abuse and violence are concealed. By contrast to these large media events, the written poetic disclosures that are my subject here are, by definition, limited to interaction between one poet and one reader. Within the larger (and, as I have suggested, problematic) cultural context of "breaking the silence," I propose to look at these poetic explorations of sexual abuse, examining in particular the function and advantages of the intimate audience enacted by the written text.

I use the term *survivor confession* because this poetic subgenre distinguishes itself very clearly from the larger category of confessional poetry. On one level, the poetry I propose to discuss *is* confessional in the way M. L. Rosenthal (1967) meant when he coined the term to describe a particular movement of post–World War II poetry in America and Britain. That is, there is indeed a focus on the poet's "private humiliations, sufferings, and psychological problems," themes which are usually developed in the first person and "intended without question to point to the author himself [or herself]" (26). This genre, then, is confessional in the way Rita Felski defines the term in relation to prose: it signals its "intention to foreground the most personal and intimate details of the author's life" (1989, 87). Characterized by a sense of intimacy, poetic survivor confessions also echo Judith Whitenack's point that the confession promises to "reveal something unknown, something that is not necessarily verifiable through recourse to the public record" (1982, 43).

And yet, while Canadian survivor poems on sexual abuse do articulate an acute, even painful intimacy, they strategically call into question traditional confessional modalities. They deliberately challenge the imbalance of power which Michel Foucault (1978) has argued is inherent in the confessional disclosure. Arguing that confession can "only reach completion in the one who assimilated and recorded it," Foucault contends that "the revelation of confession had to be coupled with the decipherment of what it said. The one who listened was not simply the forgiving master, the judge who condemned or acquitted; he was the master of truth" (1978, 66–67). As a result, the speaker of the confession is not credited with the sole production of discourse, as Jeremy Tambling (1990) notes: "The history of confession is that of power at the centre inducing people at the margins to internalize what is said about them—to accept that discourse and to live it, and thereby to live their oppression. The creation of the confessing personality may be defined as the production of the reactive spirit: focused on guilt, weakness and on the need for reparation" (6).

Indeed, shame—in large part due to the religious origin of the form—has been a central aspect of the conventional confession. Even in confessional discourse that is as far removed from the religious tradition as the poetry of Sylvia Plath and Anne Sexton, shame continues to drive the disclosure. Laurence Lerner (1987) argues, "Confession is something that causes shame. Real confession will cause shame because we have done wrong, confessional poetry deals with experience that is deeply painful to bring into public, not because it is disgusting, nor because it is sinful, but because it is intensively private" (64). I would make the case even more strongly. In poetry such as Anne Sexton's "The Double Image," the drama of the confession is precisely the poet's inability to escape blame, to move beyond a discourse that defines her (1964). This guilt may not be directly linked to religious belief or practice. Yet its power is crippling for Sexton's speaker, precisely because shame and religion's corollary, blame, are internalized.

Taken together, these definitions of confessional writing suggest that the disclosure is characterized by a sense of intimacy, while it is driven by the imbalance of power which threatens to efface the speaker (either because of her humiliation or her lack of control over her self-narrative). The survivor poems I propose to examine in this essay speak to this definition just as much as they speak from within it, while strategically challenging its dynamics. Focusing on a genre that helps women regain control over a traumatic experience of sexual violence, I will highlight two stages of this process of self-empowerment. First, the poet names the act of violence, recontextualizing it in a way that moves her from the position of object (both of violation and of discourse) to that of subject. In this act of naming, she deploys a number of strategic *distancing* devices. Having established control of the disclosure, she next reorients the blame of violence and abuse. Put bluntly, this poetry is not at all a confession of failure or psychological breakdown; rather, it is an assertion of the violation of the self as well as an articulation of its survival.

Sexual Abuse and Aesthetic Distance

I investigate poems on sexual abuse (especially childhood abuse) written by Canadian poets—female poets—in which the protagonist is closely related to the poet herself.[2] This focus on victims' disclosures of abuse first prompted me to analyze only poems that unabashedly adopted the first-person singular as a means of relating the story. But I soon realized that distancing devices are not so much poetic artifice as inevitable facilitators for the telling of the story. Indeed, the poets' reluctance to use a confessional first-person narrator, I argue, is an important strategy. The absence of the first-person pronoun, like the use of the second- and third-person singular, is a distancing tool the poet frequently uses to articulate an experience that is intensely personal and painful.

Taken as a group, these poetic disclosures of female sexual abuse reveal striking similarities in the way they articulate a sense of distance from the original experience. This distance is described as a sort of psychological evolution by the speakers themselves. Over the years, the speakers find the courage to articulate their experience and realize the importance not just of "speaking out" about their experience but also of writing it down. Libby Scheier's speaker explains in "A Poem about Rape" (1986):

> I told my friends and lover
> how I felt after it happened.
> These expressions of emotion
> were scarcely art.
> They were mainly noisy and honest
>
> . . . .
>
> In fact, it is now so many years
> (seven, I think it's seven)
> since I was raped that my anger
> has waned and cannot feed a poem.
> On the other hand, I could not
> write about rape until recently.
> My brains no longer knock against
> my skull when I think about it.

If temporal distance allows the speaker to compose a poem on her experience, her use of poetic devices helps her to control the experience. The poet's cries of anguish are not raw and unmediated. In fact, the victim's initial and raw reaction is often framed and critiqued within the poems themselves. Deploying a variety of aesthetic devices allows the speaker to reclaim her subject status. Thus survivor poetry incorporates at least two levels of communication: the disclosure itself, in which the act of sexual violence is named, and a framing narrative, in which the speaker positions herself in relation to the experience.

Libby Scheier's "A Poem about Rape," for instance, foregrounds its disturbing subject matter even in its title. The word *rape*—an unpoetic word and subject—performs an act of rhetorical violence which parallels the physical and psychological violence that is the poem's subject. The poem itself is an exploration of the speaker's relationship and responsibility both to the violence of the act and to the word itself. Similarly, Cyndia Cole's title "No Rape. No." (1980) introduces the subject, but in addition the poem offers a grammatic formulation of the shift from the poet's first position as victim (and object of rape) to that of empowered subject (who speaks the word):[3]

> the man who raped me
> was my lover
> and so it took me
> long years to name it rape.

More often, however, the poet signals the personal and troubling nature of the experience she is communicating in a complex play of gaps and absences. In "The Fall" (itself a suggestive but ultimately vague title), Claire Harris (1984) is able to name her abuser—Aggie—but names neither herself explicitly (notice the absence even of the first-person singular) nor the act of violence committed against her:

> So one day when Aggie said "I got something to show you"
> you went tingling because you were going in at last   deep into
> her enchanted place then you "shut your mouth" when she
> tugged you into her darkness shoved and flooded and washed
> over your confusion   then it was "your turn"   your face
> cracking you twisted on a corkscrew of pain
>
> When you surfaced you were still   secret in the raw heart of
> you   you never told   you never called her name

The last line highlights the victim's initial *refusal* (or inability) to name the event or the aggressor. Further, Harris's use of the second-person pronoun allows the speaker to avoid naming her younger self or situating herself at the center of the narrative: "*you* never called her name." When Aggie *is* named, then, it is not by the child victim who suffers the "secret in the raw heart" but rather by the adult survivor who, with time and distance, has arrived at a point where a disclosure is possible, albeit within the safe framework of poetic distancing devices.

Repeatedly in these poems, the pain is signaled by gaps in the victim's discourse, gaps which also allow the poet to resist a recontainment of her poetry. The words *rape* and *abuse* frequently remain unspoken in the survivor disclosure: the child is unwilling and unable to speak them, and the adult survivor knows that their absence is suggestive in a discourse that cannot easily articulate a solution.

At the same time, the poet resists the traditional power dynamics of the confessional mode. By convention, as Alcoff and Gray point out, the confession is signaled by a radical imbalance of power: "The confessional is always implicated in (both constituting of and constituted by) an unequal, nonreciprocal relation of power. And the explicit goal of the process of confession is always the normalization of the speaking subject and thus the elimination of any transgressive potential which might exist" (1993, 272). Small wonder, then, that just as some speakers inscribe gaps rather than "name" the specific abuse they have suffered, so too the poets are uncomfortable identifying too closely with such a painful experience of powerlessness. Mary di Michele, for example, makes this ambivalence explicit in "The Primer" (1990):[4]

> They think we're the same
> but we're *not*, the writer
> and the text. You see she called me in
> to interpret.

Despite this denial, however, di Michele *does* acknowledge her link with the young girl when she points out that the abused young girl becomes a writer and finds it difficult when she comes to write "this" poem:

> That the greatest gift offered
> was the gift of an English dictionary
> may sound made up when I tell
> you she grew up to write poetry.
> That she rejected this gift
> may account for her difficulty
> in getting started and her equivocation
> about the composition of *this* poem.
> (Emphasis mine)

Showing a similar reticence to link herself too closely with the abused child, Libby Scheier uses the name Jenny for her protagonist in her second book of poetry, *Second Nature* (1986). Only in "14," a poem in her subsequent collection *Sky* (1990) does she admit her "deception" explicitly:

> and I am hurt and puzzled and scared and
> alone more than anything I am alone and my name is
> Libby not Jenny and this recounts events
> that happened.

Scheier's poems, though, were about her own experience long before the publication of "14." The overlap between poems told in the third and first person—indeed, her need to go back again and again over this territory—reveals the poet's claim to this painful rite of passage.

This paradox, the simultaneous need and reluctance to name and claim experience, is at the heart of the survivor confession, and it is a function of the two levels upon which it operates. The reluctance to name abuse, moreover, conveys the shame that victims of sexual violence have felt: for the abuse, for their silence, for their speaking out. But since this reluctance to name is embedded within a poem which *does* articulate the reality of sexual violence and the responses it engenders, the poetic disclosure becomes a vehicle through which the poet invites readers to sympathize with the victim, signaling the necessity of the adult poet's overcoming of shame in order to gain control over the experience. Indeed, the survivor poet writes out of a sense of rage, not shame, and the poem invites the reader to share in that rage.

These poets argue that shame is in many ways a learned response. Libby Scheier's protagonist, Jenny, for example, is *taught* to feel ashamed by the hushed reactions of the adults around her as "Jenny's Surprise, or, Complicity" in *Second Nature* (1986) illustrates:

> No one ever does anything about it. Even though she
> tells them. She tells all the adults and they all do
> nothing. Later she makes it into a secret, learning
> from the silence that she has something to hide, that she is
> the boy's accomplice, that she should be
> ashamed.

By contrast, the first-person narrator of Susan Glickman's "The Man Next Door" (1990) finds that her story proves very effective:

> When he touched me I knew it was my fault.
> I thought about it all day and then I told
> my Dad, I told my Dad so it wouldn't be
> my fault.

Glickman's protagonist does not escape a certain twinge of shame, however, for in the following stanzas she articulates a sense of guilt ("He was nice, it was nice the way he touched me") not so much about the event, but about revealing the man's secret: "Later I told my Daddy. I know I did something wrong because / he was a nice man, he used to watch us playing. / And then he moved away." Since the little girl refuses to keep silent, her disclosure within the poem serves as a paradigm for feminist survivor poetry under examination here. Most obviously, the little girl's decision to disclose information gives her control of the situation. Her shame is very different from that felt by Scheier's Jenny: it is a function of power rather than of powerlessness.

The distance that Glickman's young speaker achieves from the event and her abuser is a dramatic enactment of the temporal, psychological, and aesthetic distance that drives the feminist survivor poetry. Interestingly, Glickman's poem "The Man Next Door" still depends upon the ironic interplay between the poet and her younger self to establish a bond between poet and reader. Glickman's adult speaker progressively distances herself from the abused child. First, there is a clear age difference between the two, creating an ironic relationship between the child who feels guilty for "telling on" the "nice" man next door and the speaker who condemns his behavior. Next, these two positions are never linked within the poem. Instead, Glickman adds a second section to the poem ("The Man Next Door II"), this one a presentation—in the third person—of the man's point of view. In this second section Glickman makes it quite clear that he is *not* nice, by anyone's definition:

> He knows
> they'd like it, he sees the way they're always
> touching themselves, and the girls, the way they
> look at him, "Hi Mister," with big eyes,
> flirting, all soft, they want it, they want it, one day
> they're really going to get it.

By adding this second section, the poet takes the task of judgment upon herself and absolves the young girl of any lingering sense of guilt or shame that she may feel. Here, the poem leaves the reader no choice but to agree.

Survivor Poetry and the Sympathetic Reader

In feminist survivor poetry, readers' responses are directed by and encoded within the poem's text. The reader is not so much addressed by the poem as she is anticipated by it. In a poem such as Claire Harris's "The Fall," for example, the use of the second-person pronoun functions not only as evidence of the poet's discomfort with the intensely personal nature of the subject matter but also to incorporate the reader into a sympathetic community. The reader is not the distant judge of the confession envisioned by Foucault, who possessed the power not only to "forgive, console, and direct" but also to "verify" the "obscure truth" of the confession (1980, 66). Rather, by adopting the second person, the poet casts the reader in the role of the victim, thereby inviting, even staging, a sympathetic response.

> When *you* surfaced *you* were still secret in the raw
> heart of *you*   *you* never told   *you* never called her name
> > (Harris 1984; emphasis mine)

"You," the reader, are also guilty of complicity in the silence. In other words, the victim position is a shared one, because the poem casts the reader in that particular role.

Somehow, at the heart of these survivor poems is a sense of a common female experience. Each woman provides her own story so that she is not alone, as Cyndia Cole illustrates in "No Rape. No." Precisely because the speaker is raped by her lover, it takes her long years to speak the word *rape*, to recognize the violation for what it is, and she ends by asking her sisters how many would join her in such a "mind fuck."

Even when a power imbalance *is* assumed to exist, as when in Betsy Warland's poem "family secrets" (1993) the speaker confides to her therapist, this poetry emphasizes the sympathetic link between speaker and listener.

> Sudden pungent smell of semen on the web of my
> hand, so strong, precise, my therapist recognized it
> too.

That Warland's speaker retains control of the narrative here poses a further challenge to Foucault's model. Although the therapist identifies with the speaker's experience, she is not given the chance to speak *for* her patient. On the contrary, the speaker gives voice to the therapist's experience.

"What would be the purpose / if I wrote a poem about rape?" asks Libby Scheier in "A Poem about Rape," a question which is central to any analysis of this confessional form. The answer Scheier provides is that the primary function is communication: "I want you to grasp the experience." In the very next sentence, though, she adds, "I don't think a poem can do that." The problem, Scheier suggests, is that it is only the initiated who can fully grasp the experience:

> How can I explain rape to someone
> who finds a one-a.m. streetcar ride alone
> boring, how can I explain that
> some people find it frightening?
> How can I explain rape to someone
> who does not worry about who gets on
> the streetcar, who looks at you,
> who gets off when you do.

So how does one communicate rape, the fear of rape, to the uninitiated? To her frustration, Scheier seems to find no perfect answer.

> A dramatic re-enactment is not the answer.
> A film about rape is not the answer.
> These usually excite you anyway
> which is not my purpose.

Raping you is not the answer.
There doesn't seem to be any answer.
There doesn't seem to be any answer right now.

That she writes and publishes the poem, though, suggests that she *does* settle on an answer. Although she recognizes that the poem will never express the fear of rape ("This poem is definitely a failure / in bringing the experience of rape / into your living room"), it does force the reader to confront the fear. After all, the subject of this poem is not the "I" who experienced the rape, but rather the way in which she can communicate the experience to "you," the reader. And the need to communicate is precisely the point.

Later in the collection, Scheier adopts three other strategies of communication in a series of poems about "Jenny," a five-year-old who is raped by a sixteen-year-old neighbor. In "Jenny's Surprise, or, Complicity," she provides a very specific account of the incident, distancing herself explicitly from the protagonist, first by calling the girl Jenny, and next by adopting an adult's perspective on the events. Consequently, the poem alternates between the impressions of a five-year-old Jenny,

She feels like a pea in a pod, the pod squeezing and
crushing her. A ball being dribbled down the court.
He is a doorless windowless brick house over her. He
does what he wants.

and the observations of the mature poet:

He only wants to feel her genitals and make her choke
a little on his cock, which feels so large to him in
her small mouth.

In this poem, Scheier communicates through painful detail, exploring the experience through the eyes of the affected child and the seemingly unaffected adult. As a result of the ironic tension between child and adult, the reader finds herself disagreeing with the adult, who seems so distant, and thereby takes on a more sympathetic role.

The subsequent poem, "Nursery Rhyme, I" (1986), suggests a further distancing between the poet and the intimate details of child rape. Here the nursery rhyme rhythm, as well as the neat couplets that open and close the poem, seem to be undercut by the complexity of the situation.

Wide-eyed and alive
she sucked cock at five.
He was sick and sixteen
and made false promises.

For years she thought cocks
were big as arms,
weapons of war and suffocation,
of mental and physical dislocation.

But this poem is far from simple. Indeed, the irony here is precisely that
the nursery rhyme cadence counters the painful subject matter and, like
the ironic double-speak of "Jenny's Surprise," invites the reader to adopt
a sympathetic stance.

In the third poem, "Jenny's Spring," Scheier adopts a different distancing
strategy. Rather than speaking in the third person, she uses an "I" narrator,
choosing instead to distance herself from the rape through changing the
subject altogether. This is a poem about a seven-year-old's thoughts—
of her boyfriend, her parents' new car, the beans she planted. Only in the
last lines does she return to the one thought that haunts her (and, as the
reader now realizes, Scheier herself):

I
was sad about moving because of the string beans and
being in love and playing with my friends in the car
but I was glad because I wouldn't have to go to the
basement any more.

In that last sentence, Scheier claims the experience of rape for herself and
her reader. In "Jenny's Spring," Scheier is finally able to communicate the
fear without, however, naming the source of that fear explicitly. The
"basement" has come to symbolize the painful rape.

Only in Scheier's next collection of poems, *Sky*, does she communicate the experience directly to the reader. In "14" of the "Earth Per Verse"
section of the volume, Scheier returns to the motifs of the earlier "Jenny"
poems, to the hated concrete basement, the rape of a five-year-old by a
sixteen-year-old neighbor, and her fear and incomprehension of the "arm-
thing." That Scheier has chosen to write a survivor poem is announced
in the first stanza as she evokes memory and shame "flaming [their] way
to anger." For the first time, Scheier names the abuser ("Alan Turchin the
child rapist / at 1504 Ocean Avenue in Brooklyn New York") and the
victim ("takes *me* by the arm and pulls *me* towards the basement again"
[emphasis mine]). But Scheier's willingness to claim the experience fully
as her own comes only at the end of the poem:

I am hurt and puzzled and scared and
alone more than anything I am alone and my name is
Libby not Jenny and this recounts
events that happened.

Here, as her use of the present tense suggests, Scheier acknowledges both the link between herself and Jenny and the way in which the horror of rape impinges on her present reality.

Besides Scheier's ability to name and claim the experience, we also see her gesture toward communicating with her audience. At first, Scheier distinguishes between "*the* hard thing"—which seems monstrous in part because it is described as a detached body part—and "*her* mouth" (emphasis mine). Consequently, the reader is already drawn to sympathize with the young female victim. Next, Scheier links the girl's experience directly with the reader's through adopting the now familiar strategy of the second-person voice:

> your eight-year-old brother has been told
> to keep him away from *you* he's been told by your
>   father who
> refuses to protect *you* and refuses to let your mother
> protect *you* and *your* mother doesn't stand up to him.

> (Emphasis mine)

Indeed, I would argue that the various strategies of communication that Scheier uses through her "Jenny" poems—namely, the use of the second-person address and the articulation of a child's incomprehension of the violence she experiences—serve to draw the reader into a sympathetic reading. Consequently, when Scheier names the abuser and herself as the abused child, she has already established an intimacy of communication which Rita Felski acknowledges as central to the feminist confession (1989, 108).

Scheier's use of the second-person pronoun is also an articulation of the adult poet's discomfort with speaking out. Indeed, Scheier's self-consciousness about her relation to the story means that words/language become a central subject, as in the early poem "A Poem about Rape": "What would be the purpose / if I wrote a poem about rape?" To be sure, her subsequent poems about rape all serve to answer the difficult question she poses. Of the many answers she suggests, the last one seems to be that it would make her seem less alone. In that final disclosure, Scheier "writes out" to a community of listeners.

Scheier's poetic engagement with confession in many ways supports Rita Felski's observations of the confessional communication. In particular, we see the "longing for intimacy" that Felski sees emerging "as a defining feature of the feminist confession at two interconnected levels: in the actual representation of the author's own personal relationships and in the relationship between author and reader established by the text" (1989, 108). The latter "level" is particularly important for Felski's argument, since she sees the feminist confession as an exercise in consciousness-raising which facilitates the "recognition that women's problems are not pri-

vate but communal," the "fundamental message underlying feminist confession" (115). Where I disagree with Felski, however, is in her refusal to
acknowledge the presence and power of irony in the feminist confession.
In order to establish the authority of the female subject, Felski argues that
"there is a conspicuous lack of interest in irony, indeterminacy, and linguistic play" (100). Yet Scheier's effective use of ironic double-speak to
engage the reader in the confessional exchange suggests otherwise. So does
Betsy Warland's very conscious play with language to which I will now
turn.

Overcoming the Impediment of Words

Whereas language provides a means of communicating with others in
Scheier's work, for Betsy Warland language is not only a tool for communication but the very site of her struggle. At the same time that she uses
language to render her personal rite of passage "in-the-visible" ("this time
there are witnesses" [1993, 10]), she focuses on the complexity of language and its relationship to the particular crimes of child abuse. Ironically, in Warland's collection, the subject of language threatens to displace
a retelling of the event itself, and Warland's survivor confession ultimately
involves her disclosing an ambivalent relationship to the medium of her craft.

Warland's sequence, *The Bat Had Blue Eyes* (1993), is an extended disclosure of the abuse the speaker received at the hands of her father and
brother. As a child, the link between abuse and language is signaled by
her difficulty with reading:

> there's another reason i forgot how to read in grade 3.
> A reason that shook my faith in the written word far
> more profoundly. I was being sexually abused.
>
> (34)

Again, in the passage where Warland acknowledges that the narrative is
her own, she links this moment of claiming with the act of reading. When
her mother returns home unexpectedly, her brother (or father?) scrambles
to cover his guilt:

> "put on your pants." spot of blood (it wasn't
> because of riding horses). hiding in the storage room
> (not supposed to be in here). his name (he's supposed
> to be in charge), then anxiously—mine (he's
> supposed to be babysitting). footsteps up the stairs,
> stop at my door, his, then straight ahead. zippers.
> he grabs an old *Life* as she flings open the door. her
> eyes—mine (this is not a dream): everything in
> that look me terrified she'll find out desperately

wanting her to (please mom, can't you *see?*). she
hesitates, glances away—then deletes. "why are you
in here?" "just reading to Betsy" he says. and she
believes him.

(76)

Language and narrative become deceptive for the young child so that
Warland's eventual ability to name the experience is a victory, not only
because it is a way of communicating with her audience, but also because
it is a step in her claiming language for herself:

> 7 years to say their names
> 11 years to write:
> father.
> brother.

(90)

What Warland describes is the need to access memory and to overcome
the impediment of words, the imperfect vehicle. "Memory is most true
when not translated into words," she writes, "With words we begin our
forgetting." What she is describing here is the inevitable distancing that
words cause. "To remember, we rely on words, words already a / substitute for the experience we seek to call up" (14). It is no wonder, then,
that when she finds out that her mother was also sexually abused she
realizes, "My mother and I are unlikely to ever speak of one of / the most
important things we share. Words would fail / us miserably" (20). Even
more disturbing, however, is Warland's knowledge that words are manipulated by her abusers.

> he told her
> it was "just a game"
> just.
> is it any wonder
> words confounded her?
>
> he willed her not to notice
> he told me "forget it."

(21)

Warland's use of "her" and "me" in this passage suggests not only the
shared victimization of mother and daughter, but also the importance of
language in achieving that victimization.

> Unlike my friend, who was abused before she had
> language, my abusers used words to secure my
> silence.

78

> which was my forgetting. mi rage.
> my mirage—no words
>
> (95)

The irony, of course, is that this passage also illustrates that Warland is herself adept at using language. For this, as well as for her willingness to forget, she feels rage.

> More motivated to recall pleasure than pain. Every
> time I was abused I didn't want to believe it.
> Doubted it. Told myself something nice was going to
> happen not something bad.
>
> In this way I contributed to my forgetting.
>
> (83)

And it is only in recognizing and acknowledging the writer's dilemma that Warland can find release.

> Can i write an i in the process of disinheriting
> itself, an i that knows an i-full isn't the whole
> story, that recognizes word as angel not servant?
>
> (85)

Warland's answer is yes, if the writer confesses to the complexity of her relationship with words and allows that language can be deceptive.

Conclusion: The Poetics of Canadian Survivors

In Canadian survivor poetry, the intimacy of the confessional form is a function of two central strategies: (a) the poet's "naming" the abuse and, drawing on a number of "safe" distancing devices in doing so, taking control of the narrative and (b) the poet's identifying herself as a survivor of abuse. Paradoxically, though, what these women poets confess is their difficulty with both. First, their ability to name the event is complicated by their distrust of language. Next, they feel unable to claim the experience because of their distance from it—both chronological and psychological. That is, the confessional reality principle is often announced in the poet's acknowledging her discomfort with disclosure.

Often this discomfort takes the form of rhetorical distancing strategies that establish an ironic interplay between protagonist, poet, and reader. If the speaker uses the third-person singular to relate the events of her childhood, the ironic distance between child and speaker allows, even encourages, a sympathetic reading on the part of the reader. Alternatively, if the speaker adopts the second-person address, the reader is cast into the role not of judge (as one might expect according to the inherited conventions of the confessional form) but of victim. That is, "you" becomes both the addressee of the poem and the protagonist of it.

In addition, the speaker's distance from the child she was and the abuse she suffered dramatically changes the power imbalance that has been (traditionally) so central to the form. No longer is the speaker a silent victim; rather, she adopts language as a vehicle for disclosing her realization that she is *not* to blame for the abuse she has suffered. In "writing out" her rage, the survivor seeks from her readers not judgment but strength and solidarity. For herself, she claims the role of judge, passing judgment on both her abuser and the appropriateness of written poetry as a context of disclosure.

Notes

For her resourcefulness in finding obscure subjects, as well as her insight, I would like to thank Rachel Rose. I am also indebted to Aaron Palmer for his frank criticism and constructive advice.

1. As I write this, however, I must acknowledge Canada's long history of "covering up" and silencing the atrocities of child sexual abuse. For example, although reports of child abuse at the Mount Cashel orphanage in Newfoundland began as early as 1974, they were systematically quashed (by the police, the media, and social services). It was not until June 1, 1990, that the orphanage was finally closed down (Harris 1991, 360).

2. Produced by victims of child sexual abuse, *Shout and Speak Out Loud* (1992) is a fascinating collection of poems, prose pieces, and illustrations. But because most of the pieces in this collection were the first attempts of victims to voice their pain and outrage, it is difficult to use them as the basis of a poetics. Nevertheless, it was an invaluable reference source. Although there are poems of child sexual abuse written by men (a notable example being bill bissett's "my first job" in *Shout and Speak Out Loud*), they are far fewer in number than those written by women. This essay focuses on poems written by women because I felt it was absolutely imperative to distinguish between male and female accounts of sexual child abuse, and I could not deal with both subjects within the scope of this work. As a first attempt to investigate the politics of survivor confessions in Canadian poetry, this essay and its sources are intended to open rather than close the subject.

3. My thanks to Aaron Palmer for this insight.

4. For a more detailed discussion of the function of confession in Mary di Michele's poetry, see Cooke (1990).

5

Not in This House: Incest, Denial, and Doubt in the White Middle-Class Family

Elizabeth A. Wilson

Survivor poets use aesthetic strategies to appeal to sympathizing readers. Yet, increasingly, the validity of stories about sexual abuse, particularly child sexual abuse, has been called into question. The essay below investigates the politics of confessional doubt, in particular the tremendous backlash against women's disclosures in the United States. The essay situates this backlash in the historical context of the middle-class ideology of the family and examines how the confessional modalities of the recovery movement both subvert and preserve elements of that ideology.

Incest has come out of the bedroom closet. In the early 1990s, it seemed that every other week another female celebrity was holding a press conference to accuse her parents of having molested her as a child. Oprah Winfrey, comedienne Roseanne Barr, former Miss America Marilyn Van Derbur Atler, Sandra Dee, and LaToya Jackson were among those who publicly told stories of incestuous sexual abuse.[1] When they came forward, Marilyn Van Derbur Atler and Roseanne were counseled by teams of therapists and social workers from the Kempe National Center for the Prevention and Treatment of Child Abuse and Neglect, based in Denver. These celebrity disclosures have apparently acted as a stimulus for other women (and other celebrities) to tell their stories. In the five months between May 1991 (the time of the Van Derbur Atler appearance) and October 1991 (the Roseanne disclosure), the Center received more than three thousand telephone calls from individuals who said they had also been sexually abused as children.[2]

These celebrity confessions represented the final mainstreaming of a testimonial strategy originating in the antirape activism of the radical feminist movement in the late 1960s and early 1970s. Radical feminists "discovered" the political salience of the issue of rape by means of informal small-group discussions in which women began to talk with one another about the experience of being a woman. These discussions eventually became more formalized; topics and format were written down and circulated and given the name of "consciousness-raising" (CR). Through CR, a form of personal testimony, women began to compare their experiences of sexual violence and to see these experiences as related to the political oppression of women rather than as idiosyncratic occurrences provoked by "seductive" behavior.[3] Although child sexual abuse was not initially the main focus of radical feminist attention, its relation to rape was quickly grasped and its affinity with personal testimony was established from the beginning. Indeed, over the years, no other form of domestic violence has lent itself to confessional storytelling like child sexual abuse.[4]

Before feminism, incestuous child sexual abuse was deemed so rare that it hardly seemed worth talking about. As late as 1975, the figure accepted by the authoritative *Comprehensive Textbook of Psychiatry*, 2d edition, was one case in a million.[5] However, more recently, new surveys and sociological studies have uncovered an unexpectedly high frequency of child sexual abuse in general and incest in particular. In 1979, David Finkelhor estimated a prevalence rate of one in five women. A Roper poll conducted in 1985 reported that one in three women and one in five men experience some form of sexual abuse as children, although these figures, like Finkelhor's, included all perpetrators, not just relatives. Diana Russell's *Secret Trauma: Incest in the Lives of Girls and Women* (1986) presented the results of a study suggesting that the true incidence rate of childhood sexual abuse is one in three women, while the rate for *incestuous* abuse is close to one in six women, with uncles and fathers the most common perpetrators.

The initial reaction to women's testimonies seemed to be collective astonishment and dismay that incest could be so ubiquitous. The pervasiveness of abuse was unprecedented, unanticipated, and turned incest from a rare occurrence perpetrated by "sick" individuals to an everyday event common to the lives of millions of children and carried out by people who must (given the arithmetic) look pretty much "just like you and me." It was often intimated that if these reports were taken seriously, they would force a profound and wide-reaching reassessment of the quality of the American family. Within the confessional spirals of America's popular media, it seemed as if a dark secret was finally seeing the light of day, a skeleton escaping from the closet

Yet almost as soon as sexual abuse was "discovered," suspicions began to arise as to whether it could actually be as frequent as alleged. It is now feared that revelations of incest, so disturbing in their intensity and so unexpectedly widespread in their frequency, do not represent the real experience of the women making them but are rather psychological artifacts created by various factors: by therapeutic interventions that do not just support a patient's recollections but direct and shape them, by aggressive and careless interrogations that involve directive questioning and undue assumptions about what the interrogation should yield, and by the patient's own possibly delusional thinking about her family. The same media outlets reporting on abuse cases have taken widely varying attitudes toward the debate, often in rapid succession, almost always with a doubtful piece following up a piece taking the disclosures seriously.[6]

The controversy about women's disclosures of child sexual abuse erupted in 1992 when the False Memory Syndrome Foundation (FMSF), an advocacy group for accused parents, was formed. Two years later, a number of current members of the Scientific and Professional Advisory Board of the FMSF published a series of scathing polemical attacks on the therapeutic and popular literature written for survivors of child sexual abuse, which, along with the skepticism generated by the more bizarre day-care trials, effected nearly overnight a change in public opinion.[7] A key figure has been memory researcher Elizabeth Loftus, who argues that it is far easier than believed to implant or create false memories in people's minds. Her skepticism has been all the more influential because of her disclosure that she herself was sexually victimized as a child.[8]

At the heart of the controversy is the psychological issue of "repressed memory." This refers to the mind's ability to "dissociate" during a traumatic experience, so that the experience does not enter normal memory but is processed differently and withheld from everyday consciousness.[9] Over the course of their lives, many of the women whose stories are in the news did not always remember being abused. But at a particular moment in adult life (in their twenties, thirties, or forties), the memory of abuse came back to them, most spectacularly in the form of flashbacks, and they made delayed accusations.[10]

Whatever its actual rate of occurrence in the population of sexual abuse survivors, the idea of repressed memory is a central feature of incest-recovery discourse. One self-help book confidently declares, "Many, if not most, incest survivors *do not know* that the abuse has even occurred! . . . This surprising phenomenon is the rule, not the exception of the post-incest experience."[11] In contrast, skeptics have argued that "robust repression" (the whole-scale expulsion of memories of prolonged trauma from consciousness) contradicts what is currently accepted about memory and thus is scientifically invalid. Advocates for alleged victims reply that traumatic memory does not operate according to the same processes as normal memory and instead brings different mental mechanisms into play. They add that denials on the part of perpetrators are to be expected and that the incidence of incest is far, far greater than the incidence of false allegations.[12]

A volatile debate has ensued, pitting parents against children, therapists against therapists, experts against experts, those who believe against those who remain skeptical. The issues raised by the current controversy about repressed memory are so complex and ambiguous, touch on so many diverse aspects of individual and social psychology, raise so many profound questions, that it would be hazardous for an outsider to the field to draw conclusions on the scientific questions being debated. What I want to do instead is comment as a cultural critic on an aspect of this debate that has rarely been noted. The horror and disbelief that attach to these stories of child sexual abuse seem intimately related to the fact that the women whose confessions have garnered the greatest amount of publicity are mainly white middle-class women. According to the FMSF, the typical profile of "false accusers" is usually a woman, in age between twenty-five and forty-five, who comes from a middle- to upper-middle-class family. Both the accuser and her parents have a high level of education: usually a university degree, and about one-fourth have postgraduate degrees. Most have good jobs.[13] In this essay, I place this debate about "repressed" or "recovered" memories of sexual abuse in a larger historical context and suggest some reasons, related to the history of the middle class, why the disclosure of sexual abuse has become the focus for such a furious debate and why the debate about the truth of "confession" is seen as having such enormous consequences.

Incest has long been regarded as a "vice of the poor." In her fascinating book on family violence, *Heroes of Their Own Lives*, Linda Gordon notes that the reformers who created the early social work agencies constructed the "meaning of incestuous sex . . . largely from a class ideology, pervaded also by anti-Catholicism. Conservatives and progressive reformers spoke of the degradation of poverty as if its victims were animalistic, lacking in standards of family life" (1989, 215).

But although the early social welfare agencies were urban phenomena and policed the domestic behavior of working-class, usually immigrant families, the most dominant American stereotype about incest, even today, is that it is a behavior of "white trash" poor families living in rural areas. In the United States, attention was directed to rural poor whites because of a remarkable "social scientific" genre, the family study, that flourished during the era of progressive reformism, from the 1870s to the 1920s. Based on assumptions drawn from eugenics, the family study was a pseudo-genealogical investigation of "degenerate clans"—large families supposedly characterized by inbreeding and undesirable traits. Poor rural whites were believed to possess especially inferior genetic stock, as indicated by their low IQs ("feeblemindedness") and their penchant for incest. A number of family studies implicated interracial marriages, with Indians, blacks, or "foreigners" in the general racial deterioration being documented.[14]

The family study was the first in a long line of sociological approaches that found supposed correlations between incest and lower socioeconomic status (usually when studying prison populations). As recently as 1979, a comprehensive review of the literature on incest by Sedelle Katz and Mary Ann Mazur concluded that "empirical evidence has confirmed the fact that most incest families are from the lower socioeconomic levels."[15]

However, the most important research on incest in the last fifteen years, Diana Russell's *Secret Trauma*, disconfirmed this prejudice resoundingly. Unlike most earlier studies, which were based on specific pools of participants, Russell surveyed a representative sample of women in San Francisco, so her conclusions are considered generalizable and thus are especially persuasive. Apart from the high level of incest discovered, the most startling aspect of the survey was the result concerning the class distribution of incest. Russell reported, "*Fewer* of the incest victims came from low-income backgrounds, and more of them came from high-income backgrounds than was the case for women who had never been incestuously abused" (1986, 113). Russell even went so far as to list "high-income background" as a "risk factor" in incest (114). She also noticed that "victims of stepfathers [are] less well represented in the upper class than the victims of biological fathers" (250), since stepfathers tended to be less frequent in the upper classes. Russell's survey also found that Latina women were slightly more likely to be incestuously abused than black or white women, but the differential rates (20, 16, and 17 percent, respectively) were not statistically significant (see 110–12). Asian women and Jewish women revealed relatively low levels of abuse (8 and 10 percent, respectively), but Russell noted that she had been warned by consultants that Asian women would simply refuse to talk about incest.

In light of the debate about repressed memory, it is significant that, as Russell herself notes, her statistics apply only to remembered abuse ("a serious though unavoidable limitation" [34]). It would seem that, even without relying on the evidence of repressed memory, there is reason to suspect that the prevalence of incestuous abuse in the white middle class is much greater than previously expected. While it may be premature to say that incest is actually *more* prevalent in the white middle class than in any other class or racial group, it does seem that incest in the middle class is frequent enough to be considered a significant social problem. Since the debate about repressed memory is taking place at a time when sociological research has begun to document a much higher prevalence of sexual abuse generally than had previously been suspected, feminist therapists and researchers feel justified in dismissing the repressed memory debate as mere "backlash."

Part of the vitriol created by the repressed memory debate is surely related to the fact that child sexual abuse accusations coming from white middle-class women pose a threat to white middle-class moral dominance. We can spell out the issues this way. White middle-class ideology implies that incest occurs more frequently in other classes or racial groups because these groups are morally *inferior* and are unable to restrain their animal impulses.[16] The flip side of this, of course, is that the white middle class abstains from incest and that this abstention makes it morally *superior*. Because the white middle class frequently justifies its dominance by referring to the putatively enlightened nature of the middle-class family and in particular to the putatively enlightened treatment of children, incest charges undermine these claims and therefore constitute a threat from within to middle-class hegemony. To illustrate more fully how incest charges threaten the core of white middle-class ideology, let me turn now to the history of middle-class attitudes toward the sexual abuse of children.

Even a cursory survey of the history of the middle-class family reveals a preoccupation with the sexual life of children and a commitment to protecting children from premature sexual experience. Beginning around 1700 and continuing until the First World War, there was a vigorous campaign in Europe and the United States to stamp out childhood masturbation, a campaign that involved frightening theories about the dire medical consequences of the practice (Neuman 1974–75, 1). This campaign involved not only misguided medical theories and a fear of childhood sexuality but a more complicated notion that adequate development required the deferral of sexual experience until adulthood. "Do you wish to put order and regularity in the nascent passions?" asks the tutor Jacques in Rousseau's *Emile* (1979, 219). "Extend the period during which they develop in order that they have the time to be arranged as they are born." For Rousseau, children in whom the passions had had a chance to develop "naturally" would be capable of attachment (marriage) when they finally emerged and would have the "first seeds of humanity" sown in their hearts (Rousseau 1979, 220).

In his two-volume *Adolescence* (1905), G. Stanley Hall acknowledged that the postponement of marriage increased the practice of masturbation "among civilized men," but the dissatisfaction created by this interval between sexual maturity and marriage could not be indulged if the higher goals of development were to be achieved. "The ideals of chastity are perhaps the very highest that can be held up to youth during this ever lengthening probationary period. This is the hard price that man must pay for full maturity" (in Neuman 1974–75, 16). Similarly, Sigmund Freud seems to have believed that sexual deprivation in the interval between puberty and civil maturity would enable individuals more easily to unite the tender and passionate sentiments in the sexual act: "In times during which no obstacles to sexual satisfaction existed, such as, may be, during the decline of the civilizations of antiquity, love became worthless, life became empty, and strong reaction-formations were necessary before the indispensable emotional value of love could be recovered" (Freud 1963a, 67). In general, the deferral of sexuality was thus perceived as crucial to the development of full physical maturity and to the formation of sentiments necessary for middle-class domestic responsibility and marriage.[17]

In his classic text *Centuries of Childhood*, French historian Philippe Ariès suggests that the modern *idea* of childhood finds its first expression in the writings of moralists who sought to protect children from adult sexuality. In a chapter titled "From Immodesty to Innocence," Ariès notes that the idea that children should not be exposed to sexuality (in the form of jokes and conversation, as well as touching) developed over the course of the seventeenth century (1962, 100–127). Prior to that, Ariès writes, children were not assumed to have sexuality before puberty, with the result that people took sexual liberties with them that would be considered astonishing today but were not then assumed to be harmful.

One of the key elements, Ariès notes, in the campaign to establish the "innocence" of childhood was the effort by moralists to alert parents to the dangers of servants (117). Individuals imported into the family from other classes and entrusted with the care of young children came to be suspected of bringing with them inappropriate attitudes and behaviors. Charles Rosenberg, in his study of nineteenth-century sexual attitudes in the United States, notes, "It was assumed . . . that domestic servants were a source of moral contagion, that they took particular pleasure in teaching masturbation and salaciousness generally to the innocents placed in their charge" (1973, 143). Jacques Donzelot, in his *Policing of Families* (1979), puts it in more abstract and general terms: "The bourgeois family was constituted by means of a *tactical constriction* of its members aimed at suppressing or controlling an internal enemy, the domestic servants" (45).[18]

As can be seen from these brief observations, the protection of the middle-class child from sexual abuse was expressed above all in the campaigns against domestic servants who, as class "others," were seen as the origin of sexual corruption in children, and against childhood sexual activity, especially masturbation. The ideology of the middle-class family thus constructs the threat as coming from *without* the family (servants) or from *within* the child (innate sexuality). There is, of course, a rather striking omission in this catalog of danger.

In general terms, white middle-class ideology holds that sexual abuse coming from within the family just *doesn't happen*. To the extent that Freudian ideas about child sexuality have become normative—or at least were normative at some time in the recent past—they have colluded powerfully with the middle-class desire to project sexual abuse onto class and racial others or to attribute it to the child's own seductive nature. In "The Passing of the Oedipus Complex" (1924), Freud notes that the "inherent impossibility" of satisfying Oedipal desires is one of the factors causing the complex to dissolve: "[T]he absence of the hoped-for gratification, the continual frustration of the wish for a child, causes the lovelorn little one to turn from its hopeless longing" (1963a, 176). A rereading of Freud's stages of sexual development, alongside his case studies, would reveal how deeply embedded in his model of psychic development is the *assumption* that the child's incestuous desires are *refused* by the parents. This refusal is conceptually rendered in the notion of castration complex, which denotes the father's law forbidding the desired incest to take place. It is interwoven, for example, with such interpretive sleights of hand as, "The obsessive thought, 'I should like to murder you,' means . . . nothing else but 'I should like to enjoy love of you'" (Freud 1935, 301).

Freud's case studies are full of examples of hostility expressed by children, not because, as we would assume today, they are angry at parental abuse but because they resent the parents' coming between their desires, whether masturbatory, incestuous, or other, and sexual (that is, often genital) satisfaction. After the Wolf-Man is seduced by his sister—a detail passed over rapidly in Freud's account—he is interpreted as trying to seduce his nurse as well as his father and as dreaming of witnessing "the primal scene"—intercourse between parents. The Rat-Man is pressured to admit that he hated his father for having interfered with his pursuit of childhood sexual pleasure in the form of masturbation. Arguably, Freud's theories, at least of sexual development, have contributed to a collective process of class denial that is potentially retraumatizing.[19]

The Freudian version of the middle-class family romance takes for granted that incest is always desired (especially by children) but almost always unconsummated. It has led to strange convolutions when clinicians are faced with evidence that incest, in some cases, has actually occurred, and then counsel their patients on the assumption that fantasies have been fulfilled. An exception to this tendency of Freudian discourse to obscure evidence of abuse is found, only momentarily to be sure, in the "seduction theory" or "traumatic theory" that Freud evolved at an early stage in his research and then precipitously abandoned, believing it to be misguided. Perhaps Freud was right to conclude that paternal seduction could not possibly be responsible for all the neurosis in the world. Undoubtedly, nonsexual traumas occur as well. Recent commentators such as Alice Miller (1986, 41) and Marianne Kruell (1979, 69–70) have suggested that Freud had another alternative before him at the point when he decided to stop believing his female patients. Rather than abandon the theory altogether, he could have broadened his notion of trauma to include physical and psychological factors and thus anticipated recent discoveries as to the role of childhood trauma in the etiology of psychiatric disturbance.

It is interesting to note that even radical reassessments of the bourgeois family, like those of French historians Michel Foucault and Jacques Donzelot, tend to assume that what the ideology says is *supposed* to happen in middle-class families is what actually happens. Foucault's seductive argument in volume one of his *History of Sexuality* (1978) is that the bourgeoisie created for themselves a "garrulous sexuality" (although a sublimated one) that was "foisted" on the lower classes "for the purpose of subjugation" (127). But consider his description of "sexuality" as "anchored" in the bourgeois family: "sexuality is 'incestuous' from the start. . . . [Incest] is constantly being solicited and refused. . . . It is manifested as a thing that is strictly forbidden in the family insofar as the latter functions as a deployment of alliance; but it is also a thing that is continuously demanded in order for the family to be a hotbed of constant sexual incitement" (108–9). Foucault notes that the middle class engaged in efforts to rout out incestuous *practices* in other classes and in rural areas at the same time that psychoanalysis was emerging to enable middle-class individuals "to express their incestuous desires in discourse" (129). In Foucault's account, confessing sexuality to the psychoanalyst was a means of sublimating it, of relegating the forbidden desire (for incest) into discourse. Thus, though noting that the family becomes a "hotbed of constant sexual incitement," Foucault takes the middle class at its word regarding the sublimation of incestuous desires and regards its campaigns against lower-class sexuality as evidence of something like hypocrisy. But if there is more incitement to incest in middle-class families than in other family units (as Foucault's analysis implies), why doesn't it follow that there is more incest, too?

Although the history of the middle class prior to the twentieth century shows a striking preoccupation with childhood "innocence" as concerns sex—for the reason that preserving children from sex was seen as necessary for their development into full adults—it is worth noting that the child was not considered innocent in other ways. As Ariès notes, the modern idea of childhood contained two quite different aspects (1962, 128–33). The first concerned the novel idea of "coddling" and "doting" on children, which is central to the modern family (and may perhaps be related to the incitement to incest that Foucault mentions). The second, arising from moralists and educators, concerned the child's immoral nature and lack of a developed rational capacity. As a result of this latter,

Ariès claims, there was a sharp rise in brutal corporal punishment used in schools; the use of physical punishment was especially harsh in England. Philip Greven's book *Spare the Child* (1991) feelingly explores the pervasiveness and unquestioned acceptance of physical punishment as a means of disciplining children in Anglo-Saxon culture and its possible social and psychological consequences.

Given the widespread tolerance of physical punishment, it is perhaps not surprising that Freud never even entertained the idea that such punishment could be a factor in the etiology of neurosis—as he did in the case of sexual abuse—even where the evidence was, so to speak, staring him in the face. In the case of the Rat-Man, for example, Freud pressures his patient to admit that he harbors hostility toward his father for interfering with his earliest efforts to achieve sexual satisfaction. The Rat-Man admits his hostility and eventually gets well, apparently proving Freud's theory correct. But Freud doesn't comment on the fact that when he does admit his hostility it is for the *wrong reason*. After a prolonged period of acting out, in which the Rat-Man "behaved like someone in desperate terror trying to save himself from castigations of boundless dimensions" (1963b, 65) and repeatedly expressed his fear that Freud would give him a beating, he eventually "recalled that his father had had a passionate temper, and sometimes in his violence had not known where to stop" (1963b, 65, 66).[20]

Quite possibly, Freud was even blinder to the role of physical violence in the etiology of neurosis than he was to seduction. But Freud's blindness reflects a class blindness. The history of the middle-class family, especially in the Anglo-Saxon world, shows comparatively little concern for the consequences of physical abuse—or for that matter psychological abuse. This is in marked contrast to its confessional obsession in the realm of sexuality, however misleading and displaced that obsession might be. Both physical abuse and psychological abuse were frequently defended as well-intentioned means of disciplining the child into adult rationality and self-control.[21]

In the current polarized climate of advocacy and suspicion, it is difficult to negotiate a middle path between the "true believer" and the "skeptical" camps. In this section I wish to examine critically a feature of incest-recovery discourse that has proved troubling to many commentators, since it encourages women to search actively for memories when they do not emerge spontaneously and thus seems to lead to a confessional spiral. Here let me begin by saying that, in my view, it is not simply a matter, as the skeptics suggest, of producing false memories of sexual abuse where there is, in fact, no abuse at all. I would like to raise a different question, namely, whether the confessional rhetoric in popular self-help books may encourage women to search for memories of sexual abuse when, in fact, there is plenty of evidence that other, less ideologically loaded forms of abuse may have been present in childhood. It is thus not a question of sexual abuse versus *no* abuse, as the false memory advocates imply, but of sexual abuse versus neglect as well as physical and psychological abuse.[22] The fact that these other forms of mistreating children may seem less spectacular than sexual abuse—and less worthy of redress—is, I would argue, related to the specific ideological history of child sexual abuse in the middle class.

The so-called Bible of the American incest-recovery movement is a self-help handbook called *The Courage to Heal* (1988), written by Ellen Bass and Laura Davis. Selling more than half a million copies and frequently quoted in critical media accounts, it bears some responsibility for fanning the flames of backlash. The reason is the apparent ease with which the book counsels adult women with symptoms to consider sexual abuse as the source of their problems. During the call-in portion of a CNN show on repressed memory, Roseanne Barr's mother telephoned to ask guest Ellen Bass the meaning of a passage on page 154 of *The Courage to Heal* where Bass, according to Mrs. Barr, allegedly says, "If you lack any facts or knowledge about the abuse, just imagine it, and you can be able to continue on with the fact that you were a victim." Through the False Memory Syndrome Foundation, Mrs. Barr said, she has heard the testimony of "hundreds and hundreds and hundreds of families" and in "every single one of them, their daughter was given the book *Courage to Heal*." When asked by the CNN host whether there was "something of that nature" in the book, perhaps not exactly what Mrs. Barr was quoting, Bass responded that there was nothing to this effect on page 154 and that she did not recommend this activity, nor did she believe that "reputable counselors" encouraged it, although she left open the possibility that "therapists make a lot of mistakes, and there are many incompetent therapists," without speculating what proportion they might make up or what they might be doing.[23]

It is noteworthy that Bass's response did not address the advice, reiterated several times in *The Courage to Heal*, that "feeling you have been abused" is as good as evidence that you have been. In the introduction, Bass and Davis state: "If you think you were abused and your life shows the symptoms, then you were" (22). Probably no line from the book has been more quoted. The problem with the advice that *The Courage to Heal* proffers, however, is evident in a controversial section of the book, entitled "But I Don't Have Any Memories," which begins on page 81: "If you don't remember your abuse, you are not alone. Many women don't have memories, and some never get memories. This doesn't mean they weren't abused."

In this section, Bass and Davis quote from the story of a woman who described her relationship with her father as "emotionally incestuous" but who had no specific memories of physical contact and was "haunted" (Bass and Davis's word) by her inability to possess solid data. Her tactic (which Bass and Davis propose as a model for other women) was to "act as if": "It's like you come home and your home has been robbed, and everything has been thrown in the middle of the room, and the window is open and the curtain is blowing in the wind, and the cat is gone. You know somebody robbed you, but you're never going to know who. So what are you going to do? Sit there and try to figure it out while your stuff lies around? No, you start to clean it up. You put bars on the windows. You assume somebody was there" (82). This woman (and through her Bass and Davis) chooses a compelling but wrong-headed metaphor for the experience in question. When a house has been robbed, there is evidence of a break-in and missing items. But the case of a woman with no memories is rather different. The accurate metaphor would be more like the following: "You come home and nothing looks disturbed. The door is locked. The windows are closed. Everything looks as you left it. But your jewelry is gone. You look everywhere. You try to remember where you left it. You look for evidence of a break-in, but you don't find any. It's a mystery." The point is that a woman with no memories *doesn't* know if she's been robbed.

It is worth dwelling here on the reasoning Bass and Davis use, since it is crucial to understanding the reception their book is generating. In both the metaphor as it appears in the book and the alternative that I have just sketched, the "something missing" could be understood as a sense of well-being, including security, calmness, and self-esteem. Their book argues that the absence of well-being must be attributable to sexual abuse; at least the reader is justified in proceeding "as if" it were. If you have the adult "symptoms," you could be a victim. Here are some of the controversial symptoms listed in E. Sue Blume's *Secret Survivors*: phobias, depression (sometimes paralyzing), anger, boundary issues, alienation from the body, and abandonment issues (1991, i–v). *The Courage to Heal* includes feeling "bad, dirty or ashamed," feeling "powerless, like a victim," having difficulty "feeling motivated," needing "to be perfect" (35).

In a much-criticized attack on the "Incest-Survivor Machine," appearing on the front page of the *New York Times Book Review* (January 3, 1993), feminist and social psychologist Carol Tavris rightly complains that "the same list could be used to identify oneself as someone who loves too much, someone who suffers from self-defeating personality disorder, or a mere human being in the late twentieth century."[24] Though I do not agree with Tavris's essay, for which she took a drubbing and which for some amounted to feminist treason, a number of the points she raises are important. Unfortunately, in their letter responding to Tavris, Bass and Davis do not specifically respond to the questions Tavris raises about the wisdom of advising women to deduce abuse from current symptoms in the absence of memories. Dismissing Tavris as part of the backlash, they merely acknowledge a few token excesses—"over-zealous therapists," "for-profit hospitals," and "desperate parents in custody cases"—but do not explore the role their book may have played in these phenomena.

For skeptics, the reasoning in *The Courage to Heal* introduces a potentially devastating indeterminacy to the question of family responsibility for personal pathology. If the confessional frame postulates that you don't have to "remember" the abuse, you are free to postulate it, reasoning like the women faced (so to speak) with the robbed house: "Why would I be feeling all of this? Why would I be feeling all this anxiety if something didn't happen?" A question raised neither by incest-recovery advocates nor by their opponents is why, for this woman, an "emotionally incestuous" relationship with her father was obviously unsatisfactory as an explanation for her adult symptoms, as if your father would have to sexually touch you in order for your relationship with him to severely and negatively affect your life.[25] This, even though Bass and Davis state at the beginning of the book that "some abuse is not even physical" (21). As yet, researchers have been unable to verify a specific cluster of symptoms that predictably appear in the wake of child sexual abuse.[26] The etiology of symptoms remains a mysterious process. It is likely that many different types of child maltreatment can leave a legacy of anger, boundary, and abandonment issues, as well as identify problems. Alienation from the body can be produced by covertly incestuous relationships. Severe sexual dysfunction is perhaps the only symptom that seems truly specific to sexual abuse.

The metaphor of the robbed house, used as it is, has the implication of suggesting that incest or sexual abuse must somehow take priority in discussions of child abuse. In an article for *Playboy*, Debbie Nathan (1992) cites the example of "Donna," who burst into tears at a retreat for victims of child abuse, saying, "I'm a survivor of emotional abuse. . . . I feel like I don't deserve to be here. I'm ashamed, because I have no memories of incest" (86). According to Nathan, the four-day retreat was advertised as a place for dealing with a variety of psychic scars, but incest and cult ritual sexual abuse quickly emerged as the dominant traumas. While it is impossible to know how accurate Nathan's account is or how representative the retreat she attended, her account of the women's responses at this retreat is consistent with what one might expect from reading the passage from *The Courage to Heal* just discussed. The way Nathan recounts it, participants were encouraged to search for memories that they didn't have, with the disturbing (and ironic) result that even those who

Elizabeth A. Wilson

did have actual memories of abuse felt invalidated, if the abuse remembered was not sexual: "Marilyn, who had been only battered, ran around raging in piteous frustration: 'No one's paying any attention to me!' Lee, a stockbroker whose mother was merely alcoholic, shrugged in disgust and vowed never again to attend a retreat. Others felt abashed but resigned. 'I have to live with the fact that I may never remember anything,' one person sighed." At the end of the four days, Donna announced to the group, "I had a dream last night . . . an incest dream." According to Nathan, "she looked relieved, calm," and Nathan concludes the article by wondering "when her parents will show up in the False Memory Syndrome Foundation files" (164).

The controversy over these anguished testimonies and angry denials, around this most private and devastating issue, apparently comes down to a question of whether the adults responsible for children in the white middle-class family—the parents or other near relatives—are morally capable of sexually abusing their children. In other words, what is at issue is the moral self-representation of the middle-class family as the biological unit of reproduction that nurtures rather than exploits its offspring. The debate over repressed memory is taking place largely within a middle class that has a deep, long-standing investment in denying that incestuous abuse can take place within its class boundaries. Despite this denial, there is good reason to believe that incest is in fact more prevalent in the white middle class than it is willing to admit. Seen in light of this evidence, all the hostile suspicion being raised about repressed memories seems like an instance of class consolidation against an internal threat to its moral self-representation (and eventually to its class power based on that self-representation).

If we look at this debate in feminist terms and ask what is being disrupted and what is being maintained, what is being lost and what is being gained, we see a complicated picture. While incest-recovery discourse reflects the previously unacknowledged extent of incestuous sexual abuse in the middle class, it also represents both a reflection and an inversion of middle-class efforts to create "childhood" by warding off sexual threats to children perceived as coming from class or racial others or from the child's own lascivious nature. The results of both of these interventions— revealing abuse and relocating the source of abuse from outside the class to within the class—are potentially disruptive. They may add up to an efficient collective strategy in that they take the worst violation the middle class is able to imagine (apropos of children) and show that the middle class itself is guilty of perpetrating it. According to the values of the middle class, a child who has been forced to be prematurely sexual has been denied the experience of childhood that is deemed so important for suc-

94

cessful middle-class adulthood. Thus, if a person wants to make it understood that they feel robbed of childhood—on the terms the middle class itself has established—a sexual abuse charge is one that is likely to be understood.

The problem is that the very ubiquity of sexual abuse charges is now helping to undermine them. Previously incest seemed to be nowhere; now it seems to be everywhere. As shown above, the middle class has historically exhibited a lack of concern for the possible ill effects of physical or psychological abuse as compared with sexual abuse. If it turns out that the incest-recovery movement is focusing on sexual abuse to the exclusion of other forms of abuse that may be indicated—and thus recapitulating within the movement the hierarchy of abuse established by the middle class itself—it may turn out that the long-term results are less disruptive than hoped for.

Notes

1. See Marilyn Van Derbur Atler (1991), Roseanne Arnold to Vickie Bane (Bane 1991), and Sandra Dee to Todd Gold (Dee 1991).

2. See Jim Coates (1991).

3. For slightly differing accounts of the origins of CR in the feminist movement, see Susan Brownmiller (1970), Alix Kates Shulman (1980), and Hester Eisenstein (1983). For early discussions of CR, see Shulamith Firestone and Anne Koedt (1970).

4. Feminist classics like *The Conspiracy of Silence* (Butler 1978) make extensive use of interviews with victims. See also the anthologies *Voices in the Night* (1982) and *I Never Told Anyone* (1983) and the book-length accounts by Katherine Brady (1979), Sylvia Fraser (1987), Louise M. Wisechild (1988), and Betsy Petersen (1991), among others. To be sure, differences exist between early feminist and later more mainstream testimonies, and a more detailed history would have to make careful distinctions. The similarities that justify my generalizations here include the assumption that the "I" of the text is identical with the author and that the focus is on linking psychological pain or self-destructive behavior occurring in adulthood with childhood sexual trauma.

5. Kluft (1990, 3).

6. Some examples. In October 1991, at the time of the Barr disclosure, *Newsweek* ran a story called "The Pain of the Last Taboo," quite sympathetic to victims and skeptical of how directly Loftus's work (which often deals with trivial memories in a laboratory situation) could be applied to incest victims. See Nina Darnton et al. (1991, 70+). Less than two years later, *Newsweek* put the grim photograph of two grandparents allegedly falsely accused on its cover, with the headline "When Does the Fight to Protect Our Children Go Too Far?" citing Loftus's work in

relation to an article questioning the credibility of child witnesses. CNN's *Sonya Live* discussed incest on August 31, 1992. Less than nine months later, on May 3, 1993, the same show treated the subject of repressed memory and featured an undercover reporter (who presented fictitious general symptoms) being diagnosed as a child sexual abuse victim by a therapist at the end of an initial consultation and being explicitly instructed as to the workings of repressed memories.

7. See Richard Ofshe and Ethan Watters (1994), Frederick Crews (1994a, 1994b), and Elizabeth Loftus (1994). Of these, Loftus is the most moderate in her tone.

8. Loftus's accounts of how she remembered her own experience of abuse have been a matter for discussion. Jennifer J. Freyd (1996) looks at them as illustrating "the paradox of traumatic memory" (1996, 28–29).

9. For overviews of the wide range of current thinking concerning repression and dissociation, see Jerome L. Singer (1990) and Steven Jay Lynn and Judith W. Rhue (1994). On traumatic memory, see the October 1995 issue of the *Journal of Traumatic Stress*, as well as Bessel van der Kolk and William Kadish (1987) and Bessel van der Kolk and Onno van der Hart (1991).

10. For a good summary of professional opinion on both sides of the repressed memory controversy, see the *Working Group on Investigation of Memories of Childhood Abuse: Final Report* (1996). Also see the exchange between Elizabeth Loftus (1993b) and Judith Herman (1993) in the *Harvard Medical School Mental Health Letter* and Elizabeth Loftus and Lucy Berlinger (1992). The August 1994 issue of *Applied Cognitive Psychology* is devoted to the controversy, as are the fall 1995 and the summer 1996 issues of the *Journal of Psychiatry and Law*. Repressed memories are often most spectacular and most incredible when they recollect what is called satanic or cult ritual abuse. For professional articles skeptical of ritual abuse claims, see George Ganaway (1989) and Susan C. van Benschoten (1990). For a fascinating account of efforts to verify one story of satanic ritual abuse, see Lawrence Wright (1993a, 1993b).

11. E. Sue Blume (1991, xxi).

12. To date, the most convincing study showing that recovered memories may be based on real events is Linda Williams (1995).

13. See Anne Mullens (1992).

14. See the introduction in Nicole Hahn Rafter (1988), esp. 7–8.

15. Quoted in Russell (1986, 113).

16. I have chosen to employ the term *ideology*, rather than *psychology*, because the former implies both the interpellation of subjects and the use of subjectivity in creating or justifying social hierarchies. It is well documented that white middle-class assumptions about the sexuality of racial others—e.g., that blacks are more strongly sexed and less able to

exert impulse control than whites—are inextricably bound up with racist attitudes. Sander L. Gilman's fascinating study, *Difference and Pathology: Stereotypes of Sexuality, Race, and Madness* (1985), shows how painting iconography often employed images of black servants to illustrate the sexual availability of the white women being portrayed. The same essay documents how Hottentot women were represented as having oversized genitals in the medical literature of the nineteenth century.

17. See also Charles Rosenberg (1973, 137).

18. See also the fine chapter on "Domestic Subversions and Children's Sexuality," in Ann Laura Stoler (1995, 1937–64).

19. Contemporary psychiatry and psychoanalysis are beginning to accumulate rereadings of Freud's case histories that highlight the abusive elements in the childhood histories of Freud's patients and offer reinterpretations. While these are limited to the data that Freud himself presents, they are indeed suggestive. The most widely known reinterpretation has been of Freud's "Psychoanalytic Notes upon an Autobiographical Account of a Case of Paranoia (Dementia Paranoides)" (1911) in *Three Case Histories* (1963b, 103–86). This case is unusual among Freud's case histories, since it did not involve an actual patient but was a diagnosis based on the published autobiography of Dr. Daniel Paul Schreber. Subsequent historical research has revealed that Schreber's father was a well-known pedagogue who advocated the use of horrific physical restraints and other devices in the disciplining of children and employed them on his own. See Morton Schatzman (1973). For a rereading of the Wolf-Man's case history, see Alice Miller (1986, 158–72). Dora's case has been reread by many. Lawrence Frank (1989) considers Dora a victim of childhood incestuous abuse. Although Anna O. was Josef Breuer's patient, her story was critical to the formation of the history of psychoanalysis. Her case is reconsidered by Richard J. Loewenstein (1993).

20. I wrote this short interpretation of the Rat-Man case based on my experience teaching Freud's 1919 text, "Notes upon a Case of Obsessional Neurosis" (in 1963b). Though independently derived, it coincides precisely with Greven's interpretation in *Spare the Child* (1991, 137–39).

21. It is fascinating to see that this blindness can sometimes be observed in researchers who are at the forefront of calling attention to childhood abuse. In an article on "Childhood Trauma in Borderline Personality Disorder," Judith Herman, Christopher Perry, and Bessel van der Kolk systematically excluded from the definition of abuse "instances of culturally-accepted corporal punishment and fighting" (1989, 491). In one of the case studies profiled, a woman who was disciplined "by means of frequent hitting with a cane or a 'bony Irish hand'" was described as enduring "harsh but nonabusive corporal punishment" (493) and was given a trauma score of zero and a Bipolar II diagnosis. It seems possible that the

subject's self-reported observation about this experience (as quoted in the case summary) influenced the rating: "It was not traumatic, [my mother] did it with everybody, it seemed all right; the nuns at school did it too" (493). But it seems likely that the subject's experience of the punishment as nonabusive was conditioned by the pervasiveness of culturally accepted physical abuse in her environment. See Herman et al. (1989, 490–95).

22. The tendency of sexual abuse to assimilate other forms of abuse is reflected in the semantics. Ian Hacking notes that today "the present primary connotation of child abuse is sexual abuse" (1991, 259), even though research into the issue began in 1962 with the question of physical abuse.

23. There is, in fact, a writing exercise on page 154 that is recommended as a form of "remembering" in which the survivor is told to write a story about "an event in your family history that you can never actually find out about"—for example, "your father's childhood or the circumstances in your mother's life that kept her from protecting you." There is no evidence that Bass and Davis recommend this exercise for the recovery of the abuse experience itself, as Mrs. Barr implies. Yet it is also true that the introductory passage describes it as "an exercise that enables you to piece together things you can't possible [*sic*] know about your history or the history of your family" (Bass and Davis, 1992, 154), thus suggesting that this foray into the imagination can produce accurate knowledge about the family experience.

24. Tavris's essay and the responses to it form a fascinating archive on this debate. See the letters responding to her column, "Real Incest and Real Survivors: Readers Respond," *New York Times*, February 14, 1993, sec. 7, pp. 3+. Her essay was widely reprinted, and many regional newspapers also published letters responding to it. See also the column in defense of Tavris's right to her opinion by Stephanie Salter (1993).

25. For research on the subject of how emotionally incestuous relationships can contribute to adult psychological symptoms, see the chapter on "seductive fathers and their families" in Judith Herman and Lisa Hirschman (1981, 109–25).

26. Joseph H. Beitchman et al. (1992, 108).

6

Raging in Tongues: Confession and Performance Art

Lynda Goldstein

In the limelight of a public arena, performance art presents a dramatic form for women to express rage about sexual trauma. On stage, the female body creates a strategic splash—externalizing anger and theatricalizing out/rage. Sexual performance art is an effective way of making the personal political, but its unsettling effects have led opponents to malign it as pornographic. Discussing the cases of Karen Finley and Holly Hughes in the United States, the essay below makes deliberate use of the term *performance confession*, highlighting the concept's appropriate double meaning: the transgressive meaning associated with the term *confession* as well as the genre's vulnerability to confessional readings in popular media.

> They speak the unspeakable, even if it manifests itself in horrifying, untidy, or esoteric matters.
>
> —Ted Weiss

> Sexual speech is forced into reticence, euphemism, and indirection. Freedom of speech about sex is a glaring exception to the protections of the First Amendment, which is not even considered applicable to purely sexual statements.
>
> —Gayle Rubin

Rehearsing History

Karen Finley, wearing a faded floral print dress, begins her "Baby Bird" monologue from *The Constant State of Desire* (1990) while seated demurely in an overstuffed chair. Her dress, posture, and comfortable chair seem to promise her audience a representation of traditionally passive femininity. "She dreams," muses Finley. "She dreams of strangling baby birds." Clearly, the initial dreaminess of this monologue has been disrupted by her articulation of violent strangulation. Here Finley has abruptly swerved off track, wrenching her audience from disingenuously comfortable cultural representations of women's lives on to a psychic journey of women's pain and self-loathing where previously "no sounds would come out of her [character's] mouth at all" (1990, 59–60). What Finley performs throughout this opening monologue is a hellish roller-coaster ride through stifling gender roles and dysfunctional family relations. The measure of woman is martyrdom, suicide, sadistic rape, and incest.

Voicing the nightmare subtending the cozy and overstuffed appearances of American culture, Finley disabuses her audience of its quiescence. And she doesn't do so softly but works into a screaming rage. Stripping off her dress in nonerotic fashion, she tosses stuffed animals and raw, colored Easter eggs into a large, clear garbage bag, repeatedly smashing it on the floor until the gooey yolks coat everything inside. Pulling the yellow-slimed stuffed animals from the bag, she uses them to sponge the eggs over her body. Next, she sprinkles silver glitter and colored paper confetti onto her egg-battered body, then drapes paper garlands around her neck. The interplay between (egg)battering and subjection to erotic expressions of femininity—nudity and party dress—highlight for Finley the double bind that women's sexuality and sexual expression inevitably effect in American culture. Too often, however, Finley's conservative critics have read her deconstruction of women's doubly-bound eroticism only as a lewd teasing of their sexual desires, not as a stripping of the cultural baggage that women's sexuality must carry.

Launching into the second movement of her performance, she under-coats her grotesque display of woman as erotic object with "I hate yellow. I hate yellow so much." As incantatory (in tone and repeated phrasing) as she is vitriolic, Finley doesn't miss a beat in her symbolic condemnation of a consumer culture that treats its citizens, especially women and children, as disposable products. Her character fantasizes revenge against Wall Street traders by "cut[ting] off their balls," rolling them in her own feces, and reselling them to gourmet chocolatiers. As she shifts characters, modulating between (female) victims and (male) abusers, her performance becomes more frenzied. Moreover, it becomes ever more graphic in its rage against incestuous rape and torturous abuse of mothers and children. Inextricably melding food imagery and problematic sexuality, her out/rage is all the more disturbing to viewers.

Like Karen Finley, Holly Hughes uses a stage set with an overstuffed chair, but she sits behind it, legs spread and facing away from the audience, to begin her 1990 monologue *World Without End:* "Okay. Here's the deal. I'm going to tell you a story. It's just a little story, nothing heavy. A story about a bird" (9). The story concerns the bird's instinctual perseverance, its perpetual return to the same disheveled nest in the tree outside "Holly's" window while her parents' fights and her father's alcoholism—"The usual family stuff, right?"—raged within the house. Thereafter, "Holly" sits in the chair wearing a silky, off-the-shoulder dress and spike heels, her voice calm and steady as she reads from a large composition book in her lap. Occasionally walking about the stage, Hughes is quietly, almost politely, sardonic as she addresses the messy politics and erotics of sexuality, particularly lesbian and bisexual, for women. While often couched in a giggling or flirtatious manner, hers is a performance that is both pointedly contemporary and insidious in its rage: "Men just kill me. They really do. They are killing us. They hate us women so deep and hard they don't even know they're doing it. They say: 'I like women, I'm all for equal rights!' But what's this antiabortion fever gripping the nation, huh? What's this unending lack of funding for the children they cared so much about as fetuses, then abandoned as children? Oh, I know what you're thinking. You're thinking there's women in the antiabortion movement. Well, that's what they *want* you to think! Those are not *women*" (24). Just as Finley abruptly shifts from dreaming to strangulation in the first two lines of her performance, Hughes shifts from "killing" as an idiomatic expression for making one laugh to "killing" as literal and metaphorical murder, sliding meaning along an out/raged trajectory of amplified abuses that culminates in the coaptation of gendered identity (and its presumptive politics): "Those are not *women*."

She later rages against the numbers of real and representational instances of battered and raped women who cannot (seem to) leave their situations, providing her audience with a sense of the scope of culturally sanctional misogyny to which women are held captive: Jennifer Levin (victim in the "Preppie" murder case and subject of a made-for-TV movie), Hedda Nussbaum (battered wife and alleged accomplice in the deadly Lisa Steinberg child abuse case), and Jodie Foster's character in *The Accused* (based on an actual pool hall gang rape in New Haven, Connecticut). She uses each case to bolster her point that the judicial system and popular media held the women, not the abusers, accountable for the sexual violence visited upon them. Within the legal and media institutions, it was the women's sexuality (the defense arguing in each case she had "asked for it") that justified the sexual abuses to which each was subjected. Characterized as "guilty," the women in these cases are used to amplify "Holly's" description of her mother's dichotomized sexuality—vamp/ "victim-waiting-to-happen"—in their small town. Taken together, these four women's stories serve as a warning that any woman's sexuality could be considered transgressive and punishable by physical battering, rape, death, and/or inscription into sensationalistic popular discourses (such as tabloids, talk shows, and made-for-TV movies).

Hughes's performance art offers a cultural critique that compresses the roles of judicial institutions and popular media together and holds them responsible for yet another level of violence upon victims of sexual assault. While her conservative critics dismiss the artistic merits of her work because it is "political," Hughes maintains that all art is politically invested; she does not categorize critique and artistic production as mutually exclusive. Rather, in Hughes's scheme, the "difference" between politics and art is that "politics" works to hide how dominant ideology operates while "art" works to expose it. While Hughes would not distinguish between "art" and "politics," she would distinguish between "art" and "popular culture," maintaining the latter, like the judicial system, operates at a level of institutional power that hides the politics of its own production. Propelled by Nielsen ratings and tabloid sales, the institution of popular culture effaces power relations in favor of sensationalized representations of women's sexuality that provokes the violence visited upon it.

In spite of the similarities of the opening sequences to *The Constant State of Desire* and *World Without End*, the performance styles of Finley and Hughes are quite distinct. However, each articulates a kind of *performance confession*, a no-holds-barred confession of/from the sexualized body that operates against the "outrage" generated by the reception of their work. Their respective modes of address (including the problematic nudity of Finley and mythologizing of Hughes to be discussed later) and incorporations of culturally taboo subject matter operate for each as a performative out/rage, a raging in tongues, against ideological systems that constrain women to victim roles. In other words, their out/rages work as oppositional modes of impassioned address to foreground the complexities of women's identity, desire, and sexualities.[1] They also articulate feminist anger at social injustices and violences perpetrated against women by the dominant culture.

The context for understanding these out/rages is, in part, a matter of performance space. Throughout the 1970s and 1980s, feminist performance art was most frequently held in small clubs and theaters in major cities or at college and university venues, often sponsored under the auspices of a women's studies program and/or a feminist-sympathetic performing arts department for a predominately female audience.[2] Significantly, this was not the case for Karen Finley's early work, which was more often performed in art spaces or nightclubs with decidedly mixed gender, and often hostile, audiences. Finley's work *is* decidedly discomfiting. Her troubling oscillation between victim and abuser is addressed to audience members, forcing them into shifting positions as abuser to her victim or victim to her abuser. Effectively, she destabilizes audience members' gendered identities and sense of power relations by directly addressing *them* as performative "hysterics" in a culture that privileges stable, gendered identities.[3]

Hughes's early ensemble work, on the other hand, played to primarily lesbian audiences at WOW Cafe in New York and worked to create a performative space for lesbian desire. That there is a presumption of certain homogenizing relations among the women audience members at WOW and similar feminist spaces is comically indicated by Hughes in *World Without End* (1990), which played to mixed audiences. "Oh I cannot tell a lie, I'm hated and I return the sentiment because it's just too big for art and I'm too old for abstraction. I think I feel okay about saying this because we're all women here tonight, right? Okay. We're not all women. But we're all lesbians. I mean anyone can be a lesbian, gender is no obstacle" (26). Though she is well aware that in a mixed gender audience all are "not women here," the strategies of her work about lesbian desire produce audience members as "lesbians." What Hughes produces in the statement above is a performative dissonance: all are not women but all could be lesbian. The unstable "lesbian" collective identity that Hughes constructs works against a reading of the mixed gender audience as "heterosexual," though many in the audience might, indeed, position themselves as such.[4]

Contesting Performance Art

What I intend to examine in this essay are the ways in which Finley and Hughes—as the "hysteric" and the "lesbian"—are contained within multiple interlocking discursive fields. Such an examination will consider the ways in which feminist performance art, as practiced by Finley and Hughes, respectively, problematizes notions of autobiography and sexuality. Further, I will investigate their modes of address and the shifting play among *rage, outrage,* and *out/rage* both within their performances and against the popular media, academic, and congressional discourses about them and their works. I read their articulations of rage as performative sexual confessions that simultaneously voice the incoherence of subject formation while constraining the confessor to a coherent identity. In each case the performance acts were recirculated in the media as symptomatic of personal failings and/or immorality rather than as strategic and performative identities with political implications on a national scale.

Michel Foucault (1978) has argued that sexual confession operates simultaneously as a foundational act of subject formation and as a mechanism of containment by dominant ideology. Given this doubled function, the use of "autobiographical" sexual disclosures in feminist performance might be "self"-defeating. Surely one place to examine how this dialectic works is at a historic juncture when it is most visible: in the domain of popular culture. Reading how Karen Finley and Holly Hughes were situated within popular culture (what we might simply collapse into the category of discourse in the public domain) means theorizing popular culture as part of an intricate system of knowledge production about subjectivities, their interrelations, and their national coherences. Further, it means acknowledging the ways in which categorical distinctions among the popular, the artistic, and the political obscure the ideological functions, as well as the production and reception histories, of all these forms.

While there are any number of moments when the workings of oppositional discourses become visible, the particular moment to which my attention will be directed here is the "crisis," as it was characterized repeatedly in press accounts, over the status of the National Endowment for the Arts (NEA) in its funding of cultural work.[5] What I intend to map out are some of the ways in which the oppositional discourses of *rage, outrage,* and *out/rage* were played out in the cultural debates attached to the NEA in and around the autobiographical feminist performance art of Karen Finley and Holly Hughes. Of special concern are the ways in which Finley and Hughes, together with their works, were situated in popular media with respect to their expressions of out/rage. Examining these funding debates through the published expressions of "outrage" and "out/rage" generated by, in, and around the performances of these two artists provides a case study of the complexly organized and ever shifting reappropriative discursive strategies governing identity politics in the domain of popular culture, particularly as inflected by sexuality in "postfeminist" America.

This essay, then, is concerned with reading the ways in which the work and identities of Finley and Hughes were discursively (re)produced, (re)circulated, and (re)contained by the debate in the popular media and in Congress, as well as in their performances throughout the debate.[6] In effect, the consumption of "Finley" and "Hughes" in popular discourse had everything to do with producing them as confessions of sexuality so "outrageous" that they required public and sustained consumption until virtually silenced.

At stake, then, are the politics of systems of knowledge production. The ability of feminist performance artists and their work to contend with other discursive systems becomes compromised by the sexual disclosures that impels much of this work. In his introduction to a volume documenting the NEA debates, Richard Bolton (1992) not only singles out Finley and Hughes as artists who have not "appropriately" used such a strategy but implies that their inappropriate usage provoked the rage against them ("they asked for it"). He situates their work/their identities as problematically and provocatively oppositional, distinguishing their performative out/rages from the more "authentic" anger of HIV+ (now deceased) David Wojnarowicz. Among other things, Bolton clearly subscribes to a notion of performative rage that is effective only when unmitigatingly autobiographical, as issuing from a subject whose experiences are "authentic," not fictionalized or reconstructed. Finley and Hughes, on the other hand, deploy a form of confessional performance that specially refuses to maintain the distinctions between a woman's personal history and the recombinant strategies of retrospective narration (Bolton 1992, 23).

Theirs is not so much a tactical error (or provocation) in assuming such modes of performative address as it is a matter of realizing the extent to which systems of knowledge production—particularly around identity formation—operate within dynamics of power. This is Peggy Phelan's reminder in her discussion of the "problem of citationality, documentation, and context" in relation to the ephemeral quality of performance art, which has had a history of resistance to reproduction and commodification (1993a, 14). Writing of the inevitability of Karen Finley's work being distorted by popular accounts, Phelan points to the "unequal economy of power-knowledge in which performers and writers find themselves. For the writer's work can be reproduced, circulated, given a kind of (temporary) permanence that performance art itself lacks. . . . Citation is always already an operation of power" (23). The power exhibited by these popular (re)citations is such that performative sexual confessions become textual reproductions of women as outrageous hysterics or lesbians. Indeed, Finley and Hughes, as the female duo of the "NEA 4," were often stereotyped as gender troublemakers, obscuring the distinctiveness of their performances.[7] In rehearsing a history of popular culture's discursive moves to produce and contain unified subject identities for Finley and Hughes, this paper risks perpetuating these operations, but it is my hope that I can write a history of the containment strategies that disrupts this history of containment.

The performance works of Karen Finley and Holly Hughes were enabled by a generic tradition of autobiographical performance art popularized in the 1970s to politicize personal experience, create empathy, and blur the line between performative and social experiences of women. This tradition encouraged the adoption of an "autobiographical" voice in an attempt to give voice to the "reality" of women's bodies. Yet since the late 1980s, feminist performance art has increasingly moved away from the notions of unified subjectivity and truthfulness implicit in autobiography. Indeed, Vivian Patraka (1992), in an essay entitled "Binary Terror and Feminist Performance," argues that "if the autobiographical is still present in feminist performance, it has mostly become a space of indeterminacy and shifting personae. . . . Thus, in contrast to realism, the audience is unable to contain these voices within individual narratives of psycho-biography or case history. And without the 'plot' of revelation attached to the life of a particular character, there can be no 'talking cure': the voice untethered from either character or performer conveys that what has to be changed is both larger and more political" (171). Recent out/raged performances of "women's experiences," then, articulate sexual subject positionings that are neither coherent nor produced from the limited number of narratives available to women within patriarchal discourse. Thus, while the speaking subject "I" appears to be unified in the bodies of Finley and Hughes through their use of autobiographical strategies, voice shifts and extraordinary fantasizing belie any sense of a unified subject for performer or audience members.

The reliance upon autobiographical subject positions has lent feminist performance art a point of leverage for its critique of American culture. Artists have incorporated the idea of "the personal is political" as a per-formative strategy to use what Jeannie Forte (1988) calls "the condition of their own lives to deconstruct the system they find oppressive. . . . [Further,] their performance practice shares concerns with recent theory interested in unmaking the system of representation and its ideological alliances" (219). Yet we need to be cautious about assuming that the deconstruction to which Forte alludes is without liabilities. Given the "confessional" status of these "autobiographical" performances, however problematized confession and autobiography are, there are necessarily containment strategies that operate counterdiscursively. As we know, indeterminacy is not a valuable commodity in popular discourses, whose work it is to delimit meaning while simultaneously embodying contradic-tions. Under a regime of determinacy, the popular, academic, and congres-sional readings of these "autobiographical" performances became insepa-rable from the performers, each of whom was precisely read as tethered to the incoherent sexuality she "confessed"—with dire political consequences.

Confessing/Sexual/Performance

Michel Foucault argues in *The History of Sexuality* that during the sev-enteenth century, the hegemony of the Catholic Church in France mobi-lized control over the "truth" of sexual discursivity through sexual con-fession, so that the "truthful confession was inscribed at the heart of the procedures of individualization by power" (1978, 59). One became an individual, a bourgeois subject of dominant power, through narration, through the avowal of one's past performances, and increasingly, Foucault maintains, through the "true" confession of one's sexual performances. Foucault defines the operations of the confession as "a ritual of discourse in which the speaking subject is also the subject of the statement; it is also a ritual that unfolds within a power relationship, for one does not confess without the presence (or virtual presence) of a partner who is not simply the interlocutor but the authority who requires the confession, prescribes and appreciates it, and intervenes in order to judge, punish, forgive, console and reconcile" (62).

The ritualization, the structural need for (an) interlocutor(s), the uneven power relations of exchange between confessor and listener (with power residing with the listener) are also, Victor Turner (1982) reminds us, characteristics of theatrical performance. Yet, broadly defined, theatrical performance is not distinguished by a mode of address that is both autobiographical and confessional as it is in performance art. In the latter, there is an intimacy between performer and material, as well as between these and the audience, that can be especially troubling when sexuality is foregrounded. Thus, the power relations established in performance art are often more fluid and destabilizing than they may be in traditional theater.

In as much as the confession operates prescriptively, it is a mechanism of authority that constructs the confessor/performer as a subject. The confessor is produced as a sexual subject within the limitations of narrative "veracity" established by the listening and viewing authority. Or, as theorist Peggy Phelan phrases it, "the performer is always in the female position in relation to power. Women and performers, more often than not, are 'scripted' to 'sell' or 'confess' something to someone who is in the position to buy or forgive" (1993b, 163). However persuasive Foucault's analysis of sexual confession is, its applicability to feminist performance art requires an adjustment. Foucault focuses on the sexual act, on the confessor's "reconstructing, in and around the act, the thoughts that recapitulated it, the obsessions that accompanied it, the images, desires, modulations, and quality of the pleasure that animated it. For the first time no doubt, a society has taken upon itself to solicit and hear the imparting of individual pleasures" (1978, 63). In his examination of the sexual confession as a regulatory discourse of sexuality, Foucault appears to place an inordinate emphasis on the "truthful" imparting of the past as a secondary sexual performance. If it is the case that confession operates to produce and contain the object of its constraint, then introducing a consideration of gender to Foucault's reading of sexual confession might lead us, as it did Judith Butler (1992), to the realization that "oppression works through . . . *exclusion* and *erasure* effected by any discursive formation, and that here the feminine is precisely what is erased and excluded in order for intelligible identities to be produced" (354).

In deploying sexual confession, feminist performance artists would seem persistently to articulate a subject always under erasure within an oppressive regime, while also producing that subject through repeated confessions. The act of confession is, Butler notes, performative in much the same way that gender is: "*performative* in the sense that it constitutes as an effect the very subject it appears to express" (1991, 24). Butler further argues that as an effect of repetitive performance, gender identity can be troubled through performances which challenge that repetition, which play with the discursive regimes that maintain identity. Since feminist performance art works to include and foreground woman's experience through discourse, its persistent and repetitive deployment of confession would seem to "trouble" hegemonic identity structures.

Finley and Hughes's performances do not simply articulate the production and regulation of pleasure under authority. Rather, they perform a much more complicated rearticulation of the dynamics of pleasure/displeasure between and among bodies: Finley through a raging exposure of the inequities of sexual politics and Hughes through a construction of lesbian sexuality in opposition to a heterosexual economy. This is not to say that "pleasure" is not imbricated in the various power dynamics of their "characters" in a variety of performances, but their works generally demonstrate the ways in which pleasure and displeasure are not mutually discrete, are always relational, and are reflective of other power inequities.

In the "Abuse" section of her solo performance, *The Constant State of Desire*, for example, Finley pushes at the permeability of the boundaries between pleasure and displeasure, enfranchisement and disenfranchisement, male and female, that so provoked anxiety among her audiences and those concerned with her funding by the NEA.[8] "After I fist fucked you with my handful of sapphires, emeralds, garnets and opals . . . I was fucking you with my aquamarines, my gold, my silver and platinum. I was fucking you with my will, my property, my esteem, and my values. I was fucking you with pearls and diamonds. Just filling your hole with everything I got. I was fucking you with my talent 'cause it's all I got left. My rings just cutting you. Your snatch on liquid fire. I just look down on you. You just look up with your doe eyes and say, 'It's better to feel abuse than to feel nothing at all'" (23). Assuming the anger of a presumably male (the fist fucking making this unclear) and certainly class-privileged voice, Finley puts into play a number of power relations. One is indicated through her reappropriation of this fisting rage by speaking it through her own vulnerable-to-abuse body (signified as much through the audience's foreknowledge of nudity in her other shows as through her body language as she delivers this monologue), so that it acts as a conduit for all those who cannot speak.[9] Another is made clear through the displeasure exhibited in the sexual confession itself, both in the moment of the sexual act (particularly for the pregnant woman) and in the performative telling by the fisting character/Finley.[10] For most audience members, the gender dissonance of Finley's female body/voice ranting such male/not male physical abuse of women strengthens the distinct sense of displeasure in listening to this confession.

Indeed, it would seem to me that such displeasure destabilizes Foucault's (and Phelan's) notion that the power relations are more securely situated with the listener, given the difficulties for most listeners in finding this exchange pleasurable. Here is an indictment of a system so violent that an abused woman would signal pleasure rather than live with no emotional or physical attention at all. Clearly, Finley's use of confession is not a simple circulation of sexual pleasures between teller and listener that empowers and gratifies only the latter.

Holly Hughes, too, reconfigures this pleasure/displeasure dynamic. In *World Without End,* she "confesses" a scene of mother instructing daughter about the nature of feminine sexuality and "the meaning of life." "Holly" recalls her mother standing naked before her "smelling of salt, and she's promising me grease, something to suck on, and she's asking me in, oh, she's asking me in. . . . I could see how wet she was! And that smell! Let me tell you about that smell! That smell made me want to do the mashed potato! Just me and my mother, my naked mother, dancing in the split level" (20). Though she instructs in the stage directions of this text that the performer's tone of voice "should be one of an initiate witnessing a sacred ritual, a mystery revealed," Hughes is well aware of how troubling this scene is to the boundaries of gender and sexuality.[11] "The tone is awe," she continues, "which can be misinterpreted as fear and lead to a reading of this passage as an incestual event. But no matter what a girl does, there will be those nuevo puritans among us who see something dirty in this. I suggest they read Joe Campbell or the Great Mother, hell, even the *World Book* probably talks about 'Fertility Rites.' See it's all in the classics" (19). Her obvious irony in these directions indicate her own pleasure at the displeasure that this scene is certain to arouse. While her performance stretches "mother" to mythic dimensions, it remains rooted in the material realities of incestuous sexuality. Where Finley's "motherfucking" is spit out in angry hatred of the mother (only to be short-circuited by the mother's belittling of the son's performance later in the scene), Hughes's is celebratory of a lesbian Earth-mother sexuality. Bound to the physicality of sexual practice by her "mother's French," an eroticized approach to the world that "Holly" has learned so well, Hughes's negotiation of sexualities is embodied in ways that some audience members are likely to find discomfiting, even outrageous, in the purposeful destabilization of power relations between confessor and listener.

Circulating Out/Rage in Popular Culture

The particular crisis surrounding Finley and Hughes was initiated in 1989 by conservative right-wing Christians and politicians who defined the funding practices of the NEA as a scandalous and outrageous underwriting of "blasphemous and obscene" photographic art with "public" monies.[12] Indeed, their attack on the NEA was rhetorically couched in terms of "outrage," which worked to seize control of the politics of cultural production, thereby policing those "unruly" artists[13] who insisted on foregrounding questions of cultural differences, power relations, and hegemonically maintained ideological systems (Davis 1990).

It was the outrage expressed by fundamentalist Christian minister Donald Wildmon, organized through massive mailings from members of his American Family Association in the spring of 1989, that prompted Senate conservatives Alfonse D'Amato and Jesse Helms and House Representative Dana Rohrabacher, among others, to question the NEA's policies of art funding that their letter-writing constituents considered blasphemous. So much did "outrage" serve as the key signifier of the New Right's cultural anxieties, that in his initial address to the Senate and subsequent letter to Hugh Southern, acting chair of the NEA (signed by twenty-two additional senators), Senator D'Amato expressly specified "outrage" five times as the justification for renewed congressional review of the NEA's funding practices.[14]

Their furious attention quickly moved, as Peggy Phelan has remarked, "from a consideration of photographic to performative transgression" (1991, 131), which repositioned performance art from the avant-garde margins to the central arena of popular culture. As the debate continued to rage in the public domain, academics and artists worked to reinscribe and recontextualize performance studies, contesting in art magazines and professional journals, but less frequently in the popular press, the "obscene" and "outrageous" terms of the debate as they were mobilized by the New Right.[15] These buzz words operated as shorthand for the ways by which variously positioned bodies and voices, in this case right-wing ideologues aligned with the state, sought to confine others' bodies and voices, particularly those confessing sexuality, that they found "outrageous" or pornographic.[16]

Perhaps the most notorious description of Karen Finley's feminist performance work persistently repeated in the popular press (and academic accounts) during the public debates represented her as a "nude, chocolate-smeared young woman," a phrase originally used by conservative commentators Rowland Evans and Robert Novak (who had not seen her perform) in their syndicated column reporting on the Bush administration's pressure on NEA chairman John Frohnmayer to revoke funding for the "NEA 4." According to the NEA memorandum leaked to them, her work is a "'solo theater piece' and what the artist herself, Karen Finley, describes as 'triggering emotional and taboo events'" (Evans and Novak 1990). "An administration insider calls the exhibit 'outrageous.'"[17]

Tags of "nudity," "chocolate," and "outrage" circulated and recirculated as the popular press picked up the story without benefit of having seen her work, though such a benefit would presumably not have altered these early citations, fueled as they were by simultaneous congressional debates about pornography.[18] These tags were supplemented by false statements (re)circulated in press accounts and, all too often, in academic critiques of her work, concerning the insertion of yams and other vegetables in anal and vaginal orifices. Although the latter were corrected by Finley's manager, Michael Overn, in *TDR*, it had little effect on the popular press, and Finley despaired of ever "correcting" the error.[19]

That there should be such concern demonstrates precisely the extent to which it was now Finley "herself" who was being produced by the collapse of sexual transgression and pornography in the popular debates, as Finley was well aware: "This was me, my individuality, and America is only defined by individuality. America is not defined by communities. My individuality was threatened, was stopped" (in Carr 1993, 160).[20] What Finley is calling her "individuality" is, I think, a sense of the integrity of the self. Her statement foregrounds the difficulties of maintaining any distinction between Finley's "real" self and her autobiographical performative selves. Yet such border maintenance is no more possible within the realm of popular discourse than it is within the context of a performance space in which the fragmented "selves" of abused/abuser are so fragilely contained by the "hysterical" body of an out/raged performer.

In contrast to the lurid descriptions of Finley's work and body—"the chocolate-smeared woman"—Hughes's, with few exceptions, remained largely imageless in the popular press. Her articulations of lesbian sexuality in the ensemble pieces and the "bourgeois" confessions of bisexuality in *World Without End* were effectively silenced.[21] Instead, the popular circulation of Hughes's work relied on a simple identification of it as "lesbian." Taking their cue from Frohnmayer's 1991 cautionary statements to the National Council on the Arts—"Holly Hughes is a lesbian and her work is very heavily of that genre. It is very tough stuff"— the press immediately reduced Hughes's work to her body.[22] Typical of the popular media's recirculation of this collapse of sexual identity politics and performance genre into "lesbian" is a *New York Times* snippet by W. Honan (1991) reporting on the revelation in NEA documents that the revocation of grants to the NEA 4 had been politically motivated: "Ms. Hughes, who is openly lesbian, has described her work as 'chock-full of good old feminist satire.'" While this description has the virtue of allowing Hughes to speak for herself, the unexamined combination of "lesbian," "feminist," and "satire" functions here as a performatively generic indictment of the "lesbian" kind by dominant heterosexual values. Just as "nudity," "chocolate," and "outrage" worked to construct

"Finley," so "lesbian," "feminist," and "satire" implicated "Hughes" in a discursive field of confessional subjectivity from which she was subjected to a debilitating notoriety as a performative lesbian.

Appropriat(iv)e Discursive Strategies

Both Finley and Hughes scavenge among the detritus of popular culture and melodramatic theatrical conventions, to name but two locations, for their discursive ammunition. They also appropriate biblical exegesis and fundamentalist religious rhetoric, which allows them to indict precisely the values held dear by New Right conservatives. While Hughes adopts the more quietly intimate tones of the self-righteous biblical revisionist, Finley's style of performance has all the appropriative fire-and-brimstone of a tent-preacher. Much has been made of the incantatory style of Finley, which has been described variously as "ranting," "trancelike," "hysterical," and "evangelical." Of course, Finley's incantations are not simply appropriative of fundamentalist rhetoric. Rather, they are also attempts to discursively construct a confessional space of healing in which she assumes the roles of both confessor and listener by taking on the audience's assumed pain. As she explains it, Finley tries to *"give* something—do work which helps people connect emotionally in a sense of *sharing and clarifying emotional pain.* . . . To me, what's important is a connection and a centering: really listening to our selves, because we're always listening to things *outside* of ourselves" (in Juno and Vale 1991, 43–44). To listen to the self is to enter a state of self-confession, one that Finley hopes to induce in her audience through her screaming, incantatory out/rages.

In deploying this rhetoric for the purpose of galvanizing an otherwise disparate and disheartened leftist response to the attacks on the arts, they deploy a playful double-edgedness. Indeed, it is this ability to "cut both ways," to refuse a stable position from which to be produced, circulated, or consumed, that enabled the rhetoric of "out/rage" to amplify the shifting relations of power within confessional modalities. What the incantations and repetitions of rage—whether from the performance stage or the Senate floor—effected was for these discourses and the subjects produced by those discourses to be heard out/side of the "private" space of the performative confessional and in the "public" space of popular culture where they could be reproduced, recirculated, and reconsumed infinitely.

Finally, one might argue that out/rageous performative confessions by women artists such as Finley and Hughes will always be countered and appropriated by other outraged discourses in American public culture. In the realm of the popular, their out/rage, as well as their "selves," will inevitably be contained as confessions, often violently. Yet the increasingly confessional nature of popular culture itself and the oppositional structures that compel it suggest that it is precisely not the case that the violences visited upon Finley and Hughes were precipitated by their sexual performances. Rather, in the discursive contests that determine identity and power relations, all who "confess" a performative sexuality that trouble stabilities will become caught up in the rages of a "world without end."

Notes

1. This gendered self designated "woman" works as a strategic negotiation between essential and socially constructed positions throughout Finley's and Hughes's work. For a theoretical discussion of the strategic advantages of mobilizing both positions simultaneously, see Diana Fuss (1989).

2. See C. Carr (1986).

3. Jill Dolan does not read Finley's performances as destabilizing for audience members, arguing that Finley remains "mired in the corporeality of her own flesh as it has been abused in the system of representation," so that she replicates, rather than deconstructs, women's cultural positioning (1988, 67).

4. Hughes's statement points to intersections of identity politics, gender, and queerness, so slippery that Axl Rose, the reconstructed homophobic leader of the heavy-metal band Guns 'n' Roses was seen sporting a "Nobody Knows I'm a Lesbian" T-shirt at one of his concerts, according to *Out* 6 (July 1993): 9.

5. The National Endowment for the Arts and the National Endowment for the Humanities were created by Congress in 1965 to fund artistic and humanities projects, yet Congress was expressly forbidden to interfere in funding decisions. Such decisions were left to peer review boards under the supervision of the respective chairs. These debates, which now appear every two years when the Endowments come under review for funding, demonstrate the extent to which politics is inextricable from cultural production and public debate is equivalent to "crisis" in American culture.

6. Miranda Joseph (1990) makes a similar argument, usefully considering Finley's work in terms of consumption rather than reception so that "the value of the performance is what is produced through its consumption, it is the effect of the performance in history rather than its self-identity" (13).

7. On June 29, 1990, NEA chairman John Frohnmayer rescinded theater program grants to four performance artists: Karen Finley, John Fleck, Holly Hughes, and Tim Miller. This was widely perceived as a politically motivated attempt to protect the NEA from further assault by cutting loose "marginal" performance artists who foregrounded sexual identity formation through the confessional form. The "NEA 4" filed suit on Sep-

tember 27, 1990, in Los Angeles Federal District Court against the NEA for revoking their grants. The NEA settled out of court in June 1993 following a flood of amicus briefs filed by what Jacqueline Trescott (1993), in the *Washington Post*, termed (but did not define) "a sweeping cross-section of the national cultural community."

8. B. Kapke (1986) similarly argues in a review of a performance of "Unspeakable Practices, Unnatural Acts," that she "pushes beyond the borders of *normal* practices and *natural* acts into an ambiguous area where we must face these boundaries, these limitations, and re-evaluate them."

9. Finley has explained, "A lot of people feel the same way I do, but they *keep it in* because it's socially unacceptable to mourn in public or to show feelings. If you did, you'd be vulnerable or abandoned—maybe no one would love you. But I have the ability to reveal my feelings—so in a sense, I'm getting even. Revenge can be art" (in Juno and Vale 1991, 41).

10. Maria Pramaggiore argues that what is truly "scandalous" about Finley is "she appropriates the power of her body and language, turning that force inward in an apparently self-destructive manner, a powerful but problematic means of communicating the pain of female oppression" (1992, 284).

11. Although the autobiographical performances of Finley and Hughes have been published, some with stage directions, allowing for performance by others, I am unaware of any artist doing so.

12. While there had been earlier "scandals" involving the NEA's funding practices of art, the most concerted mobilization of anti-NEA efforts ensued in the spring of 1989 over Andres Serrano's "Piss Christ," a photographic work depicting a crucifix submerged in a glass container of Serrano's urine. See Richard Bolton (1992, 3–26) for a discussion of the NEA crisis in terms of public access to information. See Peggy Phelan (1990) for a history of the events in terms of access to "public" funds.

13. "Unruly" in this context is borrowed from Nancy Fraser (1989).

14. Senate testimony in Richard Bolton (1992, 28–31). The New Right is a coalition between fundamentalist Christians and conservative politicians built during the administrations of Reagan/Bush (1980–1992) distinguished by their ability to mobilize public opinion by intervening in the discursive field through increasingly sophisticated technological means—cable television and direct mailing (including electronic). The political rather than moral basis of the New Right agenda is evident in Dana Rohrabacher's "trash[ing] of NEA recipients by taking works out of context and call[ing] Congressional NEA supporters proponents of pornography" in exchange for campaign donations from the American Family Association (Lehrman 1990).

15. C. Carr described Finley's performances as "obscenity in its purest form—never just a litany of four-letter expletives but an attempt to

express emotions for which there are perhaps no words, an attempt to approach the unspeakable" (1986, 17).

16. The pornography connection came about through a political collaboration between antipornography feminists and the New Right. Their reciprocal discursive relationship would have its fullest flowering in the Reagan administration's Meese Commission Report, which implicitly approved of restrictive legislation championed by antipornography feminists Catherine MacKinnon and Andrea Dworkin in 1983, particularly in Minneapolis and Indianapolis. Linda Williams similarly argues that "'normal' sexuality, the Meese Commission implies, is never violent, not even in the imagination. The attack on violence, together with the rhetoric of harm borrowed from radical feminism . . . allows this arm of the 'moral majority' to assert sexual norms under the guise of protecting pornography's victims" (1989, 19).

17. Writing two years later on the NEA's promotional film, Maurice Berger (1992) recontextualized this phrase as right-wing arts bashing: "There are no gay lovers; no women smearing their bodies with chocolate; no crucifixes soaked in urine. As candy-coated, populist propaganda, the film understandably elides all the nasty little items among the endowment's recent grant proposals that neo-conservatives love to exploit." Another revision—emphasizing Finley's intent—is evident in an Associated Press article reporting on district court judge Wallace Tashima's decision that the decency clause demanded by Congress was unconstitutional. It read in part, "Karen Finley, who has spread chocolate on her body to symbolize the degradation of women: Holly Hughes, who concentrates on lesbian issues" (Fleeman 1992).

18. For example, a discussion concerning the adoption of "National Pornography Victims Awareness Week" coincided with NEA funding discussions in September 1991, the juxtaposition of which implied a causal relationship between pornography and NEA funding that were to have such dire ramifications for Finley and Hughes.

19. Overn's response to Elinor Fuchs regarding yams and orifices indicates the extent to which academic writing was no less culpable in perpetuating a fascination with "filth": "Once and for all: *SHE HAS NEVER DONE THIS!!!!* She smeared tinned (whipped) yams on her buttocks but she has never, repeat, never put a yam up anywhere. It may seem like a petty mistake but you wouldn't believe the problems this mistake has caused Karen over the years" (Overn 1989). Fuchs's reply problematizes his implication of authenticity in Finley's performative identity: "Though I am puzzled by the vehemence with which Mr. Overn protects the image of a performer whose career was initially built on transgression, I sincerely regret any factual errors I may have made in translating the early Karen Finley through published newspaper accounts and videotapes" (9).

20. For (mis)interpretations of pornography, see Margot Mifflin (1988).

21. Kathryn Heller writes in a review of the piece staged for the National Gay and Lesbian Theater Festival:

> Holly Hughes, a self-identified "bad girl" offered the most explicit account of female sexuality and subjectivity. In her semi-autobiographical performance, *World Without End*, Hughes speaks of lesbianism, bisexuality, and her mother's pussy. Hughes's power resides in her rebellious temperament, and she dares to test how many so-called private secrets can be exposed in public. Clearly Hughes . . . situates herself quite explicitly in a contradicted relation to bourgeois liberalism. The contradiction becomes apparent as Hughes constructs herself in the manner of a private confessional, conducted from an upholstered armchair, the icon of bourgeois domestic life and privacy. In contrast to this, the incivility and confrontiveness of Hughes's diatribes expose and implicate the power of the listener/spectator position, foreclosing the role of silent voyeur usually assigned to the spectator in bourgeois theater. (1991, 243–44)

22. Reported in *Art in America* 77 (November 1991): 41.

7

TV Crisis and Confession:
The Hill-Thomas Hearings

Jessie Givner

No other case exemplifies the explosive intrusion of personal trauma into politics than the one involving the American law professor Anita Hill. In October 1991, Hill came forward during the congressional confirmation hearings of Judge Clarence Thomas to charge her former employer with sexual harassment. In contrast to the performance artists discussed earlier, Anita Hill's testimonies strategically sidestepped confessional modalities and deliberately avoided any show of emotion or rage. Given her clever political maneuver, it is all the more ironic that the public crisis caused by her disclosures prompted a rapid and effective redeployment of traditional confessional hierarchies in the political arena and in popular media. Hill's testimony on female sexual trauma was so powerful and disruptive that it could be contained only through an unrelenting deployment of confessional readings.

Of the many figures who have testified in the Senate chamber, few have taken on the monumental stature of Anita Hill. Her testimony has been credited with politicizing sexual harassment, with changing representation in the Senate, and indeed with ending a whole era of Reagan-Bush conservatism. "Anita Hill spoke for us," writes Margaret Randall (1992, 20), after Hill's powerful intervention into the political arena. "Anita Hill's voice is part of our process now. It thunders in the chorus—voices that have been raised at great personal risk, with courage, in ever-widening circles of reclaimed power" (22). Anita Hill's intrusion into the public domain made it impossible for the nation to further ignore sexual harassment as an important social and political issue. Indeed, through her intervention Hill has become an icon of massive historical change.

Susan Stewart (1993), in her study of narrative and visual scale, writes that "in contrast to the still and perfect universe of the miniature, the gigantic represents the order and disorder of historical forces" (86). Hill's televised testimony produced just such a disorder of historical forces. That Hill has indeed become a figure of gigantic significance explains the equally gigantic efforts of antifeminist forces in the United States to silence and denigrate her voice. Becoming "larger than life" was a double-edged sword in Hill's case. As Stewart demonstrates, subjects become "larger than life" not only through their historical acts but also through their medium of presentation (86). In contrast to the flow of TV news from one item to another, TV crisis repeats one image in a case of massive overexposure. If the multiple and gigantic images of Hill worked in combination with the medium of televised hearings to signal radical historical change, it also became part of a powerful containment strategy for antifeminists.

From McCarthy to Watergate to Iran Contra, televised hearings are the most traditional and recognized forms of TV crisis. Structured by an interrogation-confession format, they offer a cathartic purging of false-hood and promise a final resolution of truth. Yet the raw material that emerged during the Hill-Thomas hearings threatened to overflow this or-dered form as charges of male sexual misconduct and expressions of fe-male sexual trauma intruded. This essay argues that the disordering of TV time and space caused by that intrusion produced a political crisis and a subsequent deployment of containment strategies. Political institutions and popular media converged to frame Hill within confessional modali-ties, with the effect that public attention was strategically shifted from her powerful charges to her own sexuality.

There are temporal and spatial structures of discourse, times and places appropriate to the hearing or silencing of certain subjects. There are also certain rituals of discourse that regulate speech and silence in the public arena. These structures and rituals were transgressed during the hearings. Most striking was the disruption of the temporal and spatial organiza-tion of televised sexual testimony. The nonstop TV coverage of the hear-ings for twenty-one hours, from Friday straight through to Saturday, broke the unspoken rule that places expressions of female sexual trauma in the space of domestic weekday television time, the time slot for "women's viewing." Instead, sexual revelations emerged at night on prime-time TV, a time for "family viewing," and on Saturday morning, a slot reserved for "children's viewing."

It has been argued that crisis and catastrophe always disrupt the tem-poral organization and information flow of TV. Crisis, Mary Ann Doane (1990) notes, condenses time and implies a limitation of time in which a problem must be resolved or a decision must be made. But the hearings were a departure from previous TV crises, for they revealed that the flow of TV time is not gender neutral. TV relegates personal disclosures of sexual trauma to daytime soap operas and talk shows. Revelations of sexual "aberrations" are the material of talk shows such as *Oprah Winfrey* and *Donahue*. Produced not for family viewing but for a female audience, these shows are aired during the day, women's TV time. The genre, then, is a feminized one, linking its sexual content and confessional mode with the feminine. Far from shocking their audience, the shows' confessions are highly predictable, conventional, and routine, because of their consistent matching of feminized space, time, and audience with feminized material.

Making her charges during the political hearings, Hill strategically disrupted the gendered spaces, times, and categories that regulate sexual politics on TV, as feminine (or more precisely, what has been constructed as feminine) subject matter intruded into in a primarily "masculine" space. In a powerful historical moment, Hill drew attention to the reality of sexual harassment and the need to redress sexual trauma. The effects were explosive. Thus, *Newsweek* opens its coverage of the case by remarking on the disruption of TV time. Assessing the damage wrought by the "seismic jolt" of the hearings, *Newsweek* notes that the confrontation "preempted the game shows, it interrupted weekend plans of foliating, it transfixed a nation" (in Kaplan 1991). In a front-page piece for the *New York Times*, Andrew Rosenthal (1991a) comments that Hill's allegations "were so graphic" that they "prompted a network anchor to offer a warning for the parents of children looking for Saturday morning cartoons." Further emphasizing the hearings' disruption of TV time, Rosenthal remarks that the broadcast of the testimony, "interspersed with commercials for nail polish and long-distance telephone companies, only augmented the aura of unreality." As much as was possible, people tried to control the time structure of testimony to make the hearings conform to gendered TV time. As commentators pointed out, Hill gave her testimony during the day, whereas Thomas gave his during evening prime time, a difference that may have worked to Thomas's advantage.

It is not only the disruption of TV time but also the disjunction between TV genres and spaces that contributes to "the aura of unreality." Rosenthal (1991a) writes that the confrontation "was riveting television, the camera zooming in for soap-opera-close shots of the faces of witnesses and senators, and that helped create an overwhelming sense that the Senate judiciary committee was a manifestly unsuited forum for airing some of the most emotionally wrenching issues ever to surface in a public inquiry." In this passage, the link between the hearings and recognizably "feminine" mass culture, nail polish commercials and soap operas, suggests that it is a disjunction of gendered genres that creates the sense of "unreality." The nail polish and soap opera associations are symptomatic of the high/low, mind/body, male/female hierarchies that frame the Hill-Thomas hearings. Scheduled during the day for a domestic audience, soap opera belongs to a TV form that is denigrated precisely because it is associated with infantile, feminine spectators.[1] News titles such as "Spectacle of Degradation" and "The Ugly Circus" further weakened Hill's case by denigrating the hearings as part of feminized mass culture. As Manning Marable (1992) notes, "The media contributed to the political assassination of Hill by projecting the controversy as part soap opera" (69). In an essay entitled "Femininity as Mas(s)querade," Tania Modleski (1991) traces a broad tradition that associates "low" culture, spectacle, and mass consumerism with the feminine. The persistent characterization of the hearings as "spectacle" and "soap opera" should be seen within the context of that tradition.

It is not simply the media labels of "spectacle" and "soap opera" that are striking but also the polarization of "high" and "low," "masculine" and "feminine," genres and spaces. The *New York Times* states that there had been "nothing quite so antithetical to the pursuit of high ideals like truth and justice" (Apple 1991, 1). In a similar vein, Nancy Gibbs (1991), lamenting the debasement of "high ideals" by "low" sexuality, writes: "The U.S. Senate is a stage normally reserved for politicians debating war and peace and issues draped in high ideals. It is not a forum accustomed to interrogations about large-breasted women having sex with animals" (15). Gibbs's description clothes an implicit sexual division: the Senate is a stage for "high" ideals rather than "low" materials, for international issues rather than domestic problems, and for men rather than women. This traditional sexual division was deliberately called into question by Hill's charges against Thomas. The ensuing crisis required containment strategies as spectacular as the explosive charges themselves. Trying to regain control, conservative politicians and antifeminist media pushed Hill into the role of the confessional woman—a convenient western stereotype designed to dismantle the power of her public voice by discrediting it.

Sexual confessions usually conform to the traditional series of judge/confessor, male/female, conceptual/bodily power hierarchies. At the outset of this case, a male nominated to be a judge on the highest court in the United States was placed in the position of having to either confess to or deny sexual misconduct, when he was asked to respond to Hill's charges. Thomas, however, refused to talk about his "private life" in such "public" hearings. Also, since the hearings were not a court of law, the senators on the committee were reluctant to interrogate him on what were deemed "private" subjects. They did not have the same hesitation about Hill's private life, however. When the senators did engage in a detailed, attenuated interrogation of Thomas, they began speculating about possible "proclivities," "pathologies," and "perversions" that would drive Hill to make such charges. After suggesting that Hill lifted her story from various sources, Orrin Hatch asked Thomas, "How could this quiet, retiring woman know something like Long Dong Silver?" (Berke 1991, 29).

In contrast to Thomas, Hill was placed in the traditional role of female confessor before the authority of male interlocutors. The tables turned so that the focus was not on Thomas but on Hill, as senators probed her character for clues of "pathology" and "perversion."[2] The interrogation of Hill closely resembled the clinical, medical, and religious conventions of confessional discourse. Following clinical and medical categories established by such sexologists and psychoanalysts as Freud and Havelock Ellis, the senators questioned Hill ad nauseum about her possible "delusions," "erotomania," and "proclivities." The questioning of Hill and later summaries of the case insinuate that she was a "scorned woman," fantasist and schizophrenic. In his affidavit, John Doggett, an acquaintance of Hill's and a Yale classmate of Thomas's, claimed that "Hill was somewhat unstable, and that, in my case, she fantasized about my being interested in her romantically" (in Smolowe 1991, 20).

While issues of racism and sexism have been discussed with respect to the hearings, there has been little discussion of the pervasive heterosexism and homophobia that marked the interrogation of Hill. The homophobic elements emerged most obviously in the references to Hill's "proclivities" (read lesbianism). And the pervasive homophobia would later resurface in the hearings on gays in the military when Strom Thurmond asked a gay officer if he had ever seen a doctor or psychiatrist about his sexual orientation.

The interrogation of Hill also belongs to a tradition of medical discourse that constructs the sexuality of black women as pathological, a tradition carefully analyzed by Sander Gilman (1986) in his much-invoked essay on the iconography of female sexuality. As Wahneema Lubiano (1992) argues, the questioning of Hill produced a narrative of the pathology of black women. When Hill is referred to as a "lesbian, someone whom we are to see as unnatural in a heterosexual family romance . . . when her very 'ladylike' (another word for middle-class) behaviour is read as an aberration," Lubiano notes, then she is seen as an "indication of the pathology of African-American culture" (340–41). Like the interrogation of Hill, later summaries and interpretations of the hearings display the pathologizing classifications of clinical confessional discourse. In an article for *Time*, Jill Smolowe writes that if Hill was telling the truth, then Thomas was guilty of harassment and perjury. But if Hill's account was "a flight of fantasy," Smolowe reasons, then "she was delusional and a candidate for medical attention" (1991, 17). David Brock's 1993 book, *The Real Anita Hill*, which has been described by many as a character assassination, is pervaded by the myth that black female sexuality is the root of moral pathology. As Suzanne Moore (1993) notes in her review of the book, what is particularly abhorrent to Brock is that Anita Hill "appears to be a sexual being."

Brock's book makes explicit all of the implicit attacks on Hill's character during the Senate hearings. Brock quotes an unnamed source who claims that Hill was obsessed with pornography, sodomy, and "bestiality." In one of the few critical reviews of the book, Jill Abramson and Jane Mayer investigate Brock's construction of Hill as "a wanton sexual tease, coming on to her students in bizarre ways and engaging in kinky sexual conversations" (1993, 92). One of Brock's more outrageous stories, that Hill sprinkled pubic hairs on students' papers, is disputed by the named source. As Abramson and Mayer note, the fact that many of Brock's sources are anonymous means that most of his stories are impossible to verify. It is disturbing not only that Brock presents distortions and fictions as facts but also that his portrait of Hill is steeped in a racist mythology about black female sexuality.

The basis for Brock's cataloging of Hill's purported sexual aberrations is the myth of the "scorned woman." It is such a cataloging of details that is so central to the tradition of sexual confession. By demarcating the "normal" from the "deviant," sexual discourse constructs the heterosexual family romance. It is for this reason that the question of whether or not Hill was "a scorned woman" became a central motif of the hearings and later commentary on the confrontation. Had any of the senators charged Thomas with being a "scorned man," it would have seemed absurd. When made against Hill, however, this charge was treated seriously. While the senators questioned the racism of Hill's charges, nobody questioned the sexism and racism of the "scorned woman" label.

The theme of "the scorned woman" is reinforced by a *People* magazine interview with Virginia and Clarence Thomas that stresses the centrality of religion to their relationship. Their portrayal of their traditional marriage is defined against what was constructed as Hill's "aberrant" life. Hence, Virginia Lamp Thomas situates the debacle in the context of a dichotomy between their relationship and the single, "scorned woman," Anita Hill. The *People* article features photos of Virginia and Clarence Thomas posing at their wedding, having coffee in their kitchen, and sitting together on a couch reading the Bible. The photos thus place Thomas in the laws and spaces of the family, while the text places Hill in the margins. On the magazine cover, Virginia Lamp Thomas's words, Anita Hill "was probably in love with my husband," are displayed alongside a photo of the Thomases hugging.

In the article itself, Virginia Lamp Thomas not only continues the scorned woman motif ("I always believed she was probably someone in love with my husband and never got what she wanted"), but also links Anita Hill with one of the most potent myths of popular culture, that of the demonic, single career woman. "What's scary about her allegations," she tells *People*, "is that they remind me of the movie *Fatal Attraction*" (1991, 111). Susan Faludi (1991) notes that *Fatal Attraction* is only the most famous of a string of recent movies that have pathologized unmarried women who pursue careers. Thomas displaces the sexism of "the scorned woman" figure with the specter of racism, saying that she feared racist objections to her marriage but "knew if there were problems . . . about Clarence and me, people would get over them" (116). As many commentators on the hearings have noted, the persistent dichotomy between racism and sexism elided the more complicated combination of sexism and racism at work in the hostility toward black women. The black, single career woman is particularly demonized as the sinister counterpart of the Welfare Queen.[3] The demonic woman that emerges in the *People* interview has a long tradition and was a thread running through the interrogations and confessions of the hearings.

The mode of sexual confessional discourse, Michel Foucault (1978) argues, is based on a crucial relationship between the confessor and the subject matter confessed. And, he contends, the indisputable truth of the discourse is guaranteed by the bond between the "general baseness" of the discourse and the baseness of the person confessing (62): confessional discourse comes from below. In what is seen as the "lowest" form of television culture, confessional talk shows, there is indeed a link between the "low" material discussed and the "low" position of the person confessing. As a general rule, the confessors who appear on *Geraldo*, *Donahue*, and other talk shows to speak about sadomasochism, erotomania, or transvestism are people who belong to lower economic and social classes. The debased level of discourse, then, is closely mapped onto the speaker's position at the base of social and economic hierarchies.

Many journalists remark on the incongruity of the "prim law professor" or "poised and intelligent" Hill and the "graphic charges" she detailed. Several people, including Virginia Lamp Thomas, suggest that, by reiterating the details of bodies and sex to Thomas, Orrin Hatch somehow debased Thomas. Making Thomas speak about the charges, it is suggested, seemed to strengthen the bond between Thomas and the sexual-bodily subject matter. In the *People* interview, Virginia Lamp Thomas relates, "Once during the hearings, when Sen. Orrin Hatch was repeating the allegations, I couldn't help but cry" (112). But it was Hill, more often than Thomas, whom the senators forced to speak again and again about the details of sex and body parts. As Gayle Pemberton (1992) argues, by insisting that

Hill "repeat ad nauseum" the details of sexual harassment, the senators "reinforced notions of black vulgarity and inferiority" (1992, 180).

As popular media constructed Hill as a gigantic figure, her powerful testimony frequently moved into the background, while her own body and sexuality moved into the foreground. In an editorial on the hearings, Andrew Rosenthal (1991b) suggests that the media harassed the witnesses with TV camera close-ups. Furthermore, he suggests that women are routinely harassed by close-ups.[4] It is worth noting that in print media, Hill is photographed more often than Thomas. *Newsweek*, for example, displays a close-up only of Hill on its cover. Inside the magazine, pictures of Hill outnumber those of Thomas by two to one. The *Time* article on the confrontation displays the much reproduced photo of Hill in her teal blue dress, a photo multiplied by the numerous newsroom screens. Susan Stewart argues that media personalities, heroes, and stars become gigantic through the repetition of familiar images. Warhol's *Jackie*, a reproduction of sixteen images of Jacqueline Kennedy at the moment of John F. Kennedy's assassination, Stewart notes, exemplifies the process by which subjects become gigantic. It is significant that Warhol's most famous multiplications are of women. Perhaps more familiar than his images of Jacqueline Kennedy are his multiple photos of Marilyn Monroe, a figure who became entirely effaced by endless reproductions of her image. Stewart writes that through a "chainlike, cumulative formation" of images, a generation of "sign by means of sign," subjects become "larger than life" (91). The familiar photo of Anita Hill in her blue dress, and in particular the *Time* magazine photo of reporters watching multiple TV screens of that shot, contributed to the magnification of Hill's image.

At the beginning of the *Newsweek* article on the case is a larger-than-life close-up of Hill's face, a photo that spans two magazine pages. So magnified is the close-up of Hill, that the top of her head is cut off by the edges of the page. That the gigantic photo is not framed makes the picture all the more lifelike. More akin to the close-ups of women's faces in fashion photography than to the pictures of journalistic photography, the picture of Hill belongs to a whole code of photography. The paradigm of the close-up maps onto the woman's face a condensation of qualities—exposure, immediacy, and referentiality. In such close-ups, women's face-objects represent what Roland Barthes (1984) calls "a kind of absolute state of the flesh" (56).

Exemplifying immediacy, realism, and excess, the unframed photo of Hill moves beyond the magazine page, its edges determined only by the edges of the page. In its dimensions alone, the photo of Hill exemplifies the traditional close-up of the woman. It is a huge photo replete with details of the flesh. In a discussion of the cinematic close-up in film, Mary Ann Doane (1989) stresses the importance of dimension to the embodiment of the face. The scale of the close-up, she writes, "transforms the face into an instance of the gigantic, the monstrous: it overwhelms" (108). And this scale has a particular resonance with respect to the monstrosity in iconographies of black female sexuality. Near the center of the *Newsweek* photo is a magnification of Hill's lips which exceeds the two-page divide. We are so close to Hill's face that we can see every pore and crease in a face that seems to be pure surface.

Further emphasizing the magnification of Hill's face is a diminished two-inch inset photo of Clarence Thomas on the extreme left of the Hill close-up. Framed within a column of text entitled "A Moment of Truth," the profile photo shows Thomas's entire head supported by his hand in pensive pose. In contrast to the huge, tactile, surface close-up of Hill, we are presented with the more dimensional picture of Thomas. The role of the close-up in constructing female sexuality and female subjectivity has been frequently analyzed in discussions of film and fashion close-ups. In such images, the woman's body speaks through her face. The close-up, in fashion, film, and news media, is the photographic genre associated with women in particular, because the close-up exemplifies a split subjectivity. Although the face is the most articulate part of the body, the face, as Doane (1989) notes, is only completed by the viewer's gaze and is the only part not accessible to the subject's own gaze. Hence, the face in the close-up is paradigmatic of objectivity.

It is not surprising, then, that the close-up has come to symbolize woman as image, what Laura Mulvey (1989) calls woman's "to-be-looked-at-ness" (19). The close-up of a woman, then, places her within a gendered visual code. With her magnified face, she becomes the object of spectacle in the most literal sense of the word. *Spectacle*, the term used so much to describe the hearings, is, according to the OED, a "person or thing exhibited to the public gaze as an object either of curiosity or contempt, or of marvel or admiration." The word, then, is highly suggestive of woman's traditional position in close-ups, for its definition implies a similar objectification.

While journalists repeatedly denigrated the hearings as "spectacle," they continued to place Anita Hill, rather than Thomas, within the genre of the spectacular, by displaying gigantic and multiple reproductions of her face for the public gaze. I would argue that what seemed unfair to many commentators and journalists was that Thomas should be objectified by the camera gaze and should be subjected to elements of spectacle. The close-up of Hill, however, did not seem as disjunctive, because such objectifications are so closely associated with women and sexual confession, particularly in daytime soaps and talk shows.

The confession, as Foucault (1978) observes, is one of the primary rituals for telling the truth of sex. And the interplay of truth and sex was one of the crucial elements that marked the Hill-Thomas case. The very etymological traces of the word *confession* (*confessus*, meaning "incontrovertible, certain, beyond doubt") suggest that absolute truth is the basis of the ritual. Politicians and media dodged the responsibility of having to deal with issues of sexual trauma, by resorting to confessional parameters of truth and falsehood, parameters which further obscured rather than clarified the trauma expressed. In its lead article, *Newsweek* like most of the other newspapers and magazines, sets the two witnesses in opposition along the lines of truth and falsehood; David A. Kaplan begins his article with the statement that "one witness was telling the truth, the other was lying" (1991, 26). Jill Smolowe similarly ends her *Time* article with the assertion that there was only one certainty in the case: "One was telling the truth, and the other was lying" (1991, 20).

As early as 1959, the public was scandalized to learn that a popular TV quiz show, *Twenty One*, had been rigged. The question-and-answer format, which had once guaranteed an undisputed verification of truth, was itself betrayed as a fraud. Before a Senate committee, Charles van Doren, the symbol of knowledge and truth, confessed that he had won several rounds of *Twenty One* because the show's producers had repeatedly given him, but not his opponent, the correct answers. Nevertheless, the interrogation and confession format of the hearings offered a cathartic purging of deception and seemed to cancel out the falsehood. Ultimately, truth seemed to triumph over deception as van Doren repented and claimed to have learned much about "good and evil" from the scandal (in Ross 1989, 102).

Discussing the Thomas-Hill hearings, Virginia Lamp Thomas suggests a similar resolution to the hearings, a triumph of good over evil. In the *People* interview, she describes the hearings as "spiritual warfare. Good versus evil" (111). And yet most spectators were left with the sense that the Thomas-Hill hearings offered no such cathartic resolution. Despite the truth/falsehood polarity that marked the news commentary on the case, the interplay of truth and sex was much more complicated. Truth itself became a kind of rhetorical figure, alternately clothed and stripped bare, at times feminized and at other times racialized. During the Thomas-Hill hearings, sex was transformed into discourse through a division between literal and figurative language. While Hill became associated with the literal, Thomas became associated with the figurative. There was a sense that by speaking about sex in such literal terms, Thomas would be feminized. Indeed, Thomas strategically displaced the "feminine" discourse of sexual confession with the more masculine discourse of assassin's bullets and death.

In the 1992 collection *Race-ing Justice, En-gendering Power*, two essays suggest the extreme linguistic polarization that marks this case. While

Homi Bhabha, in an essay subtitled "Men, Metaphors, and the Common Culture," explores Thomas's figures of speech, Claudia Brodsky Lacour, in her essay, "Doing Things with Words," discusses the "unfathomable effect of literality" in Hill's testimony, a testimony stripped of linguistic detail and "embellishment" (1992, 132–33). Hill made her charges in highly literal terms, using the effective legal language of the courtroom, providing detailed and clear evidence to back up her charges that she had indeed been sexually harassed by the man who was about to be confirmed as a Supreme Court justice. Thomas, she stated, spoke of women having sex with animals, of the size of his penis, of finding pubic hair on a can of Coke. The literality of her language of evidence provided powerful testimony and proof that she had, indeed, been harassed.

In an entirely different kind of discourse, Thomas responded figuratively that he "died a thousand deaths" when the charges were made, that he was the victim of a high-tech lynching for which he refused to provide the rope, that he would prefer an assassin's bullet to "this kind of living hell," and that the hearings had become "a circus" (in Berke 1991, 1). Thomas thus wrapped the hearings in layers of linguistic clothing through familiar narratives and figures of speech, while the ferocity of Hill's literal, explicit language relentlessly disrobed what Homi Bhabha refers to as "the private parts of public discourse" (244). In an essay entitled "The Private Parts of Justice," Andrew Ross (1989) similarly points to an embodiment of the most cerebral of public spheres, the judicial branch (40). While judicial discourse was being embodied, Thomas tried to conceal its body. Hanging over the court was a decision precisely concerning private parts, women's bodies, and reproductive rights. Earlier Thomas had concealed his political position with a neutral, disembodied stance; he maintained that he had never before discussed *Roe v. Wade.*[5] Paradoxically, after all the disrobing of judicial discourse, the greatest silence to pervade the hearings was on the subject of women's bodies and the power that Thomas, as a justice of the Supreme Court, would later exercise over them.

But the extent to which the dynamic between literal and figurative language shaped the sexual politics of the hearings is evident not only in the testimony itself but also in the reports, summaries, and criticisms of the hearings. Picking up Thomas's metaphor, *Time* magazine titles its lead story "An Ugly Circus," while *Newsweek* sets Hill's words, "I had to tell the truth" in opposition to Thomas's figure of speech, "It is a high-tech lynching." In the *New York Times*, Maureen Dowd (1991) writes that the senators at the hearing remained "stunned, almost mute, at the ferocity of Clarence Thomas's language and the way his and Anita Hill's words [kept] sinking, like some kind of psychic dentist's drill, into the most sensitive, least explored parts of the national consciousness" (1). In order to convey Hill's graphic descriptions and Thomas's rebuttals, Dowd uses highly figurative language: their words are like a "dentist's drill." The only way this extremely literal language can be expressed, then, is through the figurative.

The convergence of the literary and the graphic, of the figurative and the literal, especially on the topic of sexuality, is not limited to the Thomas-Hill case. It has been discussed extensively in Linda Williams's study on pornography, *Hard Core* (1989). Williams argues that the relationship between sex and literary devices, between literal and figurative, is crucial to pornography, a medium that was central to the Thomas-Hill confrontation. According to Williams, the body in pornographic films becomes the signifier, the figure which refers to an invisible sexuality within. Sexuality is displaced onto language, and signification is in turn embodied.

Apparently, it was not uncommon for the male Yale law students to view pornographic films in their spare time. According to some students, this was a communal activity, a space in which the discourse of sex was allowed. But Thomas, himself a Yale alumnus, refused to discuss the topic of pornography in the public arena of the hearings. He did not deny the charges that he saw pornographic films and that he described those films to friends and colleagues. He argued that such issues belonged in the private sphere and hence should not be discussed in a public space such as the Senate chamber. He angrily stated that he would not talk about his private life in the hearings, thus heading off any reports by friends and supporters that he was often a patron of X-rated movie houses.

Sex, of course, has always existed in the public arena of the Supreme Court but in a concealed form. The court itself had faced the task of defining and censoring pornography. As often happens, according to Foucault, sex had been talked about ad infinitum and at the same time exploited as the secret. Years ago, Justice Potter had remarked that he could not define pornography, but he knew it when he saw it. His remark was picked up by Reagan and the moral majority when they later set about censoring pornographic materials. They could little have guessed that the Senate hearings for the confirmation of a future justice to the Supreme Court would contain material pornographic enough that the hearings themselves would be censored, labeled "not suitable for family viewing." And sex had a place in the court long before the issue of pornography came up, albeit in concealed form. Abortion appeared clothed in the abstract terms *truth* and *life*.

Of all the hearings that have taken place in the Senate chamber, the Thomas-Hill confrontation was perhaps the most shocking to the public. As I have argued, the most disconcerting aspect of the hearings was the sudden intrusion of female issues of sexual trauma into the political arena. The voicing of sexual trauma was pried from its traditional rituals, places, and spaces. Faced with this shocking displacement of proper places and spaces, Thomas replied in kind with shocking discursive displacements of his own: he cast himself in the role of the black man lynched by whites (conveniently glossing over the fact that he had been charged by a black woman). Faced with such unsettling displacements, male politicians and mainstream media formed an alliance (perhaps involuntarily) that ultimately sacrificed Hill.

And yet the temporary containment of Hill's testimony may have backfired in the long run. Although Judge Thomas was confirmed to take his position as Justice Thomas, there remained a strange feeling seeping, once again, through mainstream media that justice had not been served. As Anita Hill continued to speak publicly about sexual harassment as a social and legal issue in need of redressing, she strategically ceased to speak about her own case. In light of the Thomas-Hill hearings and the increased number of women in the Senate following the hearings, we might in the future see sexual trauma unanchored from its traditional places to intrude into the political realms of high ideals.

Notes

1. Lynn Joyrich (1990) discusses the way that mass consumerism and culture have been figured as feminine. Denigrated forms of TV culture, she argues, are linked with an audience "deemed infantile or feminine, a spectator 'not fully a man.'"

2. Nancy Fraser (1992) examines the asymmetrical power and gender relations in the interrogation of Hill and Thomas, noting that Hill's character actually became the focus of the hearings.

3. Wahneema Lubiano (1992) and Nell Irvin Painter (1992) discuss the centrality of the Welfare Queen figure to the Hill-Thomas confrontation.

4. Andrew Rosenthal (1991b) writes, "It is sexual harassment to pursue a woman's every step, leeching and leering about her. . . . The press has turned Jacqueline Onassis into a harassed, everlasting profit center for factoficto TV." Wahneema Lubiano (1992) presents an intriguing analysis of the hierarchical placement of photos of Hill and Thomas.

5. In 1973 the Supreme Court handed down the landmark *Roe v. Wade* decision. The decision, based on the right to privacy enshrined in the Fourteenth Amendment, argues that the right to privacy encompasses a woman's choice concerning abortion (see 93 *Supreme Court Reporter* 705). As many commentators on the hearings noted, it is impossible to believe that Thomas had never even discussed *Roe v. Wade*, perhaps the most controversial decision the Court has ever made and the decision that, beginning with Ronald Reagan's presidency, became crucial to all Supreme Court nominations. Linda Greenhouse (1991), for example, writes that Thomas "strained credulity" when he claimed that he had never discussed *Roe v. Wade*.

Part Three

Negotiating Identity and Confessional Inversions

In the course of the western history of sexuality, confessions of unorthodox practices have been encouraged, providing a field for effective social and sexual policing. Through confessional readings, authorities in religious, sexological, and psychological domains have passed judgment and distinguished between normal and abnormal sexual behavior; negative labels of "deviance" and "perversity" have been used strategically to dismiss unorthodox sexual practices. Part three investigates the role of confession in this process of sexual policing and normalization. Its more important concern, however, is to investigate strategies of confessional inversion in female sexual self-representations, strategies that deliberately subvert and disrupt efforts of social policing in the realm of sexuality. Confessional inversions reappropriate the very negative terms used to categorize the deviant personality and give these negative labels a positive spin; thus they celebrate the hybrid figure, imbuing the "other" sexuality—the lesbian, the sexually unclassified, the confessional cross-dresser—with pleasure and power. Part three demonstrates that if popular media encourage confessions and normalization, they also provide a rich field for its opposite. Confessional inversions abound in popular media, taking fun in inhabiting and dismantling the boundaries of the confessional practice from within. This section investigates confessional inversions in representative popular genres, including confessional pulp fiction, TV talk shows, and letters to the editor.

8

Lesbian Confession and Case History

Marylynne Diggs

Historically, sexologists in the United States and Britain have defined the lesbian as a "hybrid sex" or "third sex," relegating lesbian identity to the margins. Lesbians who desired to escape personal and social isolation were caught in a double bind of confession and normalization, on one hand, or self-imposed silence and isolation, on the other. To escape this double bind, lesbian autobiographers and writers of pulp fiction strategically appropriated the negative labels and inverted their original implications.

Lesbian confessional narrative has inherited aspects of the religious confession and the sexological case history. This history—which includes lesbian autobiographies, confessional novels, clinical confessions, case history interpretations, coming-out stories, and even appearances on popular talk shows—should be understood in the context of its relationship to the pathologizing discourse of sexology. This discourse forms the context not only for the construction of lesbian identity as a pathological, contradictory, and paradoxical subjectivity, but also for the articulation of lesbian confessional narratives which were apparently conscious of their counter-discursive political implications and, in particular, the oppositional implications of a "hybrid" subjectivity.

Reconstructing a genealogy of lesbian confession by focusing on the epistemological transformations that made this genre an ontologically significant discursive practice, I will consider several questions: In what way did confessional practices in the human sciences produce "identities" and extend control over them? In what ways do lesbian confessional texts appropriate and resist abnormalization? How have self-identified lesbians manipulated the rhetoric of confession and case history? Ultimately, I will suggest that lesbian confessional narratives have participated in a scientific discourse of hybrid identity but have also transformed that discourse by their participation. While these appropriations and transformations of hybrid lesbian subjectivity and confessional discourse often create a discursive form of identity politics, they are also vulnerable to recontainment within framing discourses of psychopathology. Understanding these implications of lesbian confessional narratives requires an understanding of the history of confession, case history, and lesbian subjectivity as it emerges through the discursive practices of the human sciences, especially sexology.

Immoral Acts and Unnatural Identities

Historians of western culture have noted the epistemological shift occurring during the eighteenth and nineteenth centuries in which theological ways of understanding and regulating human behavior were gradually displaced by scientific ones. John D'Emilio and Estelle B. Freedman address this shift in *Intimate Matters: A History of Sexuality in America* (1988). The movement to "perfect American society" and improve the American citizenry began taking a new shape when "doctors began to supplant clergymen as male authorities over sexual matters" (145). Other historians similarly note the displacement of ministers in an era of increased faith in the objective and neutral authority of the sciences, suggesting that physicians became the new confessors in American culture, creating in their consultation rooms "a sacred setting" for confidential and therapeutic discourse (Haller and Haller 1974, 29). Such discourse had long been an instrumental part of American life. Emerging from the Calvinist values of self-examination and interrogation, confessional narratives—ranging from colonial spiritual autobiographies to nineteenth-century slave narratives—have been a popular form of expression in the United States. Like Catholic confession, these Protestant confessional narratives were deployed in the newly emerging scientific discourse of the latter half of the nineteenth century, but sexology's emphasis on defining identities, rather than defining behaviors, made sexual "abnormalities" signs of an inherent identity rather than temporal transgression. Historian Nancy Leys Stepan notes that a variety of differences from middle-class, white, male heterosexuality—including women in general, homosexuals, and people of color—were constituted as "races apart," whose difference from the norm constituted a degenerative or pathological variation (1990, 40–41). While the discourse of morality relied on the definition of specific moral laws and the articulation of sins, scientific discourse more broadly cast as abnormal or unnatural anything that lay outside a narrowly defined field of normality and naturality, making possible a broader range of social control.

Thus, while the function of religious confession was ultimately to allow the wayward sinner to return to the fold, clinical confession, case history, and diagnosis in sexological discourse focused the gaze of medical technology upon the individual. These processes of examination, documentation, and interpretation placed the sexual subject almost entirely within the representational control of the physician. For, regardless of the story a sexual subject might tell, that story was constituted not as a revelation of truth but as an articulation of signs that necessitated expert interpretation.

While the powerful influence of sexology on defining and regulating human sexual differences may be indisputable, it is important to offer a caveat regarding the interests that motivated many of the early sexologists. In the United States, remnants of canon law in civil codes made sodomy a criminal act, but homosexual behavior was often prosecuted under general statutes against "indecent conduct" or "vice" as well. In Britain, the Criminal Law Amendment Act of 1885, though aimed at prostitution, also contained a clause under which gay men were prosecuted well into the twentieth century. It is not surprising, in this context, that one of the earliest claims of a biological etiology for homosexuality came from a gay lawyer rather than a scientist. Writing in the mid-nineteenth century, German attorney Karl Heinrich Ulrich was one of the first to argue that there was a physiological basis for being an "Urning" and that male homosexual practices therefore should be decriminalized (Weeks 1985, 66, 70–71, 78).

In the discourse on female inversion and lesbianism, the reform of criminal codes was less important, and the "natural" order of gender hierarchy and the health of the mothers of a nation were more crucial. A sign of degeneration of pure gender differentiation, the lesbian was constructed as a danger not only to herself but to all of western civilization. We can see this emphasis on degeneration and its eugenic implications in Richard Krafft-Ebing's *Psychopathia Sexualis* (1886). Krafft-Ebing sees sexual variation as a sign of the degeneration of "civilized" society; in his view, the breakdown of distinct gender differences coincides with "episodes of moral decay" (6). He goes on to argue that "the higher the anthropological development of the race, the stronger these contrasts between man and woman, and vice versa" (42).

Similarly informed by a transatlantic concern with moral and racial progress, American physician James Weir saw the increasing interest in women's suffrage as an atavistic movement driven by women who showed evidence of "masculo-femininity" or "psycho-sexual aberrancy" (1895, 818–19). Weir decried this process of degeneration and predicted that it would usher in the destruction of civilization.

Lesbianism, representing sexual independence from men, constituted an enormous challenge to white, male power interests. Clearly, giving voice to such a challenge without the interpretive apparatus of sexology to control, translate, and mediate its self-representation, posed a threat to the scientific construction of both "natural womanhood" and the "unnatural" variation presented by lesbianism. Thus, it is not surprising that sexologists defensively guarded their interpretive authority over the representation of lesbian identity. In his preface to the first edition of *Psychopathia Sexualis*, Krafft-Ebing, self-consciously defensive of his own authority, attempted to exclude laypeople from interpreting the discourses on sex. By addressing himself to "men engaged in serious study in the domains of natural philosophy and medical jurisprudence," he implies that women are certainly not his audience; more specifically, he suggests that only serious-minded scientific men, pursuing the subject of sexuality as professionals, not as sexual individuals themselves, are to read his book (1886, vii). The numerous letters he received from both scientists and laypeople interested in his work suggest that the early editions were unsuccessful at limiting their audience. Krafft-Ebing apparently tried to correct this in later editions. In the preface to the twelfth edition he writes, "The number of technical terms has been increased, and the Latin language is more frequently made use of than in former editions" (1929, viii).

Krafft-Ebing sought to limit not only the audience for his text but also the influence of the self-representations offered by lesbians in his case histories. Although scholars have noted that Krafft-Ebing's text enabled "the eruption into print of the speaking pervert" (Weeks 1985, 67), those eruptions were not unmediated. They were obsessively framed and recontained in the interpretive apparatus of sexological case history. Of the 238 case histories included in the 1929 English translation, fewer than half of them include first-person, autobiographical accounts. In many cases, Krafft-Ebing paraphrases the "autobiographies" that were sent to him or were included in full in other sexological studies. Even in those case histories in which the patients' own words are included, they are framed by Krafft-Ebing's own interpretations. This perhaps reflects Krafft-Ebing's sentiments about the credibility of his patients' autobiographies. He writes, "Much depends on the veracity of the patient, and that leaves in many cases much to be desired. Autobiographies are to be taken *cum grano salis*, and should be discounted." Attempting to certify the power of sexology to produce truth from these unreliable narratives, he adds, "Nevertheless the expert will soon be able to weed out exaggeration and untruth. Antipathic sexual instinct is such a complicated psychical anomaly that only the experienced specialist can quickly distinguish between truth and fiction" (444). Thus, for Krafft-Ebing, truth is the particular purview of the "experienced specialist," and the self-representational practices of lesbians are to be subjected to the truth-producing scrutiny of those who are uniquely capable of understanding them.

What emerges from this history of the clinical codification of sexual confession is a struggle for authority over the representation of sexuality. Clearly there is the conflict between theological and scientific authority which many historians have noted. But there existed as well another struggle for authority over the representation of these newly constructed sexual identities, a struggle between sexual subjects seeking to represent themselves and sexologists seeking to interpret and contain these self-representations in ways that would perhaps raise "sympathy" without necessarily creating acceptance. This containment was necessary to ensure that the self-representations of lesbians ultimately confirmed the sexologists' theories about pathology and degeneration, thus confirming their professional status as physicians of the sexually abnormal. Indeed, their authority as scientists of sex relied on the construction of sexual difference as pathology; however, when we look at lesbian confessional narratives, we can see the extent to which many of them, although informed by the rhetoric of pathology, were also able to present alternative interpretations of lesbian sexual difference.

Lesbian Confession

As early as the mid-nineteenth century, the emerging scientific discourses of health overdetermined the representation of women's intimate attachments. While historians have suggested that "romantic friendships" between women were socially acceptable and deemed compatible with heterosexual marriage until the late nineteenth century, several texts suggest that the rhetoric of confession and pathology informed representations of same-sex love between women somewhat earlier.[1] By the late nineteenth century, some women defended their relationships against the sexological representations that were gaining cultural authority. This is particularly evident in late-nineteenth- and early-twentieth-century lesbian confessional narratives, which reveal both the influence of sexological rhetoric and a struggle to elude its abnormalizing functions by offering alternative interpretations.

The rhetoric of confession and pathology in *Ethel's Love-Life* (1859), an obscure novel by little-known American writer Margaret J. M. Sweat, indicates the power of sexological rhetoric to overdetermine representations of women's intimate relationships. D'Emilio and Freedman quote *Ethel's Love-Life* to support the theory that physically intimate relations between women were an acceptable and relatively open part of nineteenth-century American life (1988, 125–26). But the novel is more appropriately read as a product of the transitional period in which it was written. Relying on the Calvinist rhetoric of self-interrogation and redemption, as well as an explicitly medical rhetoric of diagnosis and cure, *Ethel's Love-Life* is an important link in the genealogy of lesbian confessional narratives. It indicates the extent to which clinical recodifications of confession in general, and lesbian confession in particular, were transmitted in popular forms at midcentury.

The fictionalized epistolary confession from Ethel to Ernest, her future husband, is structured around a revelation of family history and external influences. Her narrative ultimately operates both as a cure and as evidence of the health of her body and soul. Ethel confesses to Ernest the effects wrought upon her system by her many romantic attachments with men and women. Her representation of Leonora, the most unequivocally queer lover in her sexual history, is profoundly informed by the emerging sexological rhetoric of "duplicity" and "contradiction" (Sweat 1859, 76–77). Such a representation implies that Leonora is one of those confusions of form alluded to by early sex scientists such as Frederick Hollick, whose popular work, *The Marriage Guide, or Natural History of Generation* (1850), addresses the uncommon but interesting phenomenon of "doubtful or double sex," one of the many physiological abnormalities of which he warns newly married couples to be aware. These persons of ambiguous sexuality are, he says, usually revealed to be female, though they may be capable of having sexual relations with other women (1974, 292–94).

Although Leonora is cast as a duplicitous and contradictory character, a seductress with a vampiric influence on Ethel, suggesting that she is informed by this early sexological discourse, Ethel apparently understands Leonora's unusual character and is sympathetic to women's intimate attachments in general. She explains, "The study and analysis of such an organism as [Leonora's] are full of interest to one who possesses the key to its contradictions" (Sweat, 82). The "key" to Leonora's unusual character is women's love for each other, "passions" which Ethel says "are of much more frequent occurrence than the world is aware of—generally they are unknown to all but the parties concerned, and are jealously guarded by them from intrusive comment" (83).

Despite this apparently sympathetic regard for the commonplace occurrence of such ties and an awareness of the need for secrecy, a healing impetus is the compelling force of Ethel's confessional narrative. Thus the reader is soon reminded that the ultimate purpose of her exhaustive self-examination, as well as her analysis of Leonora, is to purge her soul of its sexual secrets, relieve her body of its unhealthy influences, and prepare herself for marriage. After writing to Ernest about the instability that Leonora brought into her life, she writes, "And now, dear Ernest, that I have exorcised this haunting demon Leonora . . . we will turn from her and the traitorous air she breathes to our own warm and pure atmosphere of life and love and truth" (93). She sees her own sexual history, and her confession of it to Ernest, as preparation for marriage: "We have lost no strength, but have rather been disciplined to a more skilful and successful warfare" (231–32). Thus, disciplined through a varied love life and a thorough self-analysis, Ethel happily accepts marriage as that relationship which completes her own female identity.

Sweat's novel indicates that the production of a pathological lesbian identity made possible the production of the lesbian subject as a convalescing patient; however, the construction of pathological lesbian identity also made possible the production of a resistant subject of an emerging discursive identity politics. Although the sexological rhetoric of health and healing frames the representation of lesbian subjectivity as early as the mid-nineteenth century, some women were able to articulate a resisting lesbian subjectivity by appropriating the rhetoric of duplicity, hybridity, and monstrosity while undermining its negative significations. Thus, although the lesbian occupied the position of an object of medical and social analysis and a subject of confessional speech, the self-affirming lesbian subject, operating in the context of literary production, might appropriate the tools of identity production without submitting to the interpretive authority of a sexologist. Even in constituting their identities as outsiders, hybrids, or the third sex—thus using the taxonomies of scientific discourse—some writers spoke from a position that challenged the idea of the normal or the natural.

In an untitled short story, Mary E. Wilkins Freeman, a late-nineteenth-century American writer, articulates a hybrid subjectivity. Her story is excerpted extensively in Edward Foster's *Mary E. Wilkins Freeman* (1956), where Foster interprets it as an expression of Freeman's distress over having reached her forties without marrying (141–42). While the rhetoric of pathology and monstrosity may imply distress, Freeman invests the confessions of the main character with an irony that also suggests a highly rebellious spirit. Through the character of Jane Lennox, Freeman represents a woman who not only recognizes herself as an aberration of womanhood, conventionally defined, but also very clearly sees this variation from the norm as empowering. Calling herself a "rebel against the Overgovernment of all creation," she claims, "I, through my rebellion, have power. All negation has power. I, Jane Lennox, spinster, as they would have designated me a century ago, living quietly and apparently harmlessly in the old Lennox homestead in Baywater, am a power" (142).

Although Jane sees herself as deprived of every woman's "birthright" to a house, a husband, and a child, she goes on to glorify this deprivation as a source of empowerment that rises from the ashes of "negation." Claiming to be deprived of the "character of the usual woman," Jane goes on to say: "I am a graft on the tree of human womanhood. I am a hybrid. Sometimes I think I am a monster, and the worst of it is, I certainly take pleasure in it." Explaining further how she sees herself as simultaneously "other" and empowered, Jane goes on to claim that an element of self-satisfaction is a part of human nature, thus making, perhaps, the earliest expression of lesbian pride in American literature: "No mortal can exist without a certain satisfaction in herself. Satisfaction in myself I certainly have, or perhaps satisfaction may not be the right word. Perhaps pride is better, pride which intoxicates like forbidden stimulants" (143). In an articulation of the power of her hybrid identity to upset natural laws, she writes, "Here am I, a woman, rather delicately built, of rather delicate tastes, perfectly able to break those commandments, to convert to dust every one of those Divine laws. I shudder before my own power, yet I glory because of it" (143).

While nineteenth-century writers like Sweat and Freeman employed the rhetoric of sexological discourse in confessional narratives that some-times reproduced and sometimes resisted the pathological representation of lesbianism, the case history confessions of Krafft-Ebing's patients were inevitably subjected to his own interpretive apparatus. While the major-ity of those histories in *Psychopathia Sexualis* are paraphrased and nar-rated by Krafft-Ebing himself, he occasionally incorporates fragments from his patients' "autobiographies." Some of these patients appear to make sense of their sexuality within the rhetoric of scientific discourse and, through that rhetoric, absolve themselves of moral responsibility. Al-though "Miss L.," one of Krafft-Ebing's patients, presents her confessional narrative as "the history of an unhappy woman who, by the fatal caprice of nature, is deprived of all joy of life and made a victim of sorrow," she also sees her sexuality as placing her outside the moral rules of society: "It does not disturb my conscience to have had sexual intercourse with Miss A., for I succumbed to her seduction, having honestly endeavored to save her from moral ruin and to bring her up an educated and moral being. . . . Besides, I rest in the thought that the moral code is established only for normal humans, but is not binding for anomalies" (1929, 407). Krafft-Ebing, in the description and analysis that frames and interprets Miss L.'s case history confession, reestablishes the connection between the moral and physical taint, attempting to undermine the suggestions of liberation from moral codes implicit in her own narrative:

CASE 155. Homosexuality. Miss L., fifty-five years of age. No information about father's family. The parents of her mother were described as irascible, capricious and nervous. One brother of her mother was an epileptic, another eccentric and mentally abnormal.

Mother was sexually hyperaesthetic, and for a long time a messalina. She was considered to be psychopathic and died at the age of sixty-nine of cerebral disease.

Miss L. developed normally, had only slight illnesses in child-hood, and was mentally well endowed, but of a neuropathic con-stitution, emotional, and troubled with numerous fads. (404–5)

By associating Miss L.'s relatively "normal" history with her mother's fam-ily history, which includes such presumably hereditary influences as be-ing irascible, capricious, and eccentric as well as more typical nineteenth-century conditions such as nervousness and hyperaesthesia, Krafft-Ebing recontains Miss L.'s own self-representation within the realm of both the unhealthy and the immoral.

The case history confession, if not framed by the interpretive appara-tus of sexological analysis, might prove too empowering for the sexual subjects over whom Krafft-Ebing hoped to maintain control and through whom he would constitute his own professional status. While the turn of the twentieth century witnessed a consolidation of sexological author-ity over the discourse of sexuality in general, and lesbianism in particu-lar, the construction of lesbianism as a distinct identity meant that increas-ingly large numbers of women became self-identified lesbians who variously internalized the sexological discourse of pathology and appro-priated it. Thus, while there remained lesbian confessional narratives that were entrenched in the thematics of vampiric seduction and conversion, and while novels such as Radclyffe Hall's *The Well of Loneliness* (1928) attracted enormous public attention to the apparent psychological despair of lesbians, there were also lesbian confessional narratives which attempted to correct the sexologists' misrepresentations, thus making lesbianism an issue of cultural and political, rather than purely psychological, concern.

Using the confessional model as well as the sexological language of inverted or intermediate sexuality, narratives such as Mary Casal's *The Stone Wall: An Autobiography* (1930), Elisabeth Craigin's *Either Is Love* (1937), and Diana Frederics's *Diana: Strange Autobiography* (1939) high-lighted the disparity between the sexological representation of lesbians and lesbian self-perceptions. All three texts stand out as exceptions to the paradigmatic theme of 1950s and 1960s pulp novels, in which lesbians are redeemed through marriage or empowered through martyrdom (Zimmer-mann 1990, 9). Indeed, as Lillian Faderman notes, Craigin and Frederics articulate an emerging lesbian pride (1991, 102). Frederics's *Diana* is par-ticularly interesting because it so carefully appropriates the confessional rhetoric of sexology in order to present an alternative interpretation of her own case history.

As a lesbian taking control of her own representation by employing sexological rhetoric while subverting its usual diagnosis, Frederics's au-tobiography indicates the extent to which the confessional narrative and case history confession could be deployed in an articulation and affirmation of lesbian identity and pride. Using the pulp paperback, still a new form of publishing in the late 1930s, Frederics also presents her confessional case history in a decidedly antiprofessional form (Walters 1990, 87). Her autobiography did not conform to the rules of scientific authority or the conventions of literary taste. But this pulp form would provide her with fewer scientific restrictions as well as a larger, less exclusive readership, leaving her free to use the rhetoric of case history confession and the conventions of the romance together in a narrative that empowers the lesbian subject to write her own case history and her own romantic ending.

The first chapter of Frederics's autobiography, entitled "Skeletons in My Family Closet," begins much like Krafft-Ebing's case histories; however, his discussion of what he considers to be the important scientific details in a case differs greatly from the ironic tone that Frederics takes. While similarly tracing the idiosyncrasies of her relations, she strips them of any real explanatory value:

> Other than a dipsomaniac grandfather who managed to be a fair poet, and an uncle who made a fortune in mules, my family background is almost entirely without color. While my distant ancestors were among the earliest settlers in America, my immediate family did little else than earn money, establish homes and settle into comfortable living that was occasionally even plutocratic.
>
> The skeletons in our family closet are quite ordinary skeletons, neither better nor worse than those of many another average family. A great-grandfather who was a preacher exhausted three wives; and a musician cousin was killed under circumstances that focused on an outraged husband. But these suggestions of color are neutralized on the family tree alongside general blamelessness so normal as to be almost dull. Indeed, I almost resent such a respectable ancestral front; it would be a comfort to be able to explain my own shortcomings by no more than a glance at the family album.

Much like Krafft-Ebing, Frederics includes both what were typically considered medical conditions and what, even in the 1930s, might more commonly be considered mere eccentricities in her family history. By juxtaposing dipsomania with making a fortune in mules and exhausting three wives, Frederics conforms to the sexological tradition of revealing the family medical history while, in the same gesture, making fun of nineteenth- and early-twentieth-century ideas about what constitutes a pathological condition or an inheritable taint. Furthermore, she sees what Krafft-Ebing might have called a psychopathic or nervous constitution as "color," suggesting that such "abnormalities" are, in her view, more entertaining than they are pathological. Indeed, she implies that the general lack of color makes her family history regrettably boring. She even suggests that she regrets such a "respectable ancestral front," claiming that finding an excuse for her shortcomings by looking at the "family album" would be a "comfort." Although her allusion to "shortcomings" may suggest some degree of internalized homophobia, the rest of the narrative does not indicate that she sees being a lesbian as a shortcoming. This comment seems more likely to be a critique of the tendency of science to, as Krafft-Ebing would say, "trace all psychological manifestations to their anatomical and physiological sources" (1929, viii). In what may be a self-consciously normalizing gesture, Frederics also suggests that her racial and class heritage make her, if anything, entirely within the norms of white, middle-class experience.

As a self-authorized lesbian testimonial designed for popular reading, Frederics's autobiography was to be held suspect according to the parameters of sexological authority. Attempting to frame the autobiography in the authorized discourse of sexological truth production, sexologist Victor Robinson introduces the text as a "book which adds to the understanding of the lesbians in our midst." Although he seems to validate the propriety of both the writer and her autobiography by calling the text "delicate, yet enlightening; tense, but never lewd; passionate, without a word offensive to chastity," he ultimately interprets it as "the confession of one who was destined by nature to gather forbidden fruits in the garden of deviation" (Frederics 1975, ix). Thus he frames the text in the rhetoric of both the forbidden and the unnatural, in the category of that which must be interpreted by an authorized specialist.

Despite Robinson's apparent attempts to validate the credibility of the narrative, the presence of his introduction, especially its placement preceding Frederics's own prefatory remarks, presents an attempt to recontain the narrative within the parameters of sexological authority. But Frederics goes on to redefine what constitutes experience and expertise, locating them in identity, rather than scientific detachment and objectivity. In her foreword to *Diana*, Frederics constitutes her own authority over the representation of lesbianism in her identity as a lesbian: "I must write this book as if I were a person of importance. And, indeed, I can do that if I think of myself as a type, rather than an individual. As an individual, I am without importance except to myself; as a type I am quite important, for I belong to the third sex" (xi). Frederics claims to be uniquely authorized to write and interpret her own story. What is so interesting about the way she constitutes her authority is that she does it by claiming to be a "type" rather than an "individual." By constituting her identity through her status as a "type," Frederics does two things: she substitutes for individuality the notion of typicality as the constitutive element of her own identity, and she employs this notion of herself as a particular type in order to constitute her own cultural authority. In authorizing her own discourse in this way, Frederics implies that only lesbians can adequately represent lesbianism. This indicates the extent to which the rhetoric of confession and case history were manipulated to achieve a function in which lesbian identity affirmation, rather than diagnosis, cure, or repression, were the goal. In addition, her proud declaration of membership in the "third sex," like Jane Lennox's proud affirmation of hybridity and monstrosity, indicates her appropriation of the rhetoric of hybridity and its usefulness as a position from which to analyze the culture of sexuality and gender in general. Throughout her autobiography, Frederics sees her status as the "third sex" as liberating her from the gender expectations of both men and women as well as giving her the unique authority to discuss lesbianism. As Victor Robinson's introduction indicates, the scientific community greeted such gestures with mixed feelings, for these confessional narratives indicated that sexology had indeed identified a new object of study; however, the self-authorized discourse presented in popular literary autobiographies also threatened to undermine their monopoly over its representation.

We can see in both Freeman's and Frederics's representations of a self-affirming subject that the production of a specific lesbian identity through the process of confession, case history, and analysis created conditions that were oppressive as well as potentially liberating. For although the construction of lesbian identity—as hybridity or monstrosity—was clearly a pathologizing gesture, it also created a position from which lesbian subjects could constitute themselves as unbounded by the rules of nature and unequaled in their authority over lesbian representation. Even Krafft-Ebing's "Miss L." recognizes some freedom from "moral codes" as accompanying the status of "anomalies," though she hardly finds it empowering in the same way that Freeman's Jane Lennox does. Although Ethel hoped to cure herself of the unhealthy influences of Leonora, Jane and Diana both delight in the freedom from rules that results from recognizing one's very identity as an apparent transgression of pure gender difference and the rules of patriarchal authority.

Contemporary lesbian autobiographies are perhaps less self-consciously confessional and more self-consciously lesbian. Nonetheless, we can still see traces of these earlier models of confession, case history, and the rhetoric of hybridity. The late-nineteenth- and early-twentieth-century representation of hybridity and intermediacy form an important context for the work of contemporary writers, such as Gloria Anzaldúa, who represent hybrid identity or mestiza consciousness as a border consciousness that challenges the boundaries between identities. Anzaldúa's *Border-*

lands/La Frontera: The New Mestiza (1987) is unmistakably informed by the history of lesbian confessional narrative and spiritual autobiography. In the preface, Anzaldúa says that *Borderlands* is about her "preoccupations with the inner life of the Self, and with the struggle of that Self amidst adversity and violation." While these lines are reminiscent of traditional spiritual autobiography, Anzaldúa, like Freeman and Frederics, represents herself as a hybrid subject. She sees the impulse of articulating her border consciousness as an "almost instinctive urge to communicate, to speak, to write about life on the borders, life in the shadows."

Thus her interest in "the Self" turns into an interest in the confluences which constitute that self. Anzaldúa goes on to explain how this subject position of intersecting, confluent, yet paradigmatically conflicting identities produces a consciousness capable of deconstructing the dualistic paradigms that constitute mixed-race and homosexuality as problematic: "The work of mestiza consciousness is to break down the subject-object duality that keeps her a prisoner and to show in the flesh and through the images in her work how duality is transcended" (60). Mestiza consciousness, then, is a consciousness of the unworkability of the dualisms that divide one against one's self and divide people against each other. The work of the "new mestiza" is a deconstruction of those dualities—of gender, of race, of self and other or us and them—which form the foundation of oppression through normalization. Thus, Anzaldúa's *Borderlands* presents a new way of appropriating the confessional and taxonomic scientific discourses of race and sex in order to produce a new subject of identity politics that is constituted across the lines of race, class, gender, and sexuality. The "New Mestiza" suggests that perhaps the only effective appropriation of specific scientifically constituted identities is the appropriation of nonunitary, mixed-racial, and sexual identities—in short, subjectivities that confuse the boundaries of identity.

Cultural critics have questioned whether the language of sexological confession, case history, and hybridity creates the most opportune discourse for such a self-representation. As Teresa de Lauretis warns queer theorists, we do not want our own resistance discourses to be the "unwitting heir(s)" of the discourses of the unnatural, the impure, and the excessive that overdetermine us (1991, x). The pathologizing implications of this rhetoric make it strategic if used carefully. While Ethel and Miss L. are ultimately overdetermined by their own entrenchment in sexological discourse, Jane and Diana find the appropriation of scientific discourse useful. Gloria Anzaldúa, like Freeman's Jane Lennox, produces a revolutionary subject who celebrates her difference from the binaries of gender (and race) which form the basis of abnormalization. But what are the risks of appropriating this confessional and sexological discourse? The work of

Freeman, Frederics, and Anzaldúa suggests that lesbian confessional narratives have to be redeployed on new, highly politicized grounds, creating a more self-consciously empowering discourse of lesbian identity politics.

Coming Out

One might say that the twentieth-century lesbian practice of sharing "coming-out stories" evolved from these earlier spiritual autobiography and case history models, which were appropriated and parodied by late-nineteenth- and early-twentieth-century women writers. Such stories have, for generations, functioned as a kind of oral folk culture for lesbians, providing a forum for sharing both common and individual experiences. Originally told in relatively intimate, communal settings, these narratives represent autobiographical gestures shared by women who see themselves as equals and who allow each person to interpret her own experience, making the stories less a discourse of diagnosis and cure than one of testimonial and identification. As Julia Penelope and Susan J. Wolfe write in *The Original Coming Out Stories* (1989, xxi), "Our sharing defines us as participants in lesbian culture, as members of a community."

The editors and contributors who composed many of these immensely popular collections of coming-out stories would perhaps be surprised to see them placed in the context of early-twentieth-century lesbian narratives and sexological case history confessions. Throughout the 1970s and 1980s, editors of collections of coming-out stories saw themselves as "breaking a silence" rather than continuing a confessional tradition or correcting a scientific discourse. Tina Portillo's introduction to *Testimonies: A Collection of Lesbian Coming Out Stories* (1988) addresses the historical invisibility of lesbianism, saying it presents a welcome challenge: "Thanks to our invisibility, our legacy is a nice, blank page of history upon which we can now record who we are, in great numbers" (6). Penelope and Wolfe also see their collection as giving voice to an experience that has been silenced: "With the telling of these stories, the silence is shattered, and the words themselves create a new reality past and present (1989, 9–10)."

Despite differences of rhetorical context and purpose, the language of confession and case history has left unmistakable traces on contemporary lesbian autobiographies. While Bonnie Zimmerman suggests that the coming-out novel has become something of an "endangered species," we continue to see coming-out dramas played out not only in the communal settings of lesbian support groups and in widely circulated collections of personal coming-out stories but also on popular sit-coms and afternoon talk shows (1990, 209–10). While *Roseanne*'s Nancy came out to Roseanne and her sister Jackie, and provided an opportunity for the show to joke about, and dispel, the stereotype of a truck-driving dyke in a flannel shirt, the commonplace appearances of lesbians on talk shows often present a recontainment of the lesbian confessional narrative. By providing a ready-to-judge studio and viewing audience and, in many cases, a psychologist whose function it is to explain lesbianism from a scientific perspective, these talk shows—much noted for parading the sensational and grotesque—serve to reestablish the othering functions of sexological discourse in a new, more popular form. The audience itself gets a chance to interpret the stories and motives of the lesbian guests. The popularized psychiatric paradigm of such shows is highlighted by the presence of a licensed, published professional. The psychologist often frames the comments of both the lesbian guests and the studio audience with their own professional assessments and usually gets the last word as the credits begin rolling.

Finally, in the process of coming out, lesbians can significantly transform what it means to be healthy, natural, or redeemed. This transformation, however, only takes place when lesbian self-representation is self-conscious about the discourses in which it participates. The appropriated language of hybridity and the rhetoric of confession and case history tread dangerously close to recontainment in a discourse of psychopathology. Only by understanding the genealogy of lesbian autobiographical narratives, especially the elements of confession and case history that form its discursive history, can this discourse be used to reappropriate the revolutionary potential of queer difference and evade recontainment within a discourse of scientific authority. The only safeguard against such recontainment is being able to know its face when we see it.

Note

1. See Smith-Rosenberg (1975, 8); Faderman (1981, 15–16); D'Emilio and Freedman (1988, 121). I make this argument in greater detail in Diggs (1995).

9

B(e)aring It All: Talking about Sex and Self on Television Talk Shows

Cynthia J. Davis

TV talk is the confessional genre par excellence. Invited guests—the majority of them women—talk about their most intimate secrets, baring their sexualities and selves to a predominantly female public. In powerful ways, talk shows participate in the shaping of sexual and personal identities, as guests disclose secrets in hopes of finding solutions to their problems. Yet if the parade of sexualized "others" often has the effect of confirming a voyeuristic middle-class audience in its own normality, the deliberate confusions of sexual identity effectively unsettle the comfort of TV entertainment. Confessionally imposed sexual identities can be called into question through the very media that generate confessions.

In May 1990, my mother, younger sister, and I attended a taping of *Oprah Winfrey*. The topic of the program was embarrassing or "black sheep" family members. My family volunteered me as the family oddball, citing, among other things, my political views, which diverged from the conservative leanings of the six other Davises. Through this process I was "hailed" by the talk show, responding to the "Hey, you!" of the *Oprah* ad and recognizing myself in its summons. And yet, when we three found ourselves in an audience that included biker moms and preppy kids, punk kids and June Cleaver moms, drug or alcohol-addicted sisters with religious fundamentalist brothers, and so on, the lack of any significant visible difference between my mother, sister, and myself left us a bit embarrassed about our reasons for being there, wondering whether we were really the show's intended subjects.

If nothing else, our experience on *Oprah Winfrey* does suggest more complicated motivations than are commonly attributed to talk show guests by the forum's critics, who often wonder, typically condescendingly, why anyone would want to air their "dirty laundry" before an audience of thousands, even millions. In addition, it raises doubts as to whether the expectations that initially draw guests to these shows are adequately met by the time the guests leave. In this chapter, I will be taking seriously some of the reasons panelists themselves give for "baring it all" on television talk shows and using these explanations as springboards for a theoretical exploration of talk's appeal to its confessing guests.[1]

The very idea of taking talk shows "seriously" brings to the fore the fact that "talk" and the "serious" are often set up as opposing terms. Indeed, talk is frequently derided as the embodiment of lowbrow entertainment—as sensationalizing, trivializing, junk food for the masses. Recently, William Bennett, former secretary of education and author of *The Book of Virtues*, together with Democratic senators Joseph Lieberman of Connecticut and Sam Nunn of Georgia, launched a nationwide antitalk campaign to rid the airwaves of this "cultural rot." "It's time," declared Lieberman, "for a revolt of the revolted" (Luscombe 1995).

Comedians relish inventing more and more outlandish topics in their spoofs of the forum. For example, a *Saturday Night Live* skit parodying *Donahue* featured women who were attracted to abusive men; the primary gag consisted of the three panelists fighting over who would get to go home with a foul-mouthed, misogynistic male audience member who beat up his girlfriend during the show. Even a host like Jerry Springer speaks dismissively of his day job, concluding, "We are mostly silly entertainment. Our show by definition is about outrageous people and outrageous relationships. Almost every one of these subjects is something I wouldn't endorse" ("Celebrity Newsmakers" 1996).[2]

Clearly, as Rodney Dangerfield (or Andrew Ross) might say, talk shows "get no respect." Before exploring alternatives to this disrespectful response to the genre, I should first spell out what I mean by "talk shows" as well as my own views concerning their purpose and place. The talk shows I will be discussing here all loosely share the following traits: each is an hourlong forum shown five days a week, with each show devoted to a specific topic frequently involving some form of confessional divulgence by guests or audience members. Characteristically, these programs bring together—through the mediation of a host for whom the show is named—a guest panel, a studio audience, and occasionally an audience of "callers" to discuss that day's revelations and their ramifications.

In contradistinction to, say, Sunday news-in-review programs or conservative "talk shows" like Rush Limbaugh's, the talk shows I will be examining are typically viewed as "feminine" forums, a classification that stems, I believe, not simply from their status as mass cultural icons.[3] Their putative "femininity" is heightened by the fact that their hosts, guests, and audience members are so often women,[4] and their choice of topics is often geared explicitly to what have been deemed "women's concerns," including philandering spouses, secret crushes, date rape, sexual harassment, sexual incompatibility, menopause, plastic surgery, and abusive relationships. In addition, the fact that most talk shows air at 9 A.M., 10 A.M., 11 A.M., and 4 P.M. suggests that their target audiences are viewers who work at home, a population that remains predominantly female.

Although bearing their names, these talk shows are not solely vehicles for their hosts' celebrity; rather, hosts are but one component in a rich panoply of topics, guests, audience members, telephone callers, the entire *mise-en-scène*. Indeed, although certain shows may seem dominated by their hosts, a study sponsored by *Satellite Orbit* magazine finds that even the most talkative host, Montel Williams, talks an average of only 40 percent of his show. Percentages for other hosts include Winfrey, 33 percent, Joan Rivers, 29 percent, Phil Donahue, 22 percent, and Sally Jessy Raphael, 19.5 percent.

The genre is enormously popular: the April 1992 issue of the *Gallup Poll Monthly* reported that Winfrey was the top talk show host in the country and merited an 83 percent approval rating among women (43–45). Indeed, the popularity of talk shows is evidenced in the revenues they earn: according to a 1994 *NBC News at Sunrise* report, for example, Sally Jessy Raphael's show generates a yearly $40 million in sales and licensing fees (and some 4.5 million viewers) while costing less than $9 million to produce. Raphael still receives more than 2,000 letters a week from people with problems that they would like to discuss with her on future programs.

Not incidentally, the talk show's popularity plays a significant role in the dismissal of the genre as "junk" and of its guests and viewers as either "stupid," "sick," or both. While certain talk show topics may strike certain viewers as beyond the pale, the problem with much of the criticism of talk as well as of other popular forums is that it tends automatically to associate the popular with the trivial or banal and, in the process, risks representing "the people" as an un(der)educated, undifferentiated mass.[5] Such positions obviate what I believe are more useful critical strategies, wherein the popularity of specific media forms is analyzed as indicative of real, complicated needs and desires that are not being adequately met elsewhere and are sought in, on, and through such pop cultural formats.[6]

However inaccurate, talk's persistent equation with the trivial and the sordid is nonetheless worth taking into consideration when we try to account for its appeal; in fact, it could be argued that a central aspect of the desire of and for talk stems precisely from the format's implications of "lowness." As Peter Stallybrass and Allon White have suggested, "Disgust always bears the imprint of desire. These low domains, apparently expelled as 'Other,' return as the object of nostalgia, longing, and fascination" (1986, 191).

To Stallybrass and White, the history of the bourgeois subject is unfolded in the dialectic of the high- and lowbrow.[7] In order to constitute him/herself as subject, the bourgeois has to exclude that which is the negation of bourgeois values and norms: "the dirty, repulsive, noisy, contaminating" (191). But this exclusion is only overt and actually involves the inclusion of the low symbolically, "as a primary eroticized constituent of its own fantasy life" (5). This theory helps shed light on the fascination of the talk show and its audience with seemingly "taboo" topics—sex changes, incest, interracial relations, gay marriages, and so on—topics representing that which is explicitly forsaken in the construction of normative bourgeois identity, but for which, as a result of this overt rejection and covert internalization, we inevitably long. This longing may motivate viewers to turn on *Oprah, Sally, Montel, Jenny,* or *Leeza* and to watch with the powerful and complex mixture of the disgust that reaffirms our subject positions as other than these "others" and the fascination with the "other" without whom we are not ourselves, a mixture that keeps us coming back, day in and day out (and which in turn ensures the robust good health of these shows' profit margins).

Indeed, it is possible that the talk show more acutely encapsulates this dynamic because of its primary emphasis on voice, talk, confession. As Stallybrass and White argue, the singular bourgeois voice defines its individuality through its universal superiority to "the clamour of particular voices" which it differentiates itself from and sublimates (199). In particular, they maintain, "The exclusion of other social groups and classes in the struggle to achieve categorical self-identity appears as a special dialogism, an agon of voices—sometimes even an argument—within the shared Imaginary of the class in question. The very drive to achieve a singularity of collective identity is simultaneously productive of unconscious heterogeneity, with its variety of hybrid figures" (194). The seemingly endless proliferation of talk show topics, categories of difference, and "guest-experts" both acts out this "productive" process and confirms its necessity. As such, the heterogeneity that talk shows parade is in the end nonthreatening, seemingly upholding more than destabilizing bourgeois identity. Indeed, as Fredric Jameson (1979) might argue, such a parade of "hybrid figures" represents "a kind of psychic compromise or horsetrading which strategically arouses fantasy content within careful symbolic containment structures that defuse it, gratifying intolerable, unrealizable, properly imperishable desires only to the degree to which they can again be laid to rest" (141). Seen in this light, talk shows provide a sanctioned site wherein dominant bourgeois culture can safely get in touch with its hidden desires by mediating them into periodic ritual (see Stallybrass and White 19, 183–84, 200–201). In that viewing talk shows is for many— including myself—such a ritual, the extent to which it transgresses social norms may very well be the extent to which it ensures their perpetuation.

While compelling, this theory is also highly abstract and, as such, re-mains too speculative to draw from it any concrete, definitive conclusions as to the nature and appeal of talk. Although I will discuss several view-ers' reasons for watching, until a thorough ethnography of talk show view-ers similar to Janice A. Radway's 1984 study of romance readers can be conducted—through which talk show viewing and its various, often con-tradictory effects could be situated contextually—even my own conclu-sions remain largely conjectural. Ultimately, we can never fully account for the diversity and complexity of audience response and usage, nor for how such cultural forms matter in viewers' material lives. This is not to celebrate the individuality of reception, but to suggest that analyses of pop culture are insufficient without some acknowledgment of the shifting dy-namics, unevenness, and occasional quirkiness of reception.

Furthermore, I am not convinced that the containment of the "hetero-geneity," the laying to rest of the "intolerable . . . desires" staged on the talk show is always such a thorough process. Rather, it is my belief that for all its displays of "bizarre" guests and "scandalous confessions," talk is neither fully normative nor deliciously transgressive. Talk shows and their guests typically define the borders, the extremes of bourgeois subjec-tivity, and work to situate viewers safely just this side of those "extremes." However, if only because borderline sites are never foolproof, there are invariably moments when the line is crossed, when any given norm is in-terrogated, denaturalized, and even reconstituted.

In order to trace such instances and explore these dynamics in detail, I now want to return to the question of why people would participate in such forums and to offer a more concrete analysis of what guests stand to gain. In a February 1995 interview with Katie Couric on *Today*, Raphael offered an explanation when she said that her guests "want to come on. They want help. They want to clear something up. They have no other forum. Many millions of people are watching who are hoping that their lives can turn around."

When guests speak for themselves, their motivations roughly approxi-mate the ones Raphael offers. Among such guests, I have been able to roughly identify three not unrelated explanations for their televised con-fessions. Guests who discuss their reasons for revealing intimate details of their lives on and through talk shows typically claim to have done so (1) because of the confession's perceived therapeutic or cathartic benefits; (2) because, contiguously, confessing on talk shows apparently enables certain guests to wade through the lies and expose the "truth" or to get in touch with their "true" or "inner self" or with (in a nod to the influence of pop psychology within these forums) their "inner child"; (3) because such confessions allow them to reach out to others who may be experiencing similar problems, concerns, anxieties, desires, in hopes of convincing these others that they are not "all alone."

Under this last rubric, I have also placed guests who want to speak publicly (as opposed to privately or one-on-one) to those who have hurt them in the past or to those who would judge them harshly, in hopes of changing their minds, of promoting what Raphael identifies as "the purpose of what we try to do here every day": understanding (*Sally* 1989, 4). I would even put my own family's appearance in this last group—although (as evidence of the overlaps between these three rubrics) we might also fit more or less comfortably within the other two—since one of the primary reasons we went on *Oprah* was from our sense of belonging to a community, however misguided that sense proved to be.

Traditional theories of confession hold that a person discloses past troubles not only to heal the self but to reveal or find its truth; moreover, this cathartic quest eventually enables the confessee to rejoin the human community, feeling cleansed, rejuvenated, whole (Whitenack 1982). That talk show guests openly express their desire for catharsis, for a meaningful life, suggests that talk may very well serve as a substitute or even a form of religion for its devotees, something to believe in and rely on, a form of communion and community in the midst of widespread malaise, agnosticism, and isolation.

I will return to this pseudo-religious, communal aspect of talk and the confessions it inspires. For now, I want to start from specific examples of talk show confessions' three purported benefits—catharsis, uncovering self/truth, and community—and explore what such benefits reveal about the process of talking on talk, the unmet needs that may compel such confessions, and whether and to what degree such needs might be satisfied by the process. I will assess the degree to which these motives transgress as well as uphold the normalizing discourses that inform and are informed by traditional confessional practices. While I may be faulted for taking these viewers and their explanations for confessing on talk shows at face value, I do so strategically, as a compensatory gesture against those far too frequent occurrences when the reasons, the voices of these guests are perceived as lacking any value whatsoever.

Critics of talk shows often ridicule the genre's purported therapeutic function, mocking talk's superficial remedies which, they claim, depend on exploiting the pain of guests in order to pad the wallets of the show's producers and host. In her astute and thorough essay on *Oprah Winfrey*, Gloria-Jean Masciarotte comments on a *San Francisco Chronicle* article that attacked Oprah Winfrey and her show as "the apex of the TV-talk-show-as-therapy genre," with critics including Todd Gitlin decrying "the phenomenon as a display of false pain and false cure for consumer gain" (Masciarotte 1991, 82). By contrast, Masciarotte argues that the work of the talk show (of *Oprah* specifically) is not that of normative psychology, that it does not instantiate the "authentic" individualized self, that it instead produces "a coalition . . . of identities" but "in the pain rather than the cure." Indeed, Masciarotte contends that, although Winfrey's "stated message may advocate cure, her investigative method denies the importance of cure" (97).[8]

For Masciarotte to be correct, we must (once again) ignore the words of guests who insist that if they are there to speak of their pain it is not to wallow in it in the company of other sufferers but to alleviate it and hence cure themselves—who view their painful public disclosures as but a step (not a final stop) along the journey of piecing together their fragmented selves in hopes of eventually emerging healthy, functioning individuals. The issue that needs to be explored further is why confessing to a potentially painful past might be considered a form of healing.

The clearest precedent for talk's cures (talk as cure) and, indeed, for the controversy surrounding them is Josef Breuer and Sigmund Freud's early work with cathartic therapy and hysteria. The complicated genealogy of this original "talking cure" combined with its putative success suggests that all such cures are not necessarily effective or even therapeutic, nor are their normative effects necessarily permanent. Although the "talking cure" is typically credited to Breuer and publicized by Breuer and Freud in their classic early collaborative work, *Studies in Hysteria* (1895), one of Breuer's patients was instrumental in devising it as a means of self-healing and in giving the cure its name. That is, it was Breuer's patient "Anna O." (Bertha Pappenheim) who under a form of "autohypnosis" (in Breuer's presence) "talked out" the traumatic experiences undergirding her hysteric symptoms, "for which procedure she invented the good and serious name of 'talking-cure,' and humorously referred to it as 'chimney-sweeping'" (Breuer and Freud 1961, 20). As Breuer wrote in *Studies in Hysteria*, "This was not an invention of mine which I imposed on the patient by suggestion. It took me completely by surprise" (32).

Freud's interest in Pappenheim's case as described by his colleague led him to try out the "cure" on at least seventeen of his own hysterical patients. Based on these experiments, Freud developed his theory—which in "Dora's case" he later substantially (and controversially) revised as fantasy instead of reality based—that at the root of every case of hysteria examined through the cathartic method "*in the end we infallibly come to the realm of sexual experience*"—which, Freud contended, frequently amounted to early incestuous abuse (1959, 193).

The "talking cure," then, emerged as a breakthrough method by which a woman could attempt to recover from actual instances of sexual victimization, abuse, incest, and rape. Talking about such incidents enabled her to relieve some of the distress they continued to cause. And yet, the fact that it (that Breuer) ultimately failed Pappenheim—that she suffered a relapse the moment Breuer stopped seeing her despite Breuer's misleading claim that "she has since then enjoyed perfect health" (1961, 27)—suggests the imperfections of such a method. True, its ultimate failure to "cure" may stem in part from the (failed) transference and countertransference between Breuer and Pappenheim.[9] But it also has something to do with the fact that talking alone, even to a handsome, attentive doctor-listener, would not alter what Breuer deems Pappenheim's "monotonous family existence." In the end, more had to be changed than Pappenheim herself to make her lot in life less oppressive.

Pappenheim went on to become a prominent feminist, social worker, and activist, president of the Federation of Jewish Women, opponent of white slave traffic, and author of a play entitled *Women's Rights*. Her testimony at the International Congress to Fight White Slave Traffic in 1910 is just one instance among many where Pappenheim used a public forum to speak openly of the kinds of abuses that could only be hinted at privately in her early therapy. In these later instances, she also talks of cures but on behalf of other women, not simply herself. Through such public declarations, she enables and demonstrates a healing that was denied her under Breuer's supervision.

In light of such a life-path, we could read guests' appearances on talk shows as initial steps, as attempts, albeit usually depoliticized, to effect some sort of transformation in other women's lives, not simply their own. Indeed, there are guests who attribute their talk show disclosures to the desire to "heal" others and not simply themselves. For instance, one guest, whom I will call Anne, appeared on *Oprah* to discuss a lengthy history of incestuous sexual abuse beginning when she was only three. Anne explained her appearance by saying that she wanted to tell everybody what happened to her. She wanted others to know that there is help for those who have undergone similar experiences.

Indeed, the fact that the "talking cure" was devised by a woman as a way of recovering from painful experiences but was later appropriated and used against women should not distract us from its potential in a "feminine" forum like talk. This is especially true when it is used to testify to the reality of sexual abuse in the face of accusations (similar to those later raised by Freud in Dora's case) that these instances were fantasies that had at best only a psychic reality. Ironically, just as Freud later denied that the sexual abuse that lay at the heart of his patient's trauma actually occurred, Anne's disclosures of abuse occurred on a show entitled "Is Your Repressed Memory a Lie?" in which she was surrounded and frequently drowned out by irate panelists and audience members who, having suffered from apparently false accusations, were highly skeptical that Anne or the other panelists were telling the truth.

Even amid such skepticism, shows like this one nonetheless afford otherwise silenced (often female, frequently marginal) subjects the opportunity to speak publicly, and consequently they afford as well a momentary taste of equality or centrality. In turn, the antagonism produced by this contradiction between previous and present subject positioning(s) may lead the subject to struggle against the subordination that will in all probability resume the moment the show ends. It remains possible, that is, that these guests, like Pappenheim, will also eventually become politicized post-"therapy," post-(purported) "cure." Further, because this antagonism is staged before a wide audience that cuts across all demographic groups,[10] there is also the possibility that it might stir resistance in others similarly situated.

And yet, at the same time that Anne calls for a sort of radical mass "healing," her desire to help others never goes so far as to become a demand for structural healing. In fact, any notion that it is the social system that needs curing is immediately undercut when Anne subsequently asserts that every individual has his or her experience. With this position, any systemic critique implicit in her earlier explanation is evacuated; in its place, we are left with an image of a world in which abusers coexist with their victims as but two members of an infinitely diverse world, where, at the very least, diversity becomes a panoply that disavows any hierarchies and power differentials. While talk's cure may not always affirm the solipsistic self as the healthy self, rarely does its occasional critique of this equation extend to the socioeconomic forces that formulate and perpetuate it.

Pappenheim herself suggested that "psychoanalysis in the hands of the physician is what confession is in the hands of the Catholic priest. It depends on its user and its use, whether it becomes a beneficial tool or a two-edged sword" (in Rosenbaum and Muroff 1984, 20). With guests like *Oprah*'s Anne hoping to help other incest victims start on the recovery process, countered by guests who believe both the healing and the trauma she and others "like her" have experienced are shams, what results is a sort of uneasy truce that leaves, if anything, Anne's insistence on people's individuality ringing in our ears. In the end, despite Anne's desire to build connections, the way the panel was structured ultimately works to thwart any widespread identification with the panelist and the topic she discusses—a double-edged sword, indeed.

The idea that there has been for too long a "silence" about sexuality and that the time has come for that silence to be broken demonstrates that Pappenheim was most astute in comparing psychoanalysis to confession: as Freud and Breuer noted in 1895, psychoanalytic method shares with confession a displacement of (sexual) activity through language, even a replacement of action by language (see Breuer and Freud 1961, 5). In fact, both modes of inquiry share with numerous talk shows the "scheme for transforming sex into discourse" that Michel Foucault traces in *The History of Sexuality* (1978, 20).

Masciarotte (1991) argues that talk on talk shows more closely resembles "the Protestant activity of testimony or witnessing before the group, or even the more mysterious activity, speaking in tongues" (84–85) than it does a confession wherein the privatized "I" is codified and reflected in the "You" to whom and for whom s/he confesses. In fact, Masciarotte claims that there exists an "absolute opposition" between talk show's talk and Foucauldian confessions, pointing to talk's public forum, its nonhierarchical structure, its refusal to value the private self (1991, 84 n. 9).

Although it is true that talk's public nature does diverge from the sacrosanct hushed and privatized confessional, it is also true that Winfrey's constant refrain of "Mm-hmms" and her occasional "Yes?" quite revealingly mimic the sounds of the priestly confessor; the ease with which she interrupts and interrogates certain guests, soothes and even preaches to them—her constant "I'll let you speak, I'll let you speak"—certainly intimate the hierarchy of the confessional; furthermore, when, for example, an entire audience volunteers to go on *Oprah* to get in touch with their "inner child" with the help of new age guru John Bradshaw (December 2, 1992), one cannot dismiss so lightly the idea that for many even this public space serves primarily as a site for and means to private introspection. Indeed, the motives of guests like those on the "inner child" program are, demonstrably, to find themselves, to get in touch with the "truth" that is believed to lurk within.

And yet, I would also hesitantly add, talk's sanctioned pursuit of the "truth" and uncovering of some sacrosanct "inner self" may at moments, on certain shows, encounter obstacles. There are times, as in the following example, where the effort to "discover" and "reveal" this self through the confessional stage of the talk show entails examining and assessing the historic production of its gendered/"sexed" dimensions—where the exploration turns to the "what" and the "how" as opposed to simply the "who I am."

In September 1989, *Sally Jessy Raphael* featured a guest named Toby. Small, dark, bespectacled, and speaking in a distinctly nasal voice, Toby appeared on stage dressed in androgynous clothing: a neutral-colored sweater with jeans and sneakers. As Toby proudly confessed and as the show title boldly proclaimed, "I'm not a man; I'm not a woman!" He? she? it? Toby ascribes to no gender and instead identifies as a neuter. Although a chromosome test has been conducted, Toby refuses to reveal the results and instead revels in a liminal identity that, based on the host's and audience's rather tame responses, does not seem to be as disconcerting as one might expect.

For instance, one woman in the audience stands to tell Toby, "I'd like to say I'd be your friend and I'll accept you just as you are" (*Sally* 1989, 9); another finds the opportunity in Toby's appearance to say, "I think we should all be as secure in ourselves and confident that she [*sic*] . . . is going to become somebody, no matter what somebody else thinks about her" (12). Sally's concluding comment both joins in and extends these laudatory sentiments: "In a world where an awful lot of people—maybe we said this before—but a lot of people don't know who they are, don't know what's going on, you seem to have found yourself. And you're one of those people I'll never, ever forget" (14). To the extent that Toby's persistent refutations of gender identity never entail a refutation of a unique identity, Sally and her audience would seem to consider Toby worthy of respect because s/he has "found" his/her self, s/he is a "person," a "somebody," unique and unforgettable.

True, the blurb that appears on the screen whenever Toby is shown— "Says he is Neither Man nor Woman" (the use of the masculine pronoun here and the feminine in the audience member's comment above further demonstrates the difficulty as well as the need to classify Toby)—implies a third, concluding phrase: "I'm a person." Far from being pro- or transgressive, such a manifesto would approximate what Chantal Mouffe (1988) deems a central tenet of neoconservative ideology: "The conflation of pleasure and democracy under the rubric of entertainment constitutes, among other things, a central instrument in the neo-conservative deproblematization of democracy: it is analogous to saying, for instance, 'I'm not a woman, I'm a person'" (48).

The fact that Toby echoes this claim speaks to the troubled and troubling positions of such "mind-boggling" (*Sally* 1989, 14) talk show guests: while they may challenge known categories in ways that might seem potentially subversive, their unwavering embrace of individualism often simultaneously undergirds bourgeois subjectivity. As Toby tells Sally, "I like being who I am. Why should I try to be anybody else?" (4). Defiantly "true" to his/her self in the face of efforts to impose upon her/him a "false" identity, Toby's acceptance of the individualistic "I'm okay, you're okay" laissez-faire attitude of bourgeois liberalism risks leaving unchallenged the social structures that determine who is and is not "okay" and what "okay" means in the first place. From a strictly Foucauldian perspective, Toby's proud stance would follow a path wherein confessions of sexuality—even of asexuality—may seem liberating but often only further contribute to the classificatory discourse of sex and the instruments of power.

At the same time, however, although representing the truth of his/her self as "neuter" and this "neuterness" as determined by her/his body, Toby testifies that this is a "truth" arrived at after a great deal of struggle and after numerous attempts by others—doctors, specialists, family members, and now *Sally Jessy Raphael* and its audience—to classify Toby as either male or female:

> Back when I was about 16, and the professionals who were supposed to be helping me and helping my family and helping everybody to adjust and figure out what was what, had finally decided, well I obviously was not going to adjust as a female. So I should change over to a male identity and I should be supported in doing this. And their idea of how I should become a male was, since I didn't have a penis, I should wear a jock strap with some rolled-up socks inside it, to put a bulge in my pants. . . . Being a naive kid who thought the experts really knew what they were talking about, I gave it a try, and I found out a couple of interesting things. First of all, I found out, if you stand in front of the mirror and you put the socks in the jock strap, and then you look in the mirror again and you take them out, you can't tell the difference. They're not visible. But if you go about your normal, everyday activities like walking up and down the stairs and sitting and standing, they work themselves into a thoroughly unnatural-looking but quite visible conformation. And if you ride your bike to the mall two miles away, then the socks will work their way out of the jock strap, then when you get off your bike, park it and start walking across the parking lot, the socks will fall out of your pant legs, onto the ground. . . . That experiment lasted one afternoon. And the point is, all of these experts they think you have to be one way or the other, or you won't adjust. The way to adjust is to wear something attached to you that isn't a part of you. Well, I fit into my clothes just fine without that. I fit into my relationships just fine without that. (13)

Here Toby testifies at length to the "experts'" attempts to "fit" him/her within one side of the gendered divide. This anecdote and the wry tone in which it was related reveal the labor (and the occasional humor) behind the effort involved in maintaining the fiction that our dichotomous classificatory systems are both comprehensive and "natural."

Indeed, Toby's tale explores his/her "subjugated" history through a process that resembles "memory work," a term used by Frigga Haug et al. in *Female Sexualization* (1987). The contributors to this volume argue that a woman's socialization is more accurately a process of "sexualization," wherein not just the genitalia, but even the more "innocent" parts of the body—including the hair, the legs, and the "tummy"—become sexualized. In order to trace the mechanisms of the inscription of sexuality on the female body, Haug and her colleagues generate stories about these separate body parts through the collective writing process they call "memory work": "We used our own memories to review the ways in which individual parts of the body are linked with sexuality, the way gender is expressed through the body, the routines that have drilled us in a particular relationship to our bodies, and the ways in which all of this is knotted into social structures and social relations between the sexes" (34). Toby's revelations of the way gender and sexuality were (temporarily) imposed upon her/his body as well as his/her eventual rejection of such routines and classificatory attempts prove that resistance to sexualization is indeed possible, if rare; Toby's insistence on a third term—even with its sustained and sustaining relishing of individualism—opens a space for a "desexualization" of the categories of knowledge and the formation of new or at least less rigid ways of knowing.

Even guests whose appearances are not premised on speaking the "truth" may undermine the regulatory identities conferred by the talk show's confessional structure. For example, the sexual disclosures of a guest I will call Joan, who appeared twice on *Oprah*, take on a different cast in light of a subsequent confession she made in an "exclusive interview" with the *National Enquirer*. As Joan rather gleefully told "enquiring minds," some of Oprah Winfrey's guests tell fabricated stories and she herself had deceived Oprah twice (Rodeck 1993).

In the early 1990s, a "curious" Joan responded to a call for guests who had slept with their husbands' bosses. Under her own name, Joan appeared on a show that aired in the same year and told a lavish (fictional) tale about this affair which, she claimed, ended with her husband's firing. Almost to the date two years later, Joan, this time under another name, told *Oprah* audiences about how her husband had refused to have sex with her after watching her give birth—again, a total fabrication.

Joan's appearances were motivated not by a desire to get in touch with the truth or to assist in broadcasting the truth but by a rather dramatic, even exhibitionistic attempt to confirm a suspicion that the seemingly "true confessions" on talk shows are fictitious. Her three "confessions" reveal that what counts on talk shows is not the believability of the material per se but the believability of the performer, that it is possible to confess and not contribute to the discursive production of truth, knowledge, power. In short, the perceived "truth" of a confession is not adjudicated and instantiated solely by the receptive ear but depends as well on the speaking "mouth" largely forgotten by Foucault.[11]

In particular, the fact that Joan confesses to sexual "truths"—(mis)identifying first as an adulteress and later as a celibate—that are in fact fabrications underscores the manufactured nature of such discursively produced "truths" and, as did Toby's tale, the labor involved in their production. I use the term *fabrications* here to connote their constructedness; to label Joan's self-representations "falsehoods" would be to imply that there is some "true" Joan that lies outside these apparently erroneous "self-representations." In fact, what Joan's talk show performances accomplish is to interrogate rather than further instantiate such dichotomies as true/false, truth/lie. They situate subjectivity not as a function of ontology but as an effect of performativity—not in being but as the product of doing or seeming—and, in the process, unsettle any definitive location of the "truth" in the material body that confesses.

Admittedly, this truth is quickly recontained the moment Joan makes her final disclosure in the *National Enquirer*. There, she situates herself as the "truth-teller" who has ascertained talk's "falseness." Nonetheless, the hyperbolic excesses of her talk show representations—she purports to be not just an adulteress but one who sleeps with her husband's boss, not simply a celibate but forced to be one because her husband was turned off by childbirth—may, as Judith Butler (1993) argues about drag's performances, be read as revealing "the hyperbolic status of the norm itself, indeed, [such performances] can become the cultural sign by which that cultural imperative [i.e., the compulsory conformance to the heterosexual gender norm] might become intelligible" (236). Joan's exaggerated performances of these norms helps to work "the weakness in the norm"—through their very excessiveness they bring "into relief . . . the understated, taken-for-granted quality of heterosexual performativity" (236).[12] The possibility remains that the aftershocks of appearances by such guests—the disturbance and discomfort they set into motion—may cause a microscopic rupture in our seemingly automatic, nonchalant compliance with the norms that such guests if only momentarily destabilize.

The desire to bond with and/or educate others is one of the primary attractions for TV talk show guests. Winfrey's former theme song, "I'm Every Woman," and a Sally Jessy Raphael advertisement campaign, which concluded with Sally claiming, "We can face all the bumps, as long as we're together," both draw on this underlying premise of potential community, of sisterhood. Talk show guests' desire for community would seem to be matched by the viewing audience's, a community that seemingly revolves around the host but also encompasses guests, audience members, indeed, the entire process, the sharing of voices and views, the interchanged glances and supportive commentary.

Actual guests, including one named Kathy who appeared on *Sally Jessy Raphael* in hopes of finding "somebody out there for me," also document how appealing this belief in a compassionate host can be: when asked by an interviewer if she feels that Sally cares about her, Kathy responds: "Oh, very much so, very much so. . . . Her compassion. You can see it and hear it in her voice" (*NBC News at Sunrise* 1994, 8). Guests participate in talk as a means of confirming that their own alienation is not unique— "I'm not alone in my aloneness"—and because talk seems to provide a unique form of intimacy based on shared experiences that give the effect of a sort of religious commun(al)ity in the face of an overwhelming solitude.[13] Far from being motivated by a purely narcissistic urge, guests who attribute their talk show confessions to a desire for community seem less invested in reifying and authenticating the "self" than in overcoming even as they confirm its/our fragmentation and alienation.

Such utopian impulses toward community are, according to Fredric Jameson (1979), what motivates all mass cultural forms, which "have as their underlying impulse—albeit in what is often distorted and repressed, unconscious forms—our deepest fantasies about the nature of social life, both as we live it now, and as we feel in our bones it ought rather to be lived" (147–48). Even if only temporarily, talk show confessions promise what Victor Turner (1982) defines as "communitas": "a realm of direct, immediate, and total confrontations of human identities" (45). The appeal of this realm, its apparent intimacy—the opportunity to "touch" others— glimpsed at moments during the show's hour but vacated seconds after the TV set is turned off, may elucidate why viewers return the next day and why they might desire to participate as guests or audience members.

No doubt the isolation that prompts talk show appearances and viewing is only increasing in degree under the atomizing forces of late consumer capitalism and the increased sensationalistic "shock" format of the genre. Yet this is an isolation that talk alone cannot begin to alleviate. Ultimately, the talk show both stages the alienation felt by its viewers and, in its apparent inclusiveness, provides a simulacrum of actual community that proves too fleeting and insubstantial to satisfy. The interaction between host, guests, audience, and home viewers provide both an opportunity and a substitute for human relations—and, at least for my mother, sister, and myself, a far from satisfying substitute at that.

In conclusion, even while conceding talk's liabilities, it is worth noting that the longing for community that prompts talk show viewing and participation bespeaks a similar desire to the one that motivates many political groups and movements, including feminism. As Rita Felski maintains, "The recognition that women's problems are not private but communal is perhaps the most fundamental message underlying feminist confession" (1989, 115), a message that talk also frequently embraces and strives to convey. I point out this shared longing for and belief in community not to trivialize such political movements, especially since I reject the equation of talk and the trivial. In fact, one of my motives for noting it is to help dissolve the boundaries that separate "the trivial" and "the serious." This boundary often prevents dialogue between "fluff" like the talk show and "serious" political forums like feminism and tends to mask their frequently overlapping discourses, their frequently similar subject matter, confessions, and desires.[14]

This overlap, of course, has not gone unnoticed: daytime talk has evinced a nascent, often submerged feminism ever since its putative inceptor, Phil Donahue, first thrust his microphone in front of an audience member's face in 1968. It is, perhaps, no coincidence that the *Donahue* show aired then, at the outset of the second wave of American feminism (and perhaps no coincidence that Donahue signed off the air in this allegedly "post-feminist" age). From their respective beginnings, both the talk show and the feminist movement grant authority to the voice of experience—to the confession—and see such revelations as potential consciousness-raising devices. And yet in both forums, that experienced voice has been challenged by others who doubt anyone's ability to speak for everyone. As a result, both talk shows and the women's movement focus on gender as a common bond, even as they minimize its significance through a recognition of differences between similarly gendered subjects.

Acknowledging that these two forums draw audiences and converts out of similar needs and that there are many of us who participate in both simultaneously may assist in a discussion that could prove mutually beneficial. Talk's stories of victimization can certainly serve as exemplary testimonials to the reasons that feminism exists. Feminists can utilize the revelations divulged on and by talk shows and politicize them in their own arenas, providing the missing link between talk's personal confessions and the political. In turn, talk shows can teach feminism, among other things, an accessible way of speaking about crucial issues without resorting to abstraction; talk also can help instill a wariness of promoting normative definitions of womanhood, since these invariably backfire whenever attempted before talk's diverse audience.

Phil Donahue's avowed feminism implicitly permeated his every show, but at times he chose to make the connection between talk and feminism explicit. He aired programs that dealt explicitly and exclusively with feminism and its issues, several of which highlighted the diversity within feminism. In one show, "Black Women and the Feminist Movement," black feminist Loretta Ross argued that being a woman does not automatically imply being a feminist, and being a feminist does not necessarily imply a commitment to an antiracist America. In another show, entitled "Sexual Equality to Sexual Harassment: The State of American Womanhood," Donahue paired *Sexual Personae* author Camille Paglia with *Backlash* author Susan Faludi, both avowed feminists but with highly divergent, even opposing views of what feminism means.

At the very least, feminists may gain wider and more sympathetic audiences; through forums like talk shows, we can work to overturn the stigmatizing definition of feminism as elitist and unconcerned with the "real people," everyday concerns, survival issues to which the talk show is devoted. Dissolving the high/low barrier between the two sites may also help us to take seriously the frequent claims of hosts like Oprah Winfrey or Sally Jessy Raphael that they do their shows in hopes of helping, reaching, and educating people and transforming their lives for the better, goals that were and hopefully remain central to the feminist movement.

The 1996 cancellation of *Donahue*, however, provides a necessary check on my own utopian longings for community, for meaning, substance, and connection. For one thing, such connections will always have to work with and around the fact that talk shows invariably lack what feminist movements overtly possess: explicit political agendas and aims. As commodities, talk shows often function explicitly to conceal any and all political bases (including feminism) by transforming divisive, substantive issues—unemployment, wife abuse, incest, gay rights—into entertainment and larger viewer shares. And feminism, as Donahue may have proven, is hardly a best-seller within such forums.

Acknowledging the influence of market forces, however, need not force us to relinquish talk show forums as potential bully pulpits. Given the backlash against feminism in the nineties, feminists still committed to the movement cannot afford to be choosers. Talk represents a largely untapped arena, geared to a predominantly female and potentially generous audience, addressing "women's concerns," a space wherein women are sanctioned to be both speakers and viewers.[15] In lieu of such scorn, this chapter has attempted to show possible points of convergence, conversation, even perhaps conversion. As Joan Rivers famously inquired, "Can we talk?" Stay tuned.

Notes

1. Given the "dailiness" of this genre and the volatility of the talk show industry, this chapter does not claim to provide a critical commentary on the most recent developments; rather, its intent is to use representative examples from 1989 to 1996 in its exploration of confessional politics.

2. Geraldo Rivera, dubbed the "prince of sleaze" by some critics, caved under the pressure of Bennett et al. and announced that he would eliminate that which made him prince: "We're getting rid of the sleaze. It's all

history." In September 1996, a revamped *Geraldo* began airing on "stations near you." Rivera claimed that he didn't want "to be remembered as the guy who got his nose broken in an on-camera brawl with skinheads" (*Chronicle*, February 18, 1996, 5).

3. See Huyssen (1986) and Modleski (1986) for their respective arguments that mass culture itself is conceived as feminine.

4. The acknowledged first talk show host is Phil Donahue, who although not a "woman" is a sympathetic, feminist male, as is Maury Povich. Hosts like Montel Williams and Geraldo Riviera not withstanding, I agree with Gloria-Jean Masciarotte (1991), who finds "something horrifically unmasculine about the talk show's talking subject, whose origins for the most part construct and are constructed around the exploration and interpretation of issues that abut the boundaries of gender identity" (91 n. 25). Masciarotte's provocative article focuses primarily on hosts and most notably on Oprah Winfrey; my focus here will be more on guests and viewers. I will be discussing Masciarotte's take on talk shows in detail shortly.

5. This view approximates the position of critics associated with the Frankfurt School, especially Theodor Adorno. But this critique of "the culture industry" often appears in more mainstream and popular venues in the United States, including news shows like *This Week with David Brinkley*, newspaper editorials, PTA meetings, and church groups across the nation.

6. The Centre for Contemporary Cultural Studies at Birmingham is the school most credited with this approach to popular culture.

7. This is a point Fredric Jameson (1979) also hints at in his claim that "a genuinely historical and dialectical approach demands that we read high and mass culture as objectively related and dialectically interdependent phenomena, as twin and inseparable forms of the fission of aesthetic production under late capitalism" (133–34). With Stallybrass and White (1986) I would want to underscore the symbolic or psychical (as opposed to explicitly "objective") relations of the "high" and the "low."

8. Masciarotte's 1991 article and its argument may be more appropriate to the Oprah of 1991 than to her current slimmed-down, pop psychology preaching persona. Since 1997, Oprah has devoted numerous shows to gurus of various new age movements, including Deepak Chopra and John Bradshaw, even presenting herself as a kind of guru, encouraging the audience to heal themselves by finding their purpose on this planet and following it, by casting out fear and embracing love.

9. For an overview of the history of "Anna O."/Pappenheim, see Rosenbaum and Muroff (1984), esp. 1–23. All subsequent biographical facts on Pappenheim are derived from this source. Pappenheim developed an "hysterical pregnancy" exactly a year after Breuer's own wife had become pregnant, and when she named Breuer as the father, he cut off all ties with his patient, who was soon thereafter confined to a sanitorium.

10. This information on demographics was all that I could obtain from Kingworld, the distributors of *Oprah Winfrey*. Apparently, they like to keep research into audience demography under wraps, as do the folks at Nielsen, who conduct many of the studies Kingworld relies on.

11. Frances Bartkowski makes a similar point (1988).

12. In the *Utne Reader*, Joshua Gamson argues, "TV talk shows may be crass and voyeuristic, but they give a voice to those who have been silenced," particularly to lesbians and gays (1996, 79). That this is so is confirmed by a November 1995 e-mail posting from the Gay and Lesbian Alliance against Defamation (GLAD) alerting readers not only to the Bennett-sponsored "talk showdown" but also to Pat Robertson's campaign against TV talk shows. GLAD's message concludes with an "action alert" listing addresses of network CEOs who, they hoped, would soon be flooded with mail protesting censoring of TV talk.

13. Masciarotte notes this as well when she suggests that "the panelists, the on-show audience, Oprah, and the television audience talk to find a coalition, a co-respondent voice or story" (1991, 87).

14. For the classic essay on feminist approaches to popular culture, see Angela McRobbie (1982).

15. The feeling appears to be mutual: although I trace a covert feminism in the discourse of talk shows, overtly talk is a site wherein feminism is routinely dismissed for its militant, male-bashing, or "anti-male" agenda.

10

Cross-Dressing Confessions:
Men Confessing as Women

Lorraine Janzen Kooistra

Some of the men who follow the urge to confess do so, significantly, in women's clothing. The cross-dressing confession is an important subgenre of the female confession, highlighting the feminization of the genre. When men "in drag" mimic the style of women's sexual confessions, the notion of the "natural" body becomes unsettled. The confessional inversion of the cross-dressing confession playfully calls into question the essentialism that is often claimed to be a characteristic feature of the confessional genre. Through strategic confessional inversion, the cross-dressing confession reveals the female confession to be much more complex than the unmediated cry from the heart it is often claimed to be.

> And after all, what is a lie? 'Tis but
> The truth in masquerade.
>
> —Byron

Confessing the Naked Truth

When is a woman's sexual confession *not* a woman's sexual confession? What guarantees authenticity in this most naked of genres? Stripped of any pretension to "literature," the sexual confession parades in the popular marketplace, a shameless sister we secretly admire and publicly disdain. Her power resides in her "truthfulness"—in her willingness to expose the intimate details and personal traumas of her life without the assistance of art. As in all autobiographical genres, the truth-effect of women's sexual confessions relies on the reader's belief in the coincidence between the writer's body and signature—between lived and represented life. In women's confessions, the sexual identity of the speaker guarantees the truth of subjective experience within a gender-coded world.

But what if the body and the signature do *not* coincide? What happens when the woman's sexual confession is actually penned by a man? Does the identity crisis motivated by what Elizabeth Harvey (1992) calls "transvestite ventriloquism" (4) and Richard Dellamora (1990) names "cross-voicing" (71) subvert the truth-claims of the confessional narrative? Both Harvey's and Dellamora's metaphors for male writers creating a feminine persona focus more on *voice* than on *body*. But when a man confesses under a woman's name, what is foregrounded is not so much a voice as a sexualized body inscribed by a range of womanly signs. At the same time, the sign system signaling "female" appears to be supported by a socialized body of "feminine" knowledge and power. In cross-dressing confessions, both the system of female signs—breasts, clothing, and body language—and the accreditation of gender—intuition, emotion, sensitivity—are apparently contradicted if the confessor strips to reveal the naked truth of the body.

Twentieth-century culture is fascinated by the disjuncture between a feminine identity and a male body. Many television talk shows, from *Phil Donahue* to *Geraldo Rivera*, from *Sally Jessy Raphael* to *Oprah Winfrey*, have hosted cross-dressing confessions (Garber 1992, 5). Transvestism in the entertainment industry has also proven to be a popular commodity. Some rock groups, such as Guns 'n' Roses and Nirvana, and some stars, such as RuPaul and Prince, feature cross-dressing in their acts, while many others—like k. d. lang, Michael Jackson, and David Bowie—project an androgynous look. The film industry has also capitalized on the popular interest in cross-dressing, both in comedies such as *Tootsie* and *Mrs. Doubtfire*, and in the more haunting dramas of *M. Butterfly* and *Orlando*. Radio documentaries such as the CBC's "Sisters under the Skin" (1992) and newspaper coverage of the life of transvestites with headlines such as "When Clothes *Don't* Make the Man" have also interpellated this marginal discourse into mainstream culture (Cheney 1992).[1]

As the title "Sisters under the Skin" implies, what cross-dressers confess is their strong identification with women—or, perhaps more accurately, with "the feminine." This confession is primarily a gender identification unrelated to sexual orientation. Studies of cross-dressers from psychological, sociological, and cultural perspectives, as well as the testimony of transvestites themselves, indicate that most practicing cross-dressers—as opposed to drag queens—are heterosexual.[2]

At the core of the cross-dressing confession, then, is an attempt to disclose a hidden truth about sex and gender. Cross-dressing, like confession itself, is about constructing a private identity in a public space. The cross-dressing confession is an autobiographical gesture and an attempt at self-definition through representation. This is true of cross-dressing as a physical act. It is even more evident in transvestite writing, which is prolific and which seems to be intimately connected to the act of "dressing up." Language, like clothing, offers a way of representing—and re-presenting—the self. As Harry Brierley (1979) comments in his study of transvestite writing, "The act of making a statement which has a separate existence which others can read is rather like the need to appear in public for a confirmation of the fantasy of femininity" (120).

But more is at stake in the cross-dressing confession than a male fantasy of femininity. The cross-dresser does not simply hold up a distorting mirror in which we see reflected exaggerated, parodic images of our own womanliness. Rather, as I hope to demonstrate, the cross-dresser's fantasy throws into sharp relief the illusory nature of sex/gender categories as such. Precisely because its femininity is not grounded in a female body, the cross-dressing confession calls into question the necessary relationship between sex and gender. The cross-dressing confession confronts and confounds the essentialist assumption behind the theory of women's sexual confessions: that a woman's sexual confession is, by definition, written by a woman.

It is precisely along this sex/gender and sex/sexuality border that the cross-dressing confession operates. Since in the popular imagination transvestism symbolizes homosexuality,[3] a man in women's clothes challenges cultural conceptions of identity based on both biological sex and sexual orientation. A man *writing* in women's clothes—that is, confessing as a woman—disrupts these categories even further because cross-dressing confessions can mirror the *genre* of women's sexual confessions so closely that *gender* itself becomes destabilized. In art as in life, it is sometimes difficult to distinguish between the masquerade and the authentic, the female impersonator and the woman.

A man confessing as a woman is not necessarily a wolf in sheep's clothing. On the contrary, I would like to suggest that the cross-dressing confession should not be considered as a pernicious appropriation of female space, but rather as a subgenre of women's sexual confessions as such. By selecting representative texts from the early and the late twentieth century, and by crossing the border between literary and popular culture forms of confession, I hope to demonstrate that the cross-dressing confession shares a history and a tradition with women's sexual confession. As we shall see, although they perform different functions, their forms are remarkably similar.

I shall begin my examination of cross-dressing confessions with a literary text taken from the turn of the century, when the genre of women's sexual confessions was just beginning to emerge as a popular literary form. I name this disguised literary presentation "metaphoric cross-dressing" because its only "dress" is that which can be constructed rhetorically. In metaphoric cross-dressing, a male author writes an autobiographical fiction from a female subject-position in order to enact his own disguised sexual confession. Later in the chapter I shall move from the metaphoric to the real, and from the literary to the popular, in a section which leaves the early years of the century in order to examine contemporary confessions of men in skirts. In my study of the cross-dressing confession, I am neither appropriating, as Garber properly warns against, "the position of the cross-dresser for 'woman'" (1992, 174), nor endorsing the cross-dresser's appropriation of the position of "woman" for himself. Rather, I wish to investigate the implications of both the metaphoric and the literal cross-dressing confession in an attempt to "grasp," as Virginia Woolf once wrote, the elusive "truth about W" (1975, 32).

Passing as a Woman: An Englishwoman's Love-Letters

In 1900, at precisely that moment in history when the new genre of women's confessions was emerging as a best-seller, Laurence Housman (1865–1959)—the younger brother of A. E. Housman and well known in decadent circles as an illustrator and poet in his own right—published anonymously *An Englishwoman's Love-Letters*. The era was especially charged, for the rise of women's sexual confessions coincided not only with the first feminist movement, but also with the late Victorian proliferation of scientific sexual confessions (Shaw 1992, 90) and with a corresponding popular interest in, and anxiety about, the intricacies of sexuality and personal revelation. As Elaine Showalter (1990) documents in *Sexual Anarchy*, the turn of the century marks a crisis in identity formation heralded by a cultural fear "that sexuality and sex roles might no longer be contained within the neat and permanent borderlines of gender categories" (9). This identity crisis is played out in the production and reception history of Housman's cross-dressing confession. *An Englishwoman's Love-Letters* challenges fundamental assumptions about "feminine style," authentic "female experience," and "natural" sexuality because the text achieved the transvestite fantasy of "passing" as a woman.

Implicit in transvestitic discourse is the trope of writing and reading: cross-dressers "write" themselves in a certain way so that they will not be "read" as men. As a culturally determined system of signs, feminine clothing, body parts, and traits are a kind of *language*—a means of representing, or producing, the self. By invoking a particular sartorial rhetoric, the cross-dresser hopes the displayed signs will be "read" as signifiers of a feminine gender. Laurence Housman achieved this transvestite fantasy by writing from a female subject-position (an Englishwoman) and by disguising the identity of his sex and gender under the ruse of anonymity. Moreover, the love letters were properly dressed for their *femme* role when they first appeared in public. Encased within white parchment covers described as "dainty" and "slight," and tied up with green silk ribbons, *An English-woman's Love-Letters'* female-coded exterior seemed to guarantee the feminine nature of both the writing and the writer ("Tyranny of Love" 1900, 510). When the book was advertised in *The Bookman's* "New Books of the Month," the notice-writer declared he had "hesitated to loosen" the ribbons and peek inside: "It seemed an impertinence." Once unloosed and exposed, *An Englishwoman* passed even such close scrutiny—at least among male readers. It is worth noticing, however, that *An Englishwoman* had more trouble "passing" with *women* reviewers, some of whom "read" the disguised masculinity of the author.[4]

An Englishwoman's Love-Letters achieved its remarkable popularity because of its "appeal to the present appetite for 'interiors,' which," as one correspondent commented, "the publication of Mrs. Browning's letters seems to have whetted amazingly" ("Phi" 1900). According to the *Pall Mall Gazette* reviewer, "Never was there written a confession so tender, so exquisite, so tragic" (in Housman 1937, 167). Sold out in the first week, published in eight authorized and numerous pirated editions (Engen 1983, 102, 110), *An Englishwoman's Love-Letters* testifies to the enormous popular appeal of women's sexual confessions at the turn of the century.[5]

Except, of course, that this woman's sexual confession is written by a man. The publication and reception history of *An Englishwoman's Love-Letters* asks whether there is such a thing as a feminine voice or language, or whether, on the contrary, all identities—feminine, masculine, straight, gay—are cultural products constructed by historically specific social discourses. Perhaps, *Love-Letters* suggests, such identities are less *products* than they are *processes* or *performances*. By calling our attention to the stylized acts by which images of the self are produced, the cross-dresser forces us to acknowledge the degree to which our own identities are contingent and positional enactments of culturally coded scripts.

The story told in *An Englishwoman's Love-Letters* is simple. A young woman of property and culture falls in love with a man of her own class. After loving him secretly for some time (and writing him a stock of "dead" letters), she is overjoyed when he returns her love. The subsequent letters chronicle the initial happiness of the lovers; the unexpected setback occasioned by the hostility of the man's mother; the inexplicable rupture, in which the young man breaks off the engagement but refuses to explain why; and the young woman's suffering and ultimate death. In short, as a few astute reviewers noted, the melodramatic plot seems to follow a familiar fictional pattern rather than record an actual life. Yet there was clearly something in Housman's representation of femininity which found confirmation in his readers' conceptions of "real" women, for an enthusiastic public took the *Love-Letters* "for gospel truth, for pure historic record" (Cook 1901, 153).

Housman's female persona in *An Englishwoman's Love-Letters* both reflects and resists contemporary stereotypes of femininity. The writing style is effusive, replete with italics, dashes, and exclamation marks. It is also coy, playful, and metaphoric—a trait which her lover complains of. *His* letters, apparently, are typically "masculine," in that they are completely lacking in metaphor (37). Significantly, the "feminine" style of the writing is explicitly compared to women's clothing. In a self-consciously transvestitic gesture which both reveals and disguises the work itself as a cross-dressing confession, the "Englishwoman" writes that "dress . . . is but a love-letter writ large" (14). The comparison between dress-making and writing underscores the legibility trope[6] implicit in transvestitic discourse, while at the same time self-critically revealing how the feminine is caught up in representation.

In a highly charged metafictional moment, the "Englishwoman" reads "a silly 'confession book' in which a rose was everybody's favourite flower, manliness the finest quality for a man, and womanliness for a woman." Commenting that this is "as much as to say that pig is the best quality for pork, and pork for pig," the writer goes on to subvert stereotypes by reversing Byron's approbation of brave men and fair women. What she admires and loves "best in men and women [is] what they lack most often: in a man, a fair mind; in a woman, courage" (94). This critique of gender roles is supported by the Englishwoman's subversive attack on the institution of marriage throughout the book by her celebration of same-sex friendships and fulfilling relationships outside the heterosexual economy. Far from exposing the real sex of the writer, the presence of both stereotypes and subversive critique in *An Englishwoman's Love-Letters* aligns the text even more firmly with women's sexual confessions. According to Rita Felski, such contradictory elements are characteristic of the "feminist confession as a genre," which can be both radically subversive and naively reflective of cultural norms (1989, 119). As a cross-dressing confession that "passes" as the real thing, *An Englishwoman's Love-Letters* suggests that concepts of a "feminine" style and—even more troubling—a "feminist genre" are fundamentally unstable because based in a categorical, binary system of identification and definition. The limitations of such a system, which not only opposes masculine to feminine, but also (as transvestites themselves complain) uses the terms as value judgments (Lynn 1988, 23), are illuminated by the reception history of Housman's cross-dressing confession.

It is important to remember that Housman managed to keep his identity—and therefore his sex—undetected for an extended period. During this time, the unknown woman's confession was praised as the "real cries of joy and grief" of an "exquisite nature" who revealed "the fine, pure flame of her soul" in a feminine style (Housman 1937, 167; "Tyranny of Love" 1900). Critics, journalists, and readers joined in outrageous speculations about the confessor's identity, with British reviewers suggesting such unlikely (and contradictory) candidates as Queen Victoria, Alice Meynell, and Marie Corelli, and American critics naming Edith Wharton and Elizabeth von Arnim (Engen 1983, 110). When Housman was unmasked as the male author of an epistolary fiction, and the authenticity of the confession could no longer be guaranteed by a female body, *An Englishwoman's Love-Letters* was widely condemned by the same "chatter-press" which had previously "tumbled headlong into extravagant praise" (Housman 1937, 165). What is interesting here is how quickly the "exquisite" and the "tender" can change to the "unhealthy" or morbid by the simple exposure of the writer's sex. In a period in which sex, gender, and sexuality were increasingly becoming threatened categories, the revelation of the "Englishwoman's" male sex inevitably put "her" sexuality into question.

Coming Out

Turn-of-the-century sexologists such as Havelock Ellis (1936) and Edward Carpenter (1914) were fascinated by sex/gender/sexuality distinctions. Using the trope of the "Intermediate Sex" to describe the homosexual, Carpenter tried to break traditional binary oppositions by proposing a more fluid understanding of sex and gender. Carpenter based his argument on the pioneering work of Karl Heinrich Ulrichs, the first sexologist to describe the homosexual as a man with a "feminine soul enclosed in a male body" (Carpenter, 117). Ulrichs's view, which was espoused by many turn-of-the-century sexologists, promoted an understanding of homosexuality as an interior identity—a "natural" or "essential" aspect of the self—by inverting the relationships between inside and outside.[7] Since the homosexual's interior identity might logically express itself in the desire to wear the clothing of the other sex, the inversion theory encouraged an association between homosexuality and cross-dressing.[8] But even without the physical sign of cross-dressing, homosexuality was figured as a kind of psychic transvestism, for to think of the homosexual as a feminine soul inside a male body is to conceive of the body itself as "clothing" for the soul.[9] No longer the essential "ground" for either one's gender or one's sexuality, sex becomes a contingent category. The body becomes incidental: instead, *gender* and *desire* are essentialized. For turn-of-the-century sexologists, the difference between man and woman was still fundamental, but the source of that difference was located in the invisible essence of one's inner nature rather than in the visible biology of exterior anatomy.

I have been reading *An Englishwoman's Love-Letters* as a cross-dressing confession that managed to "pass" as a woman's actual emotional outpourings. Now I want to shift the focus from reception to production— to investigate more closely from what position Housman writes when he goes public as an "Englishwoman." I will be arguing that Housman's disguised self-presentation as a woman confessing her passion for a male lover constitutes a cross-dressing confession of the writer's sexual desire. The disguised confessional indicates the limitations and constraints within late Victorian discourse for the "love that dare not speak its name," especially after Oscar Wilde's public humiliation drove the homosexual subculture underground. At the same time, the text's oblique criticism of the institution of marriage indicates desires for other knowledges and pleasures, for new ways of constructing sexual and gender identity outside compulsory heterosexuality. As the autobiographical parallels between Housman's "fictional" *Love-Letters* and his "factual" memoirs, *The Unexpected Years* (1937), demonstrate, the feminine confessional form provides a stage for Housman's disguised enactment of his own sexual confession.

Housman's subject position must be understood in terms of the cultural and social discourses that shaped it. Like his contemporary, Edward Carpenter, Laurence Housman was a homosexual, a socialist, and a feminist. As a founding member and chairman of the British Society for the Study of Sex Psychology (BSSP), Housman worked with Carpenter and others for homosexual reform (Weeks 1990, 128). Housman was also a friend of Oscar Wilde. In his 1923 memoir of Wilde, *Echo de Paris: A Study from Life*, Housman appends a "Footnote" in which he offers an apologia for homosexuality and a description of the founding of the BSSP (55–60).

In a number of ways, *Echo de Paris* and Oscar Wilde are actually behind (so to speak) the writing of *An Englishwoman's Love-Letters*. Recounting how the *Love-Letters* came about, Housman explains in his autobiography that "a visit to Italy in 1899 provided me with a nucleus of material round which I had only to weave a story, or insert into it a plot" (1937, 163–64). The trip to which he refers is the trip also described in *Echo de Paris*. Returning from Italy with his friend and constant companion, the painter Herbert Alexander, Housman stopped in Paris to see Wilde (1937, 170, 182–183). He was on a commission from his friends at the Café Royal, who had collected money for Wilde's assistance and charged Housman with relieving some of Wilde's debts (Engen 1983,

100). The trip that gave Housman the "nucleus of material" for his story thus also gives the text its disguised subject: love between men.

As a cross-dressing confession, what *An Englishwoman's Love-Letters* reveals is that, in turn-of-the-century England, a man could legitimately express love for another man only from a female subject-position. If Brian Reade (1970) is right that Victorian homosexuals "found relief in the excuse to write from a woman's viewpoint" (39) in the penning of fiction, how much greater "relief" might be gained from writing love-letters which "quite a lot of people think . . . were genuine" (Housman 1937, 164)? In *An Englishwoman's Love-Letters*, Housman's anonymity allowed him to express his "feminine" nature from the safety of a woman's skirts—a campy gesture that permitted the expression of his mixed gender identity and forbidden sexual desires.

When the "Englishwoman" writes, "It is you, dearest, from the beginning who have set my head and heart free and *made me a woman*" (86; italics added), the cliché becomes first inverted, and then displaced, when the true nature of the confession is discerned. If Housman takes up a female subject-position in order to express publicly his love for Herbert Alexander, the writer's femininity seems both essential *and* constructed. Like most cross-dressers, Housman becomes a woman not only through the careful artifice of representation but also by unreservedly expressing the "femininity" of his inner nature.[10] Perhaps the point is that Alexander made Housman a "woman" in the sense of freeing his "feminine" feelings and emotions. In his autobiography, *The Unexpected Years*, Housman certainly describes his friendship with "Sandro" as a liberating one in which he was introduced to the pleasures of nude sunbathing, camping, and dressing up. Housman and Sandro took especial pleasure in dressing "in rather scanty Greek costume." Once, Sandro appeared for dinner as "a scantily clad Cupid," while Housman was dressed in traditional Greek attire (1937, 170–71). Since things Greek connoted male/male desire in the period, the choice of dress seems more than usually charged. It is, moreover, significant that Sandro, who was some nine years younger than Housman, is dressed as the very emblem of Love himself: the quintessential "pretty boy."

Unlike the fictional *Englishwoman's Love-Letters*, Housman's autobiography is not a sexual confession. On the contrary, he is very circumspect in his memoirs with regard to his own sexuality. Dominating the autobiography is the image of the bachelor whose financial situation rather than sexual orientation prevented him from marrying. But at the same time that he thus disguises his own sexuality, Housman is vociferous about the problems with Victorian repression and "taboo-morality" (1937, 62) and about the need for openness in sexual matters. If *The*

Unexpected Years is a gay autobiography of the closet, however, its secret is "outed" when the text is read alongside the "Englishwoman's" sexual confessions.

Becoming Woman

In the last twenty-five years or so, the second wave of feminism has worked to validate women's lives and experiences—to give expression to the silenced and power to the oppressed. Particularly in the early stages of the movement, feminists became empowered in confessional cliques where women told the intimate details of their lives in a context of personal support and political consciousness-raising. According to Rita Felski, it is from such roots that the genre of women's confession emerged in contemporary popular culture, and it is within this ideological framework that it derives its significance for feminists (1989, 71–72, 87–88).

The emergence of the cross-dressing confession in contemporary popular culture follows in the skirts of feminist confession. In the last twenty years, a large body of transvestitic confessional discourse has been published in magazines sponsored by cross-dressing organizations such as the International Foundation for Gender Education and the International Alliance for Male Feminism. Beginning in small support and consciousness-raising groups, the cross-dressing movement has developed into a worldwide organization with a variety of publications, services, clubs, and annual conferences. In conjunction with the self-identity, pride, and empowerment that they seek to give to the cross-dressing community, organizations such as the American Tri-Ess (the Society for the Second Self), the Australian Seahorse Club, and the British Beaumont Trust are also becoming increasingly politically active. Like feminists and gays, cross-dressers have found a political voice as they have gained a sense of identity and community.

The confessional nature of the writing in contemporary transvestite magazines is not only of interest because the cross-dressing community's development of a sense of identity as a marginal and oppressed group within a dominant culture is analogous to the development of feminist self-identity. Cross-dressing confessions also demand attention because some of the writers are self-identified "feminists," and *all* of them are self-identified "women." The men in skirts who write in transvestite magazines, signing their confessions with the female name that expresses their "femmeself," seek self-validation and community through the act of confession itself. Like the feminist confession as Felski has defined the genre, the cross-dressing confession is autobiographical, interested in both individual and communal identity, potentially both emancipatory and narcissistic, and arguably political in orientation and methodology. Unlike the metaphoric cross-dressing of Laurence Housman's confession, where male/male desire is expressed by what Dellamora calls the "rhetorical wish to be woman" (1990, 130), the "wish to be woman" as expressed in transvestite magazines is not rhetorical but literal. The majority of these men not only wish to be, but believe themselves to be, women. But this self-identity has more to do with gender than with sex: since most cross-dressers are heterosexual, their wish to be women does not usually signal male/male desire. Rather, cross-dressing confessions in contemporary popular culture are enactments of what might be called "virtual womanliness," in which both language and dress are used as systems of representation that express the truth of gender identity rather than the truth of desire.

In our valorization of Simone de Beauvoir's polemical "One is not born, but rather becomes, a woman" (1989, 267), we have often forgotten that the corollary is also true. Discussing some young boys' wish to be girls, Beauvoir emphasizes that femininity is a *choice* to which some boys—notably those oriented toward homosexuality—"obstinately" adhere (271). Beauvoir was writing in the fifties, a period in which the conceptual frameworks established by the pioneering studies of homosexuality were still widely accepted (Weeks 1992, 12). Thus Beauvoir's association of the wish-to-be woman with male/male desire is anchored in the notion that masculine and feminine are inverted in the homosexual. The inversion theory promoted by early sexologists applied both to the homosexual and to the cross-dressing heterosexual (Ellis 1936, 1–2). While the inversion theory of homosexuality is no longer the norm in queer studies, however, the notion of "psychic hermaphrodism" still dominates contemporary transvestitic discourses. Despite all the obstacles that a mature male body can present, cross-dressers "obstinately adhere" to their self-identified femininity. If turn-of-the-century sexologists described the difference between the homosexual's sexual orientation and his sex by the trope of the woman's soul trapped in a male body, present-day cross-dressers use precisely this metaphor to describe the misalignment between their sex and their gender.[11]

If one is not born, but rather becomes, a woman, how does this process take place? What is the raw material, and what is the final product? For feminists following Beauvoir, the biological female is socialized to acquire feminine traits and become a woman. For cross-dressers, however, gender, not sex, determines whether one is a man or a woman. "You don't have to be a female to be a woman," says Merissa Sherrill Lynn, founder of the International Foundation for Gender Education, and editor of *The TV-TS Tapestry Journal* (1990, 14). In transvestitic discourse, gender is not a socially acquired cultural product but an internal reality, an essential truth about the self known since childhood. This inner identity is externalized as the cross-dresser becomes a woman with the assistance of makeup, clothes, and foundation garments. Thus, although the theory of identity is based on an essentialist understanding of gender and subjectivity, in practice the cross-dresser self-consciously *constructs* himself as a woman. The tension between essential femininity and constructed femininity that exists at the heart of cross-dressing discourse duplicates the contradictions and oppositions that shape feminist thinking about sex and gender. The uncanny repetition of women's issues in the cross-dresser's masquerade motivates a reinvestigation of the concept of "woman" and what "her" confessions might be.

The cross-dresser's self-identification as a woman is both an individual and a political gesture. For this reason, the basic identity of the genre of women's sexual confessions is called into question by the privileged position of the confessional mode in transvestite magazines. Although there are also advice columns and pseudo-academic articles discussing the nature and history of transvestism, the bulk of the writing concentrates on the confessional stories of individual cross-dressers. Editorials, letters, articles, and personals—all written in the first person, all signed by a woman's name, and many accompanied by a photograph of the writer "en femme"— tend to be autobiographical "true stories" that perform the political function of consciousness-raising and the private function of self-validation. Like feminist confessions in which "the *representative* aspects" of the author's experience rather than her unique individuality are emphasized in order to establish a communal identity between writer and reader (Felski 1989, 95), cross-dressing confessions seek both to valorize individual experience by giving voice to the silenced, and to attain a mutuality and a common identity within what is called the "gender community." If, in the feminist confession, "the writing self is profoundly dependent upon . . . the projected community of female readers who will understand, sympathize, and identify with the author's emotions and experiences" (Felski 1989, 110), then this kind of "identity politics" is precisely what occurs in the pages of transvestite magazines. Readers and writers of *Tapestry*, for example—the most widely circulated transvestite publication on the continent[12]—see themselves as forming a "sisterhood" for mutual support, social reform, and political action.

The stories they tell have titles that establish the authenticity of the confession by grounding it in subjective experience: "A TV Dream Come True," "True Experience: Honeymoon over Hawaii," "Living to Tell, and Telling to Live," and "Out of the Closet for Fifteen Years and Making It in Houston, Texas." Although the authors use women's names, it "is clearly not 'female subjectivity'" we are dealing with when we read their confessions. Rather, as Garber points out, what is offered "is a man's idea of what 'a woman' is; it is male subjectivity in drag" (1992, 96). By naming their femininity, by clothing their womanliness, the writers express their desire to "pass" as women. And yet, as "Linda" ruefully confesses in a letter to the editor, "her" sex was read in a lesbian bar precisely because her "femmeself" was, the women told her, "TOO feminine! None of US walk, or act, or wear makeup like that" (*Tapestry* 59 [1991]: 17).

Like the female critics who "read" Housman's male identity, these lesbians know Linda is a fake because the masquerade is overdone. The cross-dresser is a man in a skirt acting out a male fantasy version of femininity. Despite his self-identification, the cross-dresser's experience as a "woman" can never replicate either the biological or the social experiences of actual females. And yet, paradoxically, it is precisely *as* a man in a skirt that his experience is, after all, analogous. Like women, cross-dressers have a history in western culture of invisibility, silence, and suppression. Like women they, too, have appropriated the confessional mode as a strategy of resistance against patriarchal hegemony and authority. In addition, the cross-dressing confession is, like women's sexual confession, a discourse that is personally liberating and politically subversive. In the larger cultural context, cross-dressing confessions challenge internalized norms of gender and sexuality, while at the same time disrupting and exposing the notion of "authentic" identity, both individual and generic.

Given these similarities, it is perhaps not surprising that cross-dressing confessions in transvestite magazines display features characteristic of the genre of women's confessions. Most stories—whether articles and editorials, or letters to the editor and personal ads—follow a predictable pattern. Usually, the confession begins with a direct address to the reader, to the effect that "my story is probably very similar to yours." Often, the reader is further encoded in the text by direct appeals ("Remember, up to that time I wasn't yet ready to admit to the world who and what I was") and questions ("Why not tell?"). Such engagements of the reader as a sympathetic confidante who will understand and share the writer's position are typical strategies of the feminist confession (Felski 1989, 99). After the announcement of shared experience, the writer proceeds to relate a formulaic narrative whose stock features make it more representative than individual. The writer has known of her "femmeself" since early childhood. This "inner feminine" needs to be expressed externally by the wearing of women's clothes, but because of social prohibitions, the cross-dresser experiences conflict, guilt, self-hate, and despair. A crisis occurs in which the writer brushes with death, either physical or psychological. There follows a rebirth, in which "Wanda" or "Valerie" or "Charise" is released, and the writer accepts "the woman within." The rest of the story provides the happy details of the writer's "coming out," usually with specific descriptions of outfits worn and activities pursued "en femme," and often with reference to the support of the writer's wife. The writing is emotional, but rather than being sexual or erotic, most of the emotion is directed toward the pleasure of dressing or to the joys of sisterhood in the "gender community." The exceptions to this are stories emphasizing heterosexual pleasure with a lesbian *frisson*, such as the "Honeymoon over Hawaii" story, which details the sexual and sartorial pleasures of a TV who spends his entire honeymoon as a woman (*Tapestry* 55 [1990]: 33–37).[13]

Despite such sexual escapades, most cross-dressing confessions are remarkably conventional—so conventional, indeed, that they sometimes draw on images of femininity which seem perilously close to repressive stereotypes. Cross-dressing confessions tend to reproduce the same characteristics traditionally associated with femininity as are favored in some women's confessions, such as the "belief in the moral superiority of female expressiveness" and the "assumption that women's language is more 'authentic' than that of men" (Felski 1989, 119). The cross-dressing confession is shaped as a conversion or rebirth narrative precisely because the individual's "authentic" self has been repressed by inhibiting masculine gender roles that prohibit the free expression of emotion. Women's emotional nature is apparently not only more expressive but also gentler, more nurturing, and more cooperative. One assumption, for example—shared by some female feminists—is that if more men were "feminine," we would achieve world peace. Other common assumptions are that women hug and kiss each other freely, like to get together for "girl talk" about lingerie, hose, and fashion, and enjoy such tasks as cleaning, cooking, and sewing. The "women" who write personal ads and letters to the editor often name these activities as their own. Such claims perform the same function as the accompanying photograph: corroboration of the writer's womanliness.

By visibly displaying the performative nature of gender, the cross-dresser dramatically stages the question, What is a woman? In her famous essay, "Womanliness as a Masquerade," Joan Riviere (1986; first published 1929) suggested that femininity is something acquired, something potentially detachable and transferable, something arbitrarily associated with the female. Like clothing, womanliness is, according to Riviere, nothing more than "a mask" which effectively produces the *effect* of femininity. Since she argues that "genuine womanliness and the 'masquerade' ... are the same thing" (38), Riviere "undermines the integrity of the former with the artifice of the latter," as Stephen Heath points out (1986, 50). If we accept Riviere's account of womanliness as masquerade, then the female impersonator, with all the dissimulation and artifice at "her" command, is, perhaps, as womanly as a genetic woman. Each of us performs the masquerade; each of us enacts our gender through the repetition of cultural signs, through *style*. For non-cross-dressing readers, cross-dressing confessions in transvestite magazines perform the cultural critique of pointing out "the degree to which *all* women cross-dress as women when they produce themselves as artifacts" (Garber 1992, 49).

The transvestite's assertion of the naturalness and wholeness achieved through "gender expression"—that is, through dressing in women's clothes—is contradicted by the commercial advertisements in their magazines which show exactly how "womanliness" is commodified and produced. From "Mirage Breast Forms" to "Hip Slips" to the boutiques selling "what's needed to create the feminine mystique," the cross-dressing marketplace reveals that the cross-dresser becomes a woman by laboring to produce a feminine effect. Yet, according to Riviere, one *does* become a woman precisely by such strategic performances. So the cross-dresser's effect of femininity is also, perhaps, the only way by which womanliness may be defined. If transvestite magazines reproduce characteristics traditionally associated with femininity and reinforce the image of woman as the composite of artificial parts, so too do "real" women's magazines, and "real" women's stories. The problem, in other words, is not between the "real" and the "fake," the "authentic" and the "artificial." Rather, as Judith Butler suggests, cross-dressing "destabilizes the very distinctions between the natural and the artificial . . . through which discourse about genders almost always operates" (1990, viii).

If gender is not necessarily dependent on biological sex—if, as Butler argues, "*man* and *masculine* might just as easily signify a female body as a male one, and *woman* and *feminine* a male body as easily as a female one" (6)—then theorizing women's sexual confessions seems to be artificially limited by the restrictions of an originating anatomy and a single identity. The "truth" of "W" is not something stable and universal, but rather shifting, positional, relational, enacted. In *Orlando*, her 1928 fictional biography of her friend Vita Sackville-West, Virginia Woolf could only gesture toward her "essential" subjectivity by giving Orlando two sexes, two wardrobes, two histories. Perhaps the figure of the cross-dresser forces us to confess that our dream of a single, stable point of origin is a chimera, that the body which grounds our figurations of ourselves is itself a figure. As Jacques Derrida (1987) has taught us, it is not always easy to distinguish between "the naked and natural body" and the clothing that covers it; it is not always easy to see where one leaves off and the other begins (57). Cross-dressing confessions destabilize women's sexual confessions as a generic category by disrupting the fixed poles of sex and gender and by demonstrating that the feminist confession exists on a sexual continuum. Precisely because sexual confessions like Laurence Housman's can "pass" as authentic feminine writing and womanly emotion, the essentialized grounding of the genre in a sexual subject is displaced. In addition, because the characteristic features of women's confessions are replicated in the confessions of men wearing dresses and calling themselves women, the artificial, and culturally contingent, nature of the genre is exposed. Genuine womanliness and the masquerade are the same thing, says Riviere. Perhaps a genuine woman's confession and a cross-dressing confession can also occupy the same categorical space.

Postscript: Feminist Confession

My TV friend, Kelsey, invites me to "take a walk on the Wild Side."[14] Before we go to the party, I ask about "dress-code" and worry about what to wear. I consider renting a costume and a wig (bare shoulders and big hair) so that I'll "fit in." But do I really want to fit in? Or do I want to prove I am more "womanly" than any of the woman-wannabes? Do I suffer from the *Orlando* complex? Am I secretly envious of the cross-dresser's freedom to change persona with clothing? Suddenly I realize that I would be cross-dressing in imitation of my cross-dressing friend. When a woman masquerades as a man masquerading as a woman, where *is* "W" and what is "her" truth? Kelsey clarifies my problem by referring to me throughout the evening as a *generic*—instead of a *genetic*—woman. I begin to see that it is by my genre rather than my genes—by conventionally determined and identifiable characteristics—that I become a "woman." And it is just such arbitrary and contingent features that determine the shifting identity of "women's sexual confessions."

Notes

I gratefully acknowledge the support of the Social Sciences and Humanities Research Council of Canada during the preparation of this chapter.

1. Cross-dressing is not an exclusively male phenomenon, as the female-to-male cross-dressing of Tilda Swinton in *Orlando* and the masculine attire of k. d. lang indicate. For a variety of cultural reasons, however, most self-identified cross-dressers are male. Since the focus of this chapter is on men cross-dressing in order to "pass" as women, my deployment of the terms *cross-dressing* and *homosexuality* will refer only to males unless otherwise specified.

2. Categories overlap, but a simple identification of various forms of men in women's clothing is as follows. Cross-dressers are men whose "gender dysphoria" leads them to express their "inner feminine" with the outer apparel of women. Most cross-dressers are heterosexual, many of them in long-term relationships. They prefer the term *cross-dresser* (CD) to *transvestite* (TV) because the latter is a clinical term suggestive of mental disorder, while the former indicates a lifestyle choice. Cross-dressers are, of course, "female impersonators," but this term is usually

used more precisely to describe professional entertainers. "Drag queens" are homosexual men who dress in women's clothes to parody the feminine and to declare their sexual orientation in a campy way. Unlike the cross-dresser, the drag queen's object is usually not to "pass" as a women, and the illusion is often deliberately broken with a male signifier such as facial or chest hair. Magnus Hirschfeld was the first psychologist to recognize, in 1910, that transvestism was mainly a heterosexual phenomenon. For recent work in this field, see Richard F. Docter's psychoanalytic theory of cross-gender behavior (1988), Harry Brierley's psychological case studies (1979), John T. Talamini's sociological study (1982), and the cultural studies of Peter Ackroyd (1979) and Marjorie Garber (1992). Also see Esther Newton (1972) for an anthropological study of drag.

3. Marjorie Garber's chapter, "Breaking the Code: Transvestism and Gay Identity," explores the historical interconnections between the history of transvestism and the history of homosexuality (1992).

4. It is, of course, not always obvious whether the writer is a man or a woman, as many contemporary reviews and letters to the editor were either anonymous or pseudonymous. However, the language usage—such as *The Bookman* writer's excitement in "unloosing" the ribbons, and other writers' chivalrous hopes never to meet the cad who wronged the unhappy girl—often seems to point to a male author. In January 1901, *The Bookman* published the opinions of "prominent lady writers of the day on the subject" of *An Englishwoman's* authenticity and the identity of the author. Most of the writers polled (Mrs. W. K. Clifford, Mrs. Craigie, Mrs. Beatrice Harraden, and Miss Violet Hunt) felt that it was a work of fiction. Mrs. Harrison (Lucas Malet), Miss Ellen Thorneycroft Fowler, and Miss Elizabeth Robins were less sure about the fiction/fact issue; and Miss Cholmondeley believed the author was a man ("News Notes"). *The Bookman's* reviewer, Emily Constance Cook, also thought the writer was a man, and contended that most women agreed with her (1901, 154).

5. The appeal was not merely insular; *An Englishwoman's Love-Letters* caused a sensation not only in England but also in America and France.

6. See Judith Butler for a fuller discussion of "intelligible" genders (1990, 17ff.).

7. For a good explication of the work of early sexologists, and for an historical overview of the construction of homosexuality, see Jeffrey Weeks's chapter on "Discourse, Desire, and Sexual Deviance: Some Problems in a History of Homosexuality" (1992, 10–45).

8. Early sexologists associated cross-dressing with both male and female inverts, but it was *women's* preference for masculine attire which became the privileged sign of lesbianism at the turn of the century, as Radclyffe Hall's *The Well of Loneliness* suggests.

9. In contemporary culture, this view is being popularized in RuPaul's formulation that the body is drag for the soul. I am grateful to John Kooistra for pointing out this connection.

10. The paradox inherent in the artifice of "becoming woman" through the assistance of prostheses, wigs, makeup, and clothes, and the conviction that this artificial display performs the service of expressing an essential (and hence "natural") identity, is repeated again and again in transvestitic discourse. The emblem of the International Foundation for Gender Education, which publishes the TV-TS journal, *Tapestry*, encapsulates this contradiction. The emblem depicts a masculine and a feminine hand clasping a rose, and the logo states, "The Trinity of Being: of being masculine, of being feminine, of being one with yourself and nature!" There is, apparently, nothing "unnatural" about identifying the feminine by long, painted nails.

11. The trope of the woman's soul in a man's body has different implications in these usages. As understood by early sexologists describing homosexuality, the metaphor worked to reinscribe an underlying heterosexuality within the homosexual relationship: the gay man desired men precisely because he was "really" a woman "inside." In contemporary transvestitic discourse, the trope has the opposite effect of interpellating homosexuality into a straight relationship. The heterosexual cross-dresser sexually desires women, but is himself a woman. Hence, he is "really" a lesbian trapped inside a man's body.

12. Other American magazines include *Transvestia*, a publication of Tri-Ess (the Society for the Second Self); the *Journal of Male Feminism*; and the *Femme Mirror*. The *Feminique* is published by the Seahorse Club in Australia. The *Beaumont Bulletin* is published by the Beaumont Trust in Britain.

13. *Tapestry*, the magazine on which I have largely based my study, has an explicitly "nonsexual" policy in regard to published ads, photos, and articles. That this is typical is confirmed by Brierley's study of "Transvestite Autobiographies" (chap. 5) and "Transvestite Writings" (chap. 6) (1979).

14. A private cross-dressers' club in Toronto, Ontario.

References

Contributors

Index

References

Abramson, Jill, and Jane Mayer. 1993. "The Surreal Anita Hill." *New Yorker* (May 24): 90–96.

Ackroyd, Peter. 1979. *Dressing Up: Transvestism and Drag: The History of an Obsession*. London: Thames and Hudson.

Alcoff, Linda, and Laura Gray. 1993. "Survivor Discourse: Transgression or Recuperation?" *Signs: Journal of Women in Culture and Society* 18 (2): 260–90.

Altbach, Edith Hoshino, et al., eds. 1984. *German Feminism: Readings in Politics and Literature*. Albany: State University of New York Press.

Anderson, Margaret. 1930. *My Thirty Years' War: An Autobiography*. New York: Covici, Friede.

Anzaldúa, Gloria. 1987. *Borderlands/La Frontera: The New Mestiza*. San Francisco: Aunt Lute.

Apple, R. W. Jr. 1991. "Spectacle of Degradation." *New York Times* (October 13).

Ariès, Philippe. 1962. *Centuries of Childhood: A Social History of Family Life*. Translated by Robert Baldick. New York: Vintage Books.

Atler, Marilyn Van Derbur. 1991. "The Darkest Secret." *People* (June 10): 88+.

Bane, Vickie. 1991. "A Star Cries Incest." *People* (October 7): 84–88.

Barbe, Jean. 1991. "Anne Dandurand: La chair des mots." *Lettres québécoises* 11–12.

Barreca, Regina, ed. 1988. Introduction to *Last Laughs: Perspectives on Women and Comedy*. New York: Gordon and Breach.

Barthes, Roland. 1984. "The Face of Garbo." *Mythologies*. Translated by Annette Lavers. London: Paladin.

Bartkowski, Frances. 1988. "Epistemic Drift in Foucault." In *Feminism and Foucault: Reflections on Resistance*, ed. Irene Diamond and Lee Quinby. Boston: Northeastern University Press.

Bass, Ellen, and Laura Davis. 1992 (1988). *The Courage to Heal: A Guide for Women Survivors of Child Sexual Abuse*. New York: Harper Perennial.

Bass, Ellen, and Louise Thornton, eds. 1991 (1983). *I Never Told Anyone:*

Writings by Women Survivors of Child Sexual Abuse. New York: Harper Perennial.

Beauvoir, Simone de. 1989 (1949). *The Second Sex*. Translated by H. M. Parshley. New York: Vintage Books.

Begos, Jane Dupree. 1987. "The Diaries of Adolescent Girls." *Women's Studies International Forum* 10 (1): 69–74.

Beitchman, Joseph H., Kenneth Zucker, Jane E. Hood, Granville A. DaCosta, Donna Akman, and Erika Cassavia. 1992. "A Review of the Long-Term Effects of Child Sexual Abuse." *Child Abuse and Neglect* 16: 101–18.

Berger, Maurice. 1992. *Artforum* 31 (1): 10.

Berke, Richard L. 1991. "Senators Level Additional Accusations That Law Professor Has Lied." *New York Times* (October 13).

Bernstein, Susan David. 1992. "Confessing Feminist Theory: What's 'I' Got to Do with It?" *Hypatia* 7 (2): 120–47.

———. 1997. *Confessional Subjects: Revelations of Gender and Power in Victorian Literature and Culture*. Chapel Hill: University of North Carolina Press.

Bhabha, Homi. 1992. "A Good Judge of Character: Men, Metaphors, and the Common Culture." In *Race-ing Justice, En-gendering Power*, ed. Toni Morrison. New York: Pantheon.

Biddle, George. 1939. *An American Artist's Story*. Boston: Little, Brown.

Blume, E. Sue. (1985). *Secret Survivors: Uncovering Incest and Its Aftereffects in Women*. New York: Ballantine Books.

Böhme, Margarete. 1989 (1905). *Tagebuch einer Verlorenen, von einer Toten*. Frankfurt: Suhrkamp.

Bolton, Richard. 1992. *Culture Wars*. New York: New Press.

Brady, Katherine. 1979. *Father's Days: A True Story of Incest*. New York: Seaview Books.

Breuer, Josef, and Sigmund Freud. 1961 (1895). *Studies in Hysteria*. Translated by A. A. Brill. Rev. ed. Boston: Beacon Press.

Brierley, Harry. 1979. *Transvestism: A Handbook with Case Studies for Psychologists, Psychiatrists, and Counsellors*. Oxford: Pergamon Press.

Brock, David. 1993. *The Real Anita Hill: The Untold Story*. Toronto: Maxwell Macmilliam International.

Brossard, Nicole. 1980a. *Amantes*. Montréal: Quinze.

———. 1980b. "L'écrivain/The Writer." Translated by Linda Gaboriau. *Fireweed* 5–6 (winter 1979/spring 1980): 106–17.

———. 1982a. *Picture Theory*. Montréal: Nouvelle optique.

———. 1982b. "Prendre la parole quand on est femme." *Québec français* 47 (October 1982): 31.

———. 1984. *Journal intime, ou voilà donc un manuscrit*. Montréal: Les Herbes Rouges.

———. 1985. *La lettre aérienne*. Montréal: Remue-ménage.

———. 1986. *Lovhers*. Translated by Barbara Godard. Montréal: Guernica.

———. 1988. *The Aerial Letter*. Translated by Marlene Wildeman. Toronto: Women's Press.

———. 1991. *Picture Theory*. Translated by Barbara Godard. Montréal: Guernica.

———. 1993. "Ludique critique et moderne rebelle/scribelle." In *Le discours féminin dans la littérature postmoderne du Québec*, ed. Raija Koski, Kathleen Kells, and Louise Forsyth. San Francisco: Mellen Research University Press.

Brownmiller, Susan. 1970. "Sisterhood Is Powerful." In *Women's Liberation: Blueprint for the Future*, ed. Sookie Stambler. New York: Ace Books.

Butler, Judith. 1990. *Gender Trouble: Feminism and the Subversion of Identity*. New York: Routledge.

———. 1991. "Imitation and Gender Insubordination." In *Inside/Out: Lesbian Theories, Gay Theories*, ed. Diana Fuss. New York: Routledge.

———. 1992. "Sexual Inversions." In *Discourses of Sexuality: From Aristotle to AIDS*, ed. Domna Stanton. Ann Arbor: University of Michigan Press.

———. 1993. *Bodies That Matter: On the Discursive Limits of "Sex."* New York: Routledge.

Butler, Sandra. 1978. *Conspiracy of Silence: The Trauma of Incest*. San Francisco: New Glide.

Carpenter, Edward. 1914. *Love's Coming-of-Age*. London: Methuen.

Carr, C. 1986. "Unspeakable Practices, Unnatural Acts: The Taboo Art of Karen Finley." *Village Voice* (June 24): 17–20+.

———. 1993. "'Telling the Awfullest Truth': An Interview with Karen Finley." In *Acting Out*, ed. Lynda Hart and Peggy Phelan. Ann Arbor: University of Michigan Press.

Casal, Mary. 1975 (1930). *The Stone Wall: An Autobiography*. New York: Arno.

"Celebrity Newsmakers." 1996. *State* (February 4): E2.

Cheney, Peter. 1992. "When Clothes *Don't* Make the Man." *Toronto Star* (November 17): D-1, D-3.

Coates, Jim. 1991. "Celebrity Tales of Childhood Abuse Jar Similar Memories for Many." *Chicago Tribune* (October 13): 3.

Cole, Cyndia. 1980. "No Rape. No." *Room of One's Own* 5 (4): 69–71.

Cook, Emily Constance. 1901. "A Literary Enigma." *Bookman* 19 (113): 153–56.

Cooke, Nathalie. 1990. "Mary di Michele: On the Integrity of Speech and Silence." *Canadian Poetry: Studies/Documents/Reviews* 26 (spring/summer): 43–53.

Coward, Rosalind. 1984. *Female Desire: Women's Sexuality Today*. London: Paladin.

Craigin, Elisabeth. 1975 (1937). *Either Is Love*. New York: Arno.

Crews, Frederick. 1994a. "The Revenge of the Repressed." *New York Review of Books* (November 17): 54–60.

———. 1994b. "Revenge of the Repressed, Part II." *New York Review of Books* (December 1): 49–58.

Dandurand, Anne. 1989. *Voilà c'est moi: c'est rien j'angoisse*. Montréal: Triptyque.

———. 1990. *Un coeur qui craque: Journal imaginaire*. Montréal: VLB.

———. 1991. *Petites âmes sous ultimatum*. Montréal: XYZ.

———. 1992. *The Cracks*. Translated by Luise von Flotow. Toronto: Mercury Press.

Darnton, Nina, et al. 1991. "The Pain of the Last Taboo." *Newsweek* (October 7): 70+

Davis, Doug. 1990. "Art and Contradiction: Helm, Censorship, and the Serpent." *Art in America* 178: 55–61.

Dé, Claire. 1989. *Le désir comme catastrophe naturelle*. Grenoble: Glénat.

Dee, Sandra (to Todd Gold). 1991. "Learning to Live Again." *People* (March 18): 87–93.

de Lauretis, Teresa. 1991. "Queer Theory: Lesbian and Gay Sexualities: An Introduction." *Differences* 3 (2): iii–xviii.

Dellamora, Richard. 1990. *Masculine Desire: The Sexual Politics of Victorian Aestheticism*. Chapel Hill: University of North Carolina Press.

D'Emilio, John, and Estelle B. Freedman. 1988. *Intimate Matters: A History of Sexuality in America*. New York: Harper.

Derrida, Jacques. 1987. *The Truth in Painting*. Translated by Geoff Bennington and Ian McLeod. Chicago: University of Chicago Press.

Dietze, Gabriele, ed. 1989. *Die Überwindung der Sprachlosigkeit: Texte aus der Frauenbewegung*. Frankfurt: Luchterhand Literaturverlag.

Diggs, Marylynne. 1995. "Romantic Friends or a 'Different Race of Creatures'? The Representation of Lesbian Pathology in Nineteenth-Century America." *Feminist Studies* 21: 317–40.

di Michele, Mary. 1990. "The Primer." In *Luminous Emergencies*, 3–8. Toronto: McClelland and Stewart.

Doane, Mary Ann. 1989. "Veiling over Desire: Close-ups of the Woman." In *Feminism and Psychoanalysis*, ed. Richard Feldstein and Judith Root. Ithaca: Cornell University Press.

———. 1990. "Information, Crisis, Catastrophe." In *Logics of Television*, ed. Patricia Mellencamp. Bloomington: Indiana University Press.

Docter, Richard F. 1988. *Transvestites and Transsexuals: Toward a Theory of Cross-Gender Behavior*. New York: Plenum Press.

Dolan, Jill. 1988. *The Feminist Spectator as Critic*. Ann Arbor: UMI.

Donzelot, Jacques. 1979 (1977). *The Policing of Families*. Translated by Robert Hurley. New York: Pantheon.

Dowd, Maureen. 1991. "Taboo Issues of Sex and Race Explode in Glare of Hearing." *New York Times* (October 13): 1.

Dupré, Louise. 1989. *Stratégies du vertige. Trois poètes: Nicole Brossard, Madeleine Gagnon, France Théoret.* Montréal: Remue-ménage.

Eisenstein, Hester. 1983. *Contemporary Feminist Thought.* Boston: G. K. Hall.

Ellis, Havelock. 1936 (1915). "Sexual Inversion." In *Studies in the Psychology of Sex*, pt. 4, vol. 1. New York: Random House.

Engen, Rodney. 1983. *Laurence Housman.* Stroud, Glos.: Catalpa Press.

"An Englishwoman's Love-Letters." 1900. *Athen<ae>um* 3814 (December 1): 716.

Evans, Rowland, and Robert Novak. 1990. "The NEA's Suicide Charge." *Washington Post* (May 11).

Faderman, Lillian. 1981. *Surpassing the Love of Men: Romantic Friendship and Love Between Women from the Renaissance to the Present.* New York: William Morrow.

———. 1991. *Odd Girls and Twilight Lovers: A History of Lesbian Life in Twentieth-Century America.* New York: Columbia University Press.

Faludi, Susan. 1991. *Backlash: The Undeclared War Against American Women.* New York: Anchor Books.

Felski, Rita. 1989. *Beyond Feminist Aesthetics: Feminist Literature and Social Change.* Cambridge: Harvard University Press.

Fillion, Kate. 1994. "The Age of Indiscretion." *HomeMakers* (January/February): 85–89.

Finkelhor, David. 1979. *Sexually Victimized Children.* New York: Free Press.

Finley, Karen. 1990. *The Constant State of Desire.* In *Out from Under*, ed. Lenore Champagne, 59–70. New York: Theater Communications Group.

Firestone, Shulamith, and Anne Koedt, eds. 1970. *Notes from the Second Year: Major Writings of the New York Radical Feminists.* New York: n.p.

Fleeman, M. 1992. "Court Rejects NEA Rules on Decency." *Philadelphia Inquirer* (June 10): A1.

Forte, Jeannie. 1988. "Women's Performance Art: Feminism and Postmodernism." *Theatre Journal* 40 (2): 217–35.

Foster, Edward. 1956. *Mary E. Wilkins Freeman.* New York: Hendricks House.

Foucault, Michel. 1978. *The History of Sexuality.* Vol. 1: An Introduction. Translated by Robert Hurley. New York: Vintage Books.

———. 1980. *Power/Knowledge: Selected Interviews and Other Writings, 1972–1977.* Edited by Colin Gordon. Translated by Colin Gordon et al. New York: Pantheon.

Frank, Anne. 1947. *Het Achterhuis: Dagboekbrieven van 12 juni 1942–1 augustus 1944.* Amsterdam: Contact.

———. 1952. *The Diary of a Young Girl*. Translated by B. M. Mooyaart-Doubleday. New York: Doubleday.

———. 1989. *The Diary of Anne Frank: The Critical Edition*. Translated by A. J. Pomerans and B. M. Mooyaart-Doubleday. Edited by D. Barnouw and G. Van Der Stroom. New York: Doubleday.

———. 1995. *Diary of a Young Girl: The Definitive Edition*. Edited by Otto H. Frank and Mirjam Pressler. Translated by Susan Massotty. New York: Doubleday.

Frank, Lawrence. 1989. "Freud and Dora: Blindness and Insight." In Seduction and *Theory: Readings of Gender, Representation, and Rhetoric*, ed. Dianne Hunter. Urbana: University of Illinois Press.

Franklin, P., ed. 1986. *Private Pages: Diaries of American Women, 1830s–1970s*. New York: Ballantine Books.

Fraser, Nancy. 1989. *Unruly Practices: Power, Discourse, and Gender in Contemporary Social Theory*. Minneapolis: University of Minnesota Press.

———. 1992. "Sex, Lies, and the Public Sphere: Some Reflections on the Confirmation of Clarence Thomas." *Critical Inquiry* 18 (3): 600–601.

Fraser, Sylvia. 1987. *My Father's House: A Memoir of Incest and Healing*. New York: Ticknor and Fields.

Frederics, Diana. 1975 (1939). *Diana: A Strange Autobiography*. New York: Arno.

Freud, Sigmund. 1935. *A General Introduction to Psycho-Analysis*. Translated by Joan Riviere. New York: Liveright.

———. 1959 (1896). "The Aetiology of Hysteria." In *Collected Papers: Volume I: The Early Papers*. Translated by Joan Riviere. Rev. ed. New York: Basic Books.

———. 1963a. *Sexuality and the Psychology of Love*. Edited by Philip Rieff. New York: Macmillan.

———. 1963b. *Three Case Histories*. Edited by Philip Rieff. New York: Macmillan.

Freyd, Jennifer J. 1996. *Betrayal Trauma: The Logic of Forgetting Childhood Abuse*. Cambridge: Harvard University Press.

Freytag-Loringhoven, Elsa von. [1927.] "Autobiography." Typescript prepared by Djuna Barnes. College Park: University of Maryland Archives.

———. 1992. *Baroness Elsa*. Edited by Paul Hjartarson and Douglas Spettigue. Toronto: Oberon Press.

Friday, Nancy. 1973. *Our Secret Garden: Women's Sexual Fantasies*. New York: Trident Press.

Fuchs, Elinor. 1989. "Staging the Obscene Body." *Tulane Drama Review* 33 (1): 33–58.

Fuss, Diana. 1989. *Essentially Speaking: Feminism, Nature, and Difference*. New York: Routledge.

Gammel, Irene. 1993. "No Woman Lover: Baroness Elsa's Intimate Biography." *Canadian Review of Comparative Literature* 20 (3–4): 451–67.

———. 1994. *Sexualizing Power in Naturalism: Theodore Dreiser and Frederick Philip Grove.* Calgary: University of Calgary Press.

———. 1995. "Breaking the Bonds of Discretion: Baroness Elsa and the Female Sexual Confession." *Tulsa Studies in Women's Literature* 14 (1): 149–66.

Gamson, Joshua. 1996. "Do Tell." *Utne Reader* 73 (January/February): 79–83.

Ganaway, George. 1989. "Historical versus Narrative Truth: Clarifying the Role of Exogenous Trauma in the Etiology of MPD and Its Variants." *Dissociation* 2 (4): 205–20.

Garber, Marjorie. 1992. *Vested Interests: Cross-Dressing and Cultural Anxiety.* New York: Routledge.

Germain, Georges-Hébert. 1991. "Romans à l'eau d'Éros." *L'actualité* (October 1): 90–92.

Gibbs, Nancy. 1991. "An Ugly Circus." *Time* (October 21): 15.

Gilligan, Carol. 1990. "Joining the Resistance: Psychology, Politics, Girls, and Women." *Michigan Quarterly Review* 29 (4): 501–36.

Gilman, Sander L. 1985. *Difference and Pathology: Stereotypes of Sexuality, Race, and Madness.* Ithaca: Cornell University Press.

———. 1986. "Black Bodies, White Bodies: Toward an Iconography of Female Sexuality in Late-Nineteenth-Century Art, Medicine, and Literature." In *"Race," Writing, and Difference*, ed. Henry Louis Gates. Chicago: University of Chicago Press.

———. 1988. "The Dead Child Speaks: Reading *The Diary of Anne Frank.*" *Studies in American Jewish Literature* 7 (1): 9–25.

Glickman, Susan. 1990. "The Man Next Door." In *Henry Moore's Sheep and Other Poems*, 30–33. Montreal: Signal-Véhicule.

Goettle, Gabriele. 1989. "'*Häutungen*'—eine Verwechslung von Anemone und Amazone." In *Die Überwindung der Sprachlosigkeit: Texte aus der Frauenbewegung*, ed. Gabriele Dietze. Frankfurt: Luchterhand Literaturverlag.

Gordon, Linda. 1989. *Heroes of Their Own Lives: The Politics and History of Family Violence, Boston, 1880–1960.* New York: Penguin Books.

Gould, Karen. 1990. *Writing in the Feminine: Feminism and Experimental Writing in Québec.* Carbondale: Southern Illinois University Press.

Greenhouse, Linda. 1991. "Questions about Thomas, the Man, Obscured Clues about Thomas, the Jurist." *New York Times* (October 27).

Greven, Philip. 1991. *Spare the Child: The Religious Roots of Punishment and the Psychological Impact of Physical Abuse.* New York: Alfred A. Knopf.

Grossmann, Atina. 1983. "The New Woman and the Rationalization of

Sexuality in Weimar Germany." In *Powers of Desire: The Politics of Sexuality*, ed. Ann Snitow, Christine Stansell, and Sharon Thompson. New York: Monthly Review Press.

Gulliver, Lili. 1990. *L'univers Gulliver 1*. *Paris*. Montréal: VLB.

Hacking, Ian. 1991. "The Making and Molding of Child Abuse." *Critical Inquiry* 17 (winter): 253–88.

Haller, John S., Jr., and Robin M. Haller. 1974. *The Physician and Sexuality in Victorian America*. Urbana: University of Illinois Press.

Harris, Claire. 1984. "The Fall." In *Fables from the Women's Quarters*, 31. Toronto: Williams-Wallace.

Harris, Michael. 1991. *Unholy Orders: Tragedy at Mount Cashel*. Ontario: Viking.

Harvey, Elizabeth D. 1992. *Ventriloquized Voices: Feminist Theory and English Renaissance Texts*. New York: Routledge.

Haug, Frigga, et al. 1987. *Female Sexualization: A Collective Work of Memory*. Translated by Erica Carter. London: Verso.

Heath, Stephen. 1986. "Joan Riviere and the Masquerade." In *Formations of Fantasy*, ed. Victor Burgin et al. London: Methuen.

Heller, Kathryn. 1991. Review. *Theatre Journal* 43 (2): 239–44.

Herman, Judith. 1992. *Trauma and Recovery*. New York: Basic Books.

———. 1993. "The False Memory Debate: Social Science or Social Backlash?" *Harvard Medical School Mental Health Letter* 9 (10): 4–6.

Herman, Judith, Lisa Hirschman. 1981. *Father-Daughter Incest*. Cambridge: Harvard University Press.

Herman, Judith, Christopher Perry, and Bessel van der Kolk. 1989. "Childhood Trauma in Borderline Personality Disorder." *American Journal of Psychiatry* 146 (4): 490–95.

Hessel, Helen. 1991. *Journal d'Helen, Lettres à Henri-Pierre Roché, 1920–1921*. Marseille: André Dimanche.

Hollick, Frederick. 1974 (1850). *The Marriage Guide, or Natural History of Generation*. New York: Arno.

Honan, W. 1991. "U.S. Documents Said to Show Endowment Bowed to Pressure." *New York Times* (September 18): C13.

Housman, Laurence. 1901. *An Englishwoman's Love-Letters*. Authorized ed. New York: Doubleday, Page.

———. 1923. *Echo de Paris: A Study from Life*. London: Jonathan Cape.

———. 1937. *The Unexpected Years*. London: Jonathan Cape.

Hughes, Holly. 1990. *World Without End*. In *Out from Under*, ed. Lenore Champagne, 3–32. New York: Theater Communications Group.

Huyssen, Andreas. 1986. "Mass Culture as Woman: Modernism's Other." In *Studies in Entertainment: Critical Approaches to Mass Culture*, ed. Tania Modleski, 188–206. Bloomington: Indiana University Press.

Irigaray, Luce. 1985. *This Sex Which Is Not One*. Translated by Catherine Porter with Carolyn Burke. Ithaca: Cornell University Press.

———. 1991. "The Bodily Encounter with the Mother." Translated by D. Macey. In *The Irigaray Reader*, ed. M. Whitford. Cambridge, Mass.: Basil Blackwell.

Iskander, Sandra Patterson. 1991. "Anne Frank's Autobiographical Style." *Children's Literature Association Quarterly* 16 (2): 78–81.

Jameson, Fredric. 1979. "Reification and Utopia in Mass Culture." *Social Text* 1: 130–48.

Joseph, Miranda. 1990. "Letter to the Editor." *Tulane Drama Review* 34 (4): 13–16.

Joyrich, Lynn. 1990. "Critical and Textual Hypermasculinity." In *Logics of Television*, ed. Patricia Mellencamp. Bloomington: Indiana University Press.

Juno, Andrea, and V. Vale, eds. 1991. *Angry Women*. San Francisco: Re/Search Publications.

Kapke, B. 1986. *High Performance* 36: 66.

Kaplan, David. 1991. "Anatomy of a Debacle." *Newsweek* (October 21): 26.

Keitel, Evelyne. 1983. "Recent Literary Trends: Verständigungstexte— Form, Funktion, Wirkung." *German Quarterly* 55 (3): 431–55.

———. 1996. "Anne Sexton: Der Tanz mit dem Tod." In *WahnsinnsFrauen, zweiter Band*, ed. Sibylle Duda and Luise F. Pusch. Frankfurt: Suhrkamp.

Kluft, Richard P., ed. 1990. Introduction to *Incest-Related Syndromes of Adult Psychopathology*. Washington, D.C.: American Psychiatric Press.

Kolkenbrock-Netz, Jutta, and Marianne Schuller. 1982. "Frau im Spiegel: Zum Verhältnis von autobiographischer Schreibweise und feministischer Praxis." In *Entwürfe von Frauen in der Literatur des 20. Jahrhunderts*, ed. Irmela von der Lühe. Berlin: Argument Verlag.

Krafft-Ebing, Richard von. 1929. (1886) *Psychopathia Sexualis, with Especial Reference to the Antipathic Sexual Instinct*. 12th ed. Chicago: Login Brothers.

Kruell, Marianne. 1979. *Freud and His Father*. Translated by Arnold J. Pomerans. New York: W. W. Norton.

Kulessa, Hanne. 1989. Afterword to *Tagebuch einer Verlorenen, von einer Toten*, by Margarete Böhme. Frankfurt: Suhrkamp.

Lacour, Claudia Brodsky. 1992. "Doing Things with Words: 'Racism' as Speech Act and the Undoing of Justice." In *Race-ing Justice, Engendering Power*, ed. Toni Morrison. New York: Pantheon.

Lehrman, K. 1990. "The Dope on Dana." New Republic (November 5): 18.

Lejeune, Philippe. 1975. *Le pacte autobiographique*. Paris: Seuil.

Lerner, Laurence. 1987. "What Is Confessional Poetry?" *Critical Quarterly* 29 (2): 46–66.

"Linda." 1991. Letter to the Editor. *Tapestry* 59: 17.

Loewenstein, Richard J. 1993. "Anna O: Reformulation as a Case of Multiple Personality Disorder." In *Rediscovering Childhood Trauma: Historical Casebook and Clinical Applications*, ed. Jean M. Goodwin, 139–67. Washington, D.C.: American Psychiatric Press.

Loftus, Elizabeth. 1993. "Repressed Memories of Childhood Trauma: Are They Genuine?" *Harvard Medical School Mental Health Letter* 9 (9): 4–5.

Loftus, Elizabeth, and Lucy Berliner. 1992. "Sexual Abuse Accusations: Desperately Seeking Reconciliations." *Journal of Interpersonal Violence* 7 (4): 570–78.

Loftus, Elizabeth, with Katherine Ketcham. 1994. *The Myth of Repressed Memory: False Memory and Allegations of Sexual Abuse*. New York: St. Martin's Press.

Lubiano, Wahneema. 1992. "Black Ladies, Welfare Queens, and State Minstrels." In *Race-ing Justice, En-gendering Power*, ed. Toni Morrison. New York: Pantheon.

Luscombe, Belinda. 1995. "Target: Trash." *Time* (November 6): 74.

Lydon, Mary. 1988. "Foucault and Feminism: A Romance of Many Dimensions." In *Feminism and Foucault: Reflections on Resistance*, ed. Irene Diamond and Lee Quinby, 135–47. Boston: Northeastern University Press.

Lynn, Merissa Sherrill. 1988. "Definitions of Terms Commonly Used in the Transvestite-Transsexual Community." *Tapestry* 51: 19–36.

———. 1990. "Symbiotic Synergism with the Gay Community and the Woman's Movement." *Tapestry* 55: 5–14.

Lynn, Steven Jay, and Judith W. Rhue, eds. 1994. *Dissociation: Clinical and Theoretical Perspectives*. New York: Guilford.

Mallon, Thomas. 1984. *A Book of One's Own: People and Their Diaries*. New York: Ticknor and Fields.

Marable, Manning. 1992. "Clarence Thomas and the Crisis of Black Political Culture." In *Race-ing Justice, En-gendering Power*, ed. Toni Morrison. New York: Pantheon.

Masciarotte, Gloria-Jean. 1991. "C'mon Girl: Oprah Winfrey and the Discourse of Feminine Talk." *Genders* 11 (fall): 81–110.

Maynes, Mary Jo. 1989. "Gender and Narrative Form in French and German Working-Class Autobiographies." In *Interpreting Women's Lives: Feminist Theory and Personal Narrative*, ed. Joy Webster Barbre et al. Bloomington: Indiana University Press.

McNaron, Toni A. H., and Yarrow Morgan. 1982. *Voices in the Night: Women Speaking about Incest*. Minneapolis: Cleis Press.

McRobbie, Angela. 1982. "Politics of Feminist Research: Between Talk, Text, and Action." *Feminist Review* 12 (October): 46–57.

Merian, Svende. 1988 (1980). *Der Tod des Märchenprinzen*. Reinbeck bei Hamburg: Rowohlt.

———. 1994. *Sehnsucht hat lange Beine.* Hamburg: Hoffmann und Campe.

Meulenbelt, Anja. 1979. *Voor Onszelf (For Ourselves).* Amsterdam: Feministische Uitgeverij Sara.

———. 1980. *The Shame Is Over: A Political Life Story.* Translated by Ann OOsthuizen. London: Women's Press.

Mifflin, Margot. 1988. Interview. *High Performance* 41/42: 87.

Miller, Alice. 1986. *Thou Shalt Not Be Aware: Society's Betrayal of the Child.* Translated by Hildegarde and Hunter Hannum. New York: Meridian Books.

Miller, Nancy. 1988. "Writing Fictions: Women's Autobiographies in France." In *Life/Lines: Theorizing Women's Autobiography*, ed. Bella Brodzki and Celeste Schenck. Ithaca: Cornell University Press.

———. 1991. *Getting Personal: Feminist Occasions and Other Autobiographical Acts.* New York: Routledge.

Modleski, Tania. 1986. "Femininity as Mas(s)querade: A Feminist Approach to Mass Culture." In *High Theory, Low Culture*, ed. Colin McCabe. Manchester: University of Manchester Press.

———. 1991. "Femininity as Mas(s)querade." In *Feminism Without Women: Culture and Criticism in a "Postfeminist" Age.* New York: Routledge.

Moore, Suzanne. 1993. "Who's Afraid of Anita Hill?" *Guardian*, reprinted in the *Globe and Mail* (May 22): D5.

Mouffe, Chantal. 1988. *Marxism and the Interpretation of Culture.* Urbana: University of Illinois Press.

Mullens, Anne. 1992. "Doubt Cast on Memories of Child Sex Abuse." *Vancouver Sun* (November 26): A1.

Mulvey, Laura. 1989. "Visual Pleasure and Narrative Cinema." In *Visual and Other Pleasures.* Bloomington: Indiana University Press.

Nathan, Debbie. 1992. "Cry Incest: Victims of Childhood Sexual Abuse." *Playboy* 39 (10): 84.

Neuman, R. P. 1974–75. "Masturbation, Madness, and the Modern Concepts of Childhood and Adolescence." *Journal of Social History* 8 (spring): 1–27.

"New Books of the Month." 1900. *Bookman* 19 (111): 104.

Newton, Esther. 1972. *Mother Camp: Female Impersonators in America.* Englewood Cliffs, N.J.: Prentice Hall.

Ofshe, Richard, and Ethan Watters. 1994. *Making Monsters: False Memories, Psychotherapy, and Sexual Hysteria.* New York: Scribner.

Overn, Michael. 1989. "Letter to the Editor." *Tulane Drama Review* 33 (winter): 9.

Painter, Nell Irvin. 1992. "Hill, Thomas, and the Use of Racial Stereotype." In *Race-ing Justice, En-gendering Power*, ed. Toni Morrison. New York: Pantheon.

Patraka, Vivian. 1992. "Binary Terror and Feminist Performance: Reading Both Ways." *Discourse* 14 (2): 163–85.

Pemberton, Gayle. 1992. "The Sentimental Journey: James Baldwin and the Thomas-Hill Hearings." In *Race-ing Justice, En-gendering Power*, ed. Toni Morrison. New York: Pantheon.

Penelope, Julia, and Susan J. Wolfe, eds. 1989. *The Original Coming Out Stories*.Freedom, Calif.: Crossing Press.

Petersen, Betsy. 1991. *Dancing with Daddy: A Childhood Lost and a Life Regained*. Toronto: Bantam Books.

Phelan, Peggy. 1990. "Serrano, Mapplethorpe, the NEA, and You." *Tulane Drama Review* 34 (1): 4–15.

———. 1991. "Money Talks, Again." *Tulane Drama Review* 35 (3): 131–41.

———. 1993a. "Reciting the Citation of Others." In *Acting Out*, ed. Lynda Hart and Peggy Phelan. Ann Arbor: University of Michigan Press.

———. 1993b. *Unmarked: The Politics of Performance*. New York: Routledge.

"Phi." 1900. "Correspondence: 'An Englishwoman's Love-Letters.'" *Academy* 1493 (December 15): 610.

Portillo, Tina. 1988. Introduction to T*estimonies: A Collection of Lesbian Coming Out Stories*, ed. Sarah Holmes. Boston: Alyson.

Pramaggiore, Maria. 1992. "Resisting/Performing/Femininity: Words, Flesh, and Feminism in Karen Finley's *The Constant State of Desire*." *Theatre Journal* 44 (3): 269–90.

Presse canadienne. 1991. "Anne Dandurand, écrivaine rêveuse." *La presse* (April 8): B-4.

Prin, Alice [Kiki de Montparnasse]. 1930. *Kiki's Memoirs*. Translated by Samuel Putnam. Introduction by Ernest Hemingway. Paris: Edward W. Titus.

Radway, Janice A. 1984. *Reading the Romance: Women, Patriarchy, and Popular Literature*. Chapel Hill: University of North Carolina Press.

Rafter, Nicole Hahn, ed. 1988. *White Trash: The Eugenic Family Studies, 1877–1919*. Boston: Northeastern University Press.

Randall, Margaret. 1992. "Doublespeak and Doublehear: Anita Hill in Our Lives." In *Sexual Harassment: Women Speak Out*, ed. Amber Coverdale Sumrall and Dena Taylor. Freedom, Calif.: Crossing Press.

Reade, Brian. 1970. *Sexual Heretics: Male Homosexuality in English Literature from 1850 to 1900*. London: Routledge and Kegan Paul.

Riviere, Joan. 1986 (1929). "Womanliness as a Masquerade." In *Formations of Fantasy*, ed. Victor Burgin et al. London: Methuen.

Roché, Henri-Pierre.. 1990. *Carnets: Les Années Jules et Jim, Première Partie, 1920–1921*. Marseille: André Dimanche.

———. 1992. *Jules et Jim: A Novel*. Translated by Patrick Evans. London: Marion Boyars.

Rodeck, Jeffrey. 1993. "Oprah Fans Fooled by Her Phony Guests." *National Enquirer* (June 8): 42–43.

Rosenbaum, Max, and Melvin Muroff, eds. 1984. *Anna O.: Fourteen Contemporary Reinterpretations.* New York: Free Press.

Rosenberg, Charles E. 1973. "Sexuality, Class and Role in Nineteenth-Century America." *American Quarterly* 25 (2): 131–53.

Rosenthal, Andrew. 1991a. "Theater of Pain." *New York Times* (October 13).

———. 1991b. "Harassment by Press." *New York Times* (October 15): 26.

Rosenthal, M. L. 1967. *The New Poets: American and British Poetry since World War II.* New York: Oxford University Press.

Ross, Andrew. 1989. *No Respect: Intellectuals and Popular Culture.* New York: Routledge.

Rousseau, Jean-Jacques. 1979 (1762). *Emile; or, On Education.* Translated by Allan Bloom. New York: Basic Books.

Roy, Monique. 1990. "Anne et Claire: la volupté d'écrire." *Châtelaine* 31 (11): 30.

Rubin, Gayle. 1993. "Thinking Sex: Notes for a Radical Theory of the Politics of Sexuality." In *The Lesbian and Gay Studies Reader.* ed. Henry Abelove, Michelle Barale, and David Halperin. New York: Routledge.

Russell, Diana E. H. 1986. *The Secret Trauma: Incest in the Lives of Girls and Women.* New York: Basic Books.

Saint-Martin, Fernande. 1967. *La femme et la société cléricale.* Montréal: Mouvement laïque de langue française.

Saint-Martin, Lori. 1986. "Nicole Brossard." *Le magazine littéraire* 234 (October): 103–4.

———. 1989. "Anne Hébert et Nicole Brossard, de la poésie à la prose." *Études de lettres* 3 (July/September): 67–77.

———. 1992. "Le métaféminisme et la nouvelle prose féminine au Québec." *Voix et images* 18 (1): 78–88.

Sally Jessy Raphael. 1989. "I'm Not a Man; I'm Not a Woman." Transcript #280 (September 29). Copyright 1989 Multimedia Entertainment.

Salter, Stephanie. 1993. "Intellectual Fascism Does Not Serve Women." *Star Tribune* (April 15): 27A.

Schatzman, Morton. 1973. *Soul Murder: Persecution in the Family.*

Scheier, Libby. 1986. *Second Nature.* Toronto: Coach House.

———. 1990. "14. Earth Per Verse, A Catalogue of Suspicions and Dreams." In *Sky*, 48–50. Stratford, Ontario: Mercury-Aya.

Schwarzer, Alice. 1992 (1975). *Der "kleine Unterschied" und seine grossen Folgen.* Frankfurt: Fischer.

Sexton, Anne. 1964. *Selected Poems.* London: Oxford University Press.

Shaw, Marion. 1992. "'To Tell the Truth of Sex': Confession and Abjection in Late Victorian Writing." In *Rewriting the Victorians: Theory, History, and the Politics of Gender*, ed. Linda M. Shires. New York: Routledge.

Showalter, Elaine. 1990. *Sexual Anarchy: Gender and Culture at the Fin de Siècle.* New York: Viking.

Shulman, Alix Kates. 1980. "Sex and Power: Sexual Bases of Radical Feminism." *Signs* 5 (4): 590–604.

Simons, Judy. 1990. *Diaries and Journals of Literary Women from Fanny Burney to Virginia Woolf.* Houndsmills: Macmillan.

Singer, Jerome L. 1990. *Repression and Dissociation: Implications for Personality Theory, Psychopathology, and Health.* Chicago: University of Chicago Press.

"Sisters under the Skin: Exploring the World of Transvestites." 1992. *Centrepoint.* Toronto: Canadian Broadcasting Corporation (March 15).

Smith, Sidonie. 1990. "Construing Truths in Lying Mouths: Truthtelling in Women's Autobiography." *Studies in the Literary Imagination* 23 (2): 145–63.

Smith, Sidonie, and Julia Watson, eds. 1996. *Getting a Life: Everyday Uses of Autobiography.* Minneapolis: University of Minnesota Press.

Smith-Rosenberg, Carroll. 1975. "The Female World of Love and Ritual: Relations Between Women in Nineteenth-Century America." *Signs: Journal of Women in Culture and Society* 1: 1–29.

Smolowe, Jill. 1991. "He Said, She Said." *Time* (October 21): 16–20.

Spender, Stephen. 1980. "Confessions and Autobiography." In *Autobiography: Essays Theoretical and Critical,* ed. James Olney. Princeton: Princeton University Press.

Stallybrass, Peter, and Allon White. 1986. *The Politics and Poetics of Transgression.* Ithaca: Cornell University Press.

Stefan, Verena. 1975. *Häutungen.* Munich: Frauenoffensive.

———. 1978. *Shedding.* Translated by Johanna Moore and Beth Weckmueller. New York: Daughters.

Stekel, Wilhelm. 1943 (1926). *Frigidity in Woman in Relation to Her Love Life.* Vol. 2. Translated by James S. Van Teslaar. New York: Liveright.

Stepan, Nancy Leys. 1990. "Race and Gender: The Role of Analogy in Science." In *Anatomy of Racism,* ed. David Theo Goldberg. Minneapolis: University of Minnesota Press.

Stewart, Susan. 1993. *On Longing: Narratives of the Miniature, the Gigantic, the Souvenir, the Collection.* Durham, N.C. : Duke University Press.

Stoler, Ann Laura. 1995. *Race and the Education of Desire: Foucault's History of Sexuality and the Colonial Order of Things.* Durham, N.C.: Duke University Press.

Stone, Albert, ed. 1981. *The American Autobiography: A Collection of Critical Essays.* Englewood Cliffs, N.J.: Prentice Hall.

Sweat, Margaret J. M. 1859. *Ethel's Love-Life: A Novel.* New York: Rudd and Carleton.

Talamini, John T. 1982. *Boys Will Be Girls: The Hidden World of the Heterosexual Male Transvestite.* Washington, D.C.: University Press of America.

Tambling, Jeremy. 1990. *Confession*. Manchester: Manchester University Press.

Tavris, Carol. 1993. "Beware the Incest-Survivor Machine." *New York Times Book Review* (January 3): 1+.

Thomas, Virginia Lamp. 1991. "Breaking Silence." *People* (November 11): 111–16.

Trescott, Jacqueline. 1993. "Artists Add Voices on Decency." *Washington Post* (June 4): C10.

Tünnermann, Simone. 1996. "Ida Bauer: Rebellin der Ohnmacht." In *WahnsinnsFrauen, zweiter Band*, ed. Sibylle Duda and Luise F. Pusch. Frankfurt: Suhrkamp.

Turner, Victor. 1982. *From Ritual to Theater: The Human Seriousness of Play*. New York: Performing Arts Journal.

TV-TS Tapestry: The Journal for All Persons Interested in Cross-dressing and Transsexualism. Wayland, Mass.: International Foundation for Gender Education.

"Tyranny of Love." 1900. (Review of *An Englishwoman's Love-Letters*.) *Academy* 1491 (December 1): 510–11.

van Benschoten, Susan C. 1990. "Multiple Personality Disorder and Satanic Ritual Abuse: The Issue of Credibility." *Dissociation* 3 (1): 22–30.

Vance, Carole S., ed. 1984. *Pleasure and Danger: Exploring Female Sexuality*. London: Routledge and Kegan Paul.

van der Kolk, Bessel, and William Kadish. 1987. "Amnesia, Dissociation, and the Return of the Repressed." In *Psychological Trauma*, ed. Bessel van der Kolk, 173–90. Washington, D.C.: American Psychiatric Press.

van der Kolk, Bessel, and Onno van der Hart. 1991. "The Intrusive Past: The Flexibility of Memory and the Engraving of Trauma." *American Image* 48: 425–54.

Van Der Stroom, Gerrald. 1989. "The Diaries, *Het Achterhuis*, and the Translations." In *The Diary of Anne Frank: The Critical Edition*, 59–77. Translated by A. J. Pomerans and B. M. Mooyaart-Doubleday. Edited by D. Barnouw and G. Van Der Stroom. New York: Doubleday.

von Flotow, Luise. 1992. "Women's Desiring Voices from Quebec: Nicole Brossard, Anne Dandurand, and Claire Dé." In *US/THEM*, ed. Collier Gordon, 109–19. Amsterdam: Cross-Culture 6.

Walters, Suzanna Danuta. 1990. "As Her Hand Crept Slowly Up Her Thigh: Ann Bannon and the Politics of Pulp." In *Sexual Politics and Popular Culture*, ed. Diane Raymond. Bowling Green, Ohio: Bowling Green State University Popular Press.

Warland, Betsy. 1993. *The Bat Had Blue Eyes*. Toronto: Women's Press.

Weeks, Jeffrey. 1985. *Sexuality and Its Discontents: Meanings, Myths, and Modern Sexualities*. London: Routledge and Kegan Paul.

———. 1990. *Coming Out: Homosexual Politics in Britain from the Nineteenth Century to the Present*. London: Quartet Books.

———. 1992. *Against Nature: Essays on History, Sexuality, and Identity*. London: Rivers Oram Press.

Weigel, Sigrid. 1984. "'Woman Begins Relating to Herself': Contemporary German Women's Literature (Part One)." *New German Critique* 31: 53–94.

Weir, James. 1895. "The Effects of Female Suffrage on Posterity." *American Naturalist* 29 (345): 815–25.

Whitenack, Judith. 1982. "A New Look at Autobiography and Confession." *Ball State University Forum* 23 (3): 40–48.

Williams, Linda. 1989. *Hard Core: Power, Pleasure, and the "Frenzy of the Visible."* Berkeley: University of California Press.

———. 1995. "Recovered Memories of Abuse in Women with Documented Child Sexual Victimization Histories." *Journal of Traumatic Stress* 8 (4): 649–73.

Williams, William Carlos. 1967 (1948). "The Baroness." In *The Autobiography of William Carlos Williams*. New York: New Directions.

Wisechild, Louise M. 1988. *The Obsidian Mirror: An Adult Healing from Incest*. Seattle: Seal Press.

Wolfe, Susan, and Julia Penelope Stanley, eds. 1980. *The Coming Out Stories*. Watertown, Mass.: Persephone Press.

Women's Research Centre, ed. 1989. *Recollecting Our Lives: Women's Experience of Childhood Sexual Abuse*. Vancouver: Press Gang.

Woolf, Virginia. 1975. *A Room of One's Own*. Harmondsworth, Middlesex: Penguin Books.

———. 1986 (1928). *Orlando: A Biography*. London: Grafton Books.

Working Group on Investigation of Memories of Childhood Abuse: Final Report. 1996. N.p.: American Psychological Association.

Wright, Lawrence. 1993a. "Remembering Satan—Part I." *New Yorker* (May 17): 60–81.

———. 1993b. "Remembering Satan—Part II." *New Yorker* (May 24): 54–76.

Zimmerman, Bonnie. 1990. *The Safe Sea of Women: Lesbian Fiction, 1969–1989*. Boston: Beacon Press.

Contributors

Marion Bishop is an assistant professor of English at Bentley College in Waltham, Massachusetts. She holds a Ph.D. in English from New York University, where her doctoral dissertation focused on women's journals. Her approach challenged traditional rhetorical definitions of the writer-audience relationship, particularly in her reading of Anne Frank's diaries. Her research will be published in forthcoming book chapters.

Nathalie Cooke, an associate professor of English at McGill University and senior editor of the Hugh MacLennan Poetry Series, has researched and published extensively on women's fictive confessions. Her specific focus is on Canadian fictive and poetic confessions. She is the coeditor of Oxford's revised and abridged *Anthology of Canadian Literature in English* and the author of *Lorna Crozier and Her Work* and *Margaret Atwood: A Biography*.

Cynthia J. Davis, an assistant professor of English at the University of South Carolina, specializes in American literature and feminist theory. She is the coauthor of *American Women Writers: A Timeline of Literary, Cultural, and Social History*. She has published her research in many academic journals, book chapters, and encyclopedia entries.

Marylynne Diggs teaches English and cultural studies at Clark College. She has published articles on romantic friendship and sexual identity in *Feminist Studies* and the *Journal of Homosexuality*, as well as in book collections. She has recently completed a literary biography on Mary Wilkins Freeman for *The Dictionary of Literary Biography*.

Irene Gammel, an associate professor of English at the University of Prince Edward Island, has published widely on early-twentieth-century representations of women's sexuality in Canadian and American fiction and life writing. She is the author of *Sexualizing Power in Naturalism: Theodore Dreiser and Frederick Philip Grove* and coeditor of *L. M. Montgomery and Canadian Culture*. She is currently writing a book on Baroness Elsa von Freytag-Loringhoven.

Jessie Givner is completing her dissertation on autobiographical forms in literature, politics, and theory at Brown University. She has published several of her research projects in academic journals.

Lynda Goldstein, an associate professor at Pennsylvania State University, Wilkes-Barre, teaches American studies and popular culture courses. She has published on documentary filmmaking, MTV, consumer politics of body building, and queer theory. With Virginia Smith, she is writing *Reading Martha Stewart*, a study of Stewart as cultural force and icon.

Lorraine Janzen Kooistra, an associate professor of English at Nipissing University, specializes in the interrelationship between visual and verbal texts in both high art and popular culture. She has published her research in numerous book chapters and academic journals and is researching a book-length study on Christina Rossetti and the visual imagination. She is the coeditor, with Mary Arseneau and Antony H. Harrison, of *The Culture of Christina Rossetti: Female Poetics and Victorian Contexts*. She is the author of *The Artist as Critic: Bitextuality in Fin-de-Siècle Illustrated Books*, a study that lays the foundation for her exploration of confessional politics in this collection.

Lori Saint-Martin, an associate professor at the Université du Québec à Montréal, specializes in feminist theory and women's writing. She has edited two collections of essays on Québec women's writing, *Lettre imaginaire à la femme de mon amant* and *L'Autre Lecture: La critique au féminin et les textes québécois*, and is the author of several books, most notably *Malaise et révolte des femmes dans la littérature québécoise depuis 1945*, *Contre-Voix: Essais de critique au féminin*, and *Le Nom de la Mère: Maternité et textualité dans l'écriture des femmes québécoises*. She has also published a collection of short stories and, with Paul Gagné, two literary translations of novels by Daphne Marlatt and Keith Oatley.

Elizabeth A. Wilson is a visiting professor in gender studies and American studies at Humboldt University in Berlin. She worked as an assistant professor at Yale University before becoming a research fellow with the Bunting Institute at Harvard University, where she was also a fellow in the Research Training Program in Family Violence at Children's Hospital. She has published on sociological, feminist, and comparative issues in such journals as *Diacritics*. She is also the author of a book on the repressed memory controversy, *Not in This House: Child Sexual Abuse and the White Middle-Class Family*.

Index